Praise for War Story

Army Ranger Sergeant Steven Elliott has written one of the most compelling and moving personal narratives on war-stress injury; moral pain; and the long, twisted road to recovery that I have ever read! *War Story* is a must-read for active-duty personnel, veterans, family members, friends of veterans, clergy, healthcare professionals, and mental health clinicians alike.

> **MARK C. RUSSELL, PHD, ABPP**
> Commander, US Navy (Ret.)

Steven Elliott is a determined warrior who volunteered to serve his country out of a sense of duty—a sacred obligation he felt was his as an American citizen. This book, *War Story*, recalls a tragic event in one of the world's best-trained and most capable combat units, an American Ranger battalion. More important, Steve courageously shares the deeply personal effects of posttraumatic stress from this combat action that nearly destroyed him and his family. This is an absolute must-read for every professional soldier. *War Story* should make leaders reexamine how the unseen wounds of war are addressed within the Department of Defense!

> **JAY W. HOOD**
> Major General, US Army (Ret.)

Steven Elliott's *War Story* includes the final day of combat for Pat Tillman. Steve discovered how hard it is to ask for help in bearing the fog and the wounds war. This book is about courage, facing the past, and winning the future. It is an inspiration to all of us who bore the battle.

> **CHARLES R. FIGLEY, PHD**
> Distinguished Chair and Professor and Traumatology Institute Director, Tulane University, New Orleans

STEVEN ELLIOTT

WAR STORY

SOMETIMES THE REAL FIGHT STARTS AFTER THE BATTLE

TYNDALE
MOMENTUM®

The nonfiction imprint of
Tyndale House Publishers, Inc.

All proceeds from the writing of this book that would otherwise be payable to the author will be donated to the Elliott Fund, a nonprofit organization dedicated to meeting the mental health needs of the active-duty and veteran community. Visit www.elliottfund.org.

Visit Tyndale online at www.tyndale.com.

Visit Tyndale Momentum online at www.tyndalemomentum.com.

TYNDALE, Tyndale Momentum, and Tyndale's quill logo are registered trademarks of Tyndale House Publishers, Inc. The Tyndale Momentum logo is a trademark of Tyndale House Publishers, Inc. Tyndale Momentum is the nonfiction imprint of Tyndale House Publishers, Inc., Carol Stream, Illinois.

War Story: A Memoir

Designed by Dean H. Renninger

Published in association with the literary agency of Tandem Sports + Entertainment, 2900 Crystal Drive, Suite 420, Arlington, VA 22202.

For information about special discounts for bulk purchases, please contact Tyndale House Publishers at csresponse@tyndale.com, or call 1-800-323-9400.

Library of Congress Cataloging-in-Publication Data
Names: Elliott, Steven (Steven V.), date- author.
Title: War story : a memoir / Steven Elliott.
Description: Carol Stream, Illinois : Tyndale Momentum, the nonfiction imprint of Tyndale House
    Publishers, Inc., [2019] | Includes bibliographical references.
Identifiers: LCCN 2018051246 | ISBN 9781496429919 (hc : alk. paper) | ISBN 9781496429926 (sc :
    alk. paper)
Subjects: LCSH: Elliott, Steven (Steven V.), date- | Afghan War, 2001—Personal narratives, American.
    | Tillman, Pat, 1976-2004—Death and burial. | Friendly fire (Military science)–Psychological
    aspects. | Soldiers–United States–Biography. | United States. Army. Ranger Regiment, 75th–
    Biography. | Healing–Religious aspects–Christianity. | Redemption.
Classification: LCC DS371.413 .E45 2019 | DDC 958.104/742 [B] –dc23 LC record available at https://
    lccn.loc.gov/2018051246

Printed in the United States of America

25	24	23	22	21	20	19
7	6	5	4	3	2	1

To the warrior who is fallen

the heart that is broken

and the wanderer, lost and longing for home

A special thanks to writer, editor, and friend Jim Lund. You helped me find the story and write it down. Thank you for your commitment to this work and for being a part of our story, a story that continues to be written.

Contents

Author's Note

Wars take many shapes and sizes, and the field of battle can be found both without and within. This memoir, *War Story*, represents my attempt to accurately capture the events leading up to, during, and following my time as an Army Ranger in Afghanistan. My deployment in 2004 was brief—a mere six weeks. The time I spent revisiting the battlefield in my mind and experiencing the pains of war was much longer. This is a story of a war that began on foreign soil but followed me home. If this story is worth reading, it is worth reading not because it is unique but precisely because it is ordinary. *War Story* is one of many stories of hope, pain, and loss that leave us with questions. Why do we choose to fight for any country or any cause, military or otherwise? What happens when the cost of that fight overwhelms and destroys? Can we forgive? Can we be forgiven? Is there such a thing as hope? While I don't pretend to have simple, conclusive answers to any of these questions, it is for the purpose of posing and wrestling with these thoughts that this story of war, fought both at home and abroad, was written down.

At certain points within this work you will find instances of what could be called "strong language." Please know that such language is employed in an effort to accurately represent the context and interactions of real people, particularly within the military environment. The work of the military, specifically the Army Ranger community of which I was once a part, is harsh to say the least, and the language used within that environment is consistent with that reality. Conveying truth is the goal, not the shock value that such language can sometimes create. I hope the commitment to accuracy as it relates to the language used, strong or otherwise, serves as an insight into the story and not a barrier to understanding.

Finally, unless otherwise noted, the material for this book comes from my memories, journal, and personal records. As deemed appropriate, some names have been changed to protect the privacy of the individuals. I have reconstructed the times, dates, events, and conversations portrayed in this book to the best of my recollection. When possible, I have cross-checked my memories with reliable sources. Any errors that have resulted are mine alone.

Foreword

You hold in your hands an amazing and critically important book that captures a critical time and a critical event in our nation's history. I have read many books to come out of the wars in Iraq and Afghanistan, and *War Story* has touched and moved me like no other.

I graduated from Ranger School in 1979, class 8-79. Ranger School was the hardest thing I have ever done in my life, with endless days of food deprivation and sleep deprivation, combined with the constant demand of small-unit combat leadership positions.

We who graduated were a hollow-cheeked, sunken-eyed, emaciated band who could have been mistaken for survivors of some terrible concentration camp. The greater the challenge, the greater the pride in wearing the "tab" on our left shoulder—above our unit patch, above all other identification, one word that said it all: *RANGER*. No matter how bad the situation should ever get in our lives, we could always say, "I've had worse. At least I'm not still in Ranger School."

In 1974, I was just a young private in the 82nd Airborne Division when, for the first time since World War II, the US Army created a Ranger battalion. The major difference from all previous Ranger units was that this battalion would be composed, ideally, entirely of graduates of Ranger School.

And Pat Tillman's response to 9/11 was to give up his football career to serve in this most prestigious and elite unit.

I remember our nation's pride when we heard that Pat Tillman, in the aftermath of the 9/11 terrorist attacks, had turned down a multimillion-dollar paycheck in professional football in order to serve our nation as a US Army Ranger. Then came our sadness when we heard that Pat Tillman had died on the field of battle. Next was our horror when we heard that Tillman was killed by a tragic train of misunderstanding, the same kind of mistake that saw Confederate General "Stonewall" Jackson killed by friendly fire in the US Civil War—the kind of tragedy that is an inextricable part of all war.

Then came the shame, the deep and burning shame, when we heard that the leadership of our Army had tried to cover up that Pat Tillman had been killed by his own brother Rangers. As always, the cover-up did far more harm than the actual incident.

Steven Elliott's intensely personal account of his experience as one of the shooters in the friendly fire incident and its aftermath is all too familiar. My professional expertise is in researching the effects of combat on the human mind. I am a former West Point psychology professor, and I have written extensively about my findings in my books *On Killing* and *On Combat*, which are read in colleges, military academies, and police academies around the world. Today I train military and law enforcement organizations about the reality of combat.

Part of that reality is a myriad of unseen wounds that our service members may endure as a result of their wartime service, which includes posttraumatic stress disorder (PTSD). PTSD is a condition in which, essentially, every time you remember a traumatic event, you relive it. The fear, horror, and shame you experience in an event can come back to haunt you for a lifetime. Each time can be just as traumatic and devastating as the first time. Indeed, it can be even worse than the first time, because now you live in a constant state of fear and dread that can amplify the impact across the years. This disorder can be debilitating and devastating, and Steven Elliott's

War Story is a powerful and accurate depiction of an individual struggling with PTSD. An experience in which a person has killed one of his own beloved comrades is one of the most devastating trials anyone could imagine.

The National Health Study for a New Generation of US Veterans, a systematic scientific study of more than 20,000 veterans, tells us that 15.7 percent of the veterans of Iraq and Afghanistan have PTSD, and 10.9 percent of service members who did not deploy have PTSD. There are currently more than three million veterans of the wars in Iraq and Afghanistan, and 15.7 percent of this population is almost half a million people. To me, the key point here is that Steven's experiences, his journey from PTSD to healing, can apply to our veterans and to the many civilians who have experienced traumatic events in our general population. They *all* need this book and the lessons from this *War Story*.

Awareness and understanding of the unseen wounds of war, including PTSD, are critical, but it is likewise absolutely essential to know that we can treat PTSD. In Steven's case we see the value of EMDR and other tools in his path to healing. Medical science moves on, we get better every year, and we have hundreds of thousands of cases where PTSD has been treated and individuals have recovered completely. Indeed, you can be even stronger afterward; this is called posttraumatic growth. The goal, therefore, is not simply PTSD awareness but that those who are suffering the unseen wounds of war find a path to healing and strength.

The war story that Steven Elliott has courageously shared in this book is a tale of shame, of failure, and of one individual caught up in tragic events. But it is also a story of some people who did the right thing and stood behind a young Sergeant Elliott. And most important, this book provides powerful and redeeming evidence of that greatest and most important of truths: God's ability to heal us, his power to take us when we are most broken and to make us stronger in the broken places. From the depths of human despair to the supremacy of God's healing and redemption, this story is told with such grace and authority that I was personally moved to tears.

In the end, the greatest achievement of this *War Story* is to tell that most ancient, powerful, and vital of all truths: "It is no secret what God can do / What He's done for others, He'll do for you."

Dave Grossman
Lt. Colonel, US Army (Ret.)
Author of *On Killing, On Combat,*
and *Assassination Generation*
Director, Killology Research Group,
www.killology.com

Prologue

The shovel scraped the rock of the canyon floor, carving a hole in the Afghan landscape. Dust sprang out like the last dirty breath of a dying man as a small cavern emerged in the soil.

I took a green ammo can, now full of empty brass shells, and laid it to rest in the miniature grave I had just dug. No eulogy was offered as the flat, drab lid sank below the earth's surface. No songs were sung as the final burial approached.

I returned to our vehicle and continued to place spent shell casings from the .50-caliber machine gun mounted in the turret and from my own weapon, the M240B machine gun, into yet another ammo can, laying the hollow brass casualties to rest and finally covering them with dirt. Hundreds of rounds had been fired the previous day by me and my fellow Rangers who called this vehicle "home" while on mounted patrol on the Afghanistan/Pakistan border in the Taliban-ridden Khost Province. If only brass shells were all that needed burying.

"Get her cleaned up, boys. We'll be moving back to the FOB once it's dark." This was the simple order given to us by our squad leader and vehicle commander, Staff Sergeant Greg Baker.

"Roger, Sarn't" was our collective reply as we continued to

remove the metal remnants of yesterday's engagement. Save for removing spent shell casings, there was little else we could do to make the Humvee truly clean. The doorless, roofless machine would always bear some trace of this canyon's dirt, but at least some element of yesterday's memory could be cleansed.

Yesterday. April 22, 2004. Our platoon had been split, one half to clear a village and look for the Taliban, and the other half to escort a broken Humvee back to Forward Operating Base Salerno—a Humvee we would have happily left behind if our commander at the FOB would have allowed it. Our vehicle drove behind the useless Humvee as it was towed by an Afghan local. It was stupid and we all knew it. Splitting the unit and thereby severing communications between the two elements, moving at dusk, following a civilian through a narrow, nearly impassable canyon. Stupid.

We entered the darkening canyon on the evening of April 22, 2004, shadows growing longer by the minute as daylight faded. An explosion erupted from the hillside. We stopped, stuck behind the broken Humvee as the Afghan driver fled. Muzzle flashes sparked to life from the graying cliffs, and we returned fire, confident that we would die and now, the day after, thankful we hadn't. Not everyone in our platoon was as fortunate.

Having survived the kill zone, with darkness upon us, we stopped, checked for casualties, took stock of our ammo, and pulled security.

Two. That was the number of men who had been wounded. Our platoon leader, Lieutenant David Uthlaut, caught shrapnel in his face. Amazingly, he would be okay. Our radio transmission operator, Specialist Jade Lane, was next to him and took rounds to his chest, shoulder, and knee. His body armor saved his life, though his knee was torn to pieces. Both had been part of Serial One, the half of the platoon sent to clear the village.

Two. That was the number of men who had been killed. The first was Sayed Farhad. He was part of the Afghan Military Force, and he and a handful of his comrades had been on patrol with us. He was hit with six rounds in the chest. He wore no body armor and died from his wounds.

The second man to die was an American, a Ranger like us, a member of our platoon. Specialist Pat Tillman. Before joining the army and venturing into the Afghan wilderness, Pat had played football in the NFL. He had turned down a $3.6 million football contract in favor of military service. Pat was struck in the head with multiple rounds. His body armor did no good.

Now, the day after, the brass had been buried and our weapons cleaned as we waited again for the sun to set and for the order to move out. The air cooled quickly.

I climbed onto the back of the vehicle and sat on ration cases. I opened the feed tray cover of my weapon to ensure it was clean and unobstructed so that more brass rounds—these still filled with lead and powder—could be fired if need be.

I looked up to the turret of the vehicle and saw my immediate superior, Specialist Stephen Ashpole, sitting in the turret where he manned the .50-cal machine gun, the largest and most formidable weapon in our Ranger platoon. As he sat, he seemed to slump, the weight of his head pressing hard into his chest.

"What's up, Specialist?" I asked.

He lifted his head and turned toward me, his face barely visible in the gray light. "I was talking to Arreola a few minutes ago," he said. "He was with the first sergeant and some of the other guys over where Pat got hit. He said the first sergeant was pulling .50-cal rounds out of the rock where Pat died."

The words were as heavy to hear as they must have been to speak. Our enemies didn't have a .50 cal. The only weapon of that caliber was the one Ashpole was sitting behind. I understood why it was difficult for him to raise his head.

"I'm sure it wasn't you, Specialist," I offered. "I'm sure you didn't hit him." But how could I be sure?

His head nodded with anxious labor as he sought to receive my words knowing, as I did, that they were based on nothing more than a desire to comfort.

Our vehicle's engine sprang to life. "Load up, fellas, we're movin' out!" was the word from Sergeant Baker.

I turned on my night vision, staring at the now hazy green land-scape.

I can't believe it. I wondered, *Could Ashpole have hit Pat?*

What about me? I fired where he fired last night.

But how could we have hit him?

He couldn't have been there. We were firing at the enemy, weren't we?

The vehicle lurched forward as we began our four-hour ride back to the FOB. I stared intently into the green darkness as the thoughts continued to flow.

What if Ashpole killed him?

What if we killed him?

What if I killed him?

The darkness of the Afghan night offered no reply.

1

LEAVING HOME

Home is the nicest word there is.
LAURA INGALLS WILDER

The day had been full. Relatives descended upon the home place situated on the plains of northwest Kansas, five and a half miles from the nearest town. The home place had been built by my great-grandfather Carl Luhman, and it was where one of his sons, Hugo, now lived in retirement along with my grandma Irene. Every Memorial Day weekend, Grandma and Grandpa hosted a family reunion at the home place. Relatives gathered while the kids eagerly engaged in water-gun fights of epic proportions. Only darkness could halt the activity.

At nine years old, I lay in one of the guest rooms upstairs waiting for sleep to come. I glanced at a portrait of Grandpa on the dresser, which was partially illuminated by a night-light sitting next to the frame. He was a handsome twenty-year-old with wavy black hair. He offered neither smile nor frown while wearing his army dress uniform, khaki tie neatly tucked into his khaki shirt. The picture itself was printed in a dreamy sepia hue, and it was as if a silver-screen war hero had descended from the altar of victory and become my grandpa. He was once Corporal Luhman, a gunner on a 155 Howitzer cannon, and he served on the Italian front in World War II for a full year and a half. He returned from the war and spent his life as a farmer, raising wheat and cattle. He was now my grandpa, the closest I would come to a father, and a man of endless vibrancy and joy whose wartime service provided no hint of burden that I could see.

I could hear frogs croaking through the open window. It began to rain gently as I fell asleep.

Memorial Day 1990 dawned fair and clear. Grandpa exchanged his farmer's overalls for black slacks, a black tie, a white short-sleeved button-down shirt, and an American Legion cap emblazoned with the organization's gold emblem. His service in World War II was both normal and extraordinary—normal in that he never embellished or avoided conversations about the war, which I as his grandson was endlessly curious about; extraordinary, because he was a living, breathing member of the Greatest Generation that had sailed to Europe and helped defeat the Axis powers. The more humbly he acknowledged his service, the more brightly his heroic halo seemed to shine.

Grandma had dutifully and joyfully fulfilled her role as part of the American Legion Auxiliary, women whose husbands had served and who themselves served the community. Today their service would come in the form of song and food.

The men of the local American Legion, Grandpa included, were part of a color guard that would visit each surrounding cemetery and provide a twenty-one-gun salute, firing blank rounds from bolt-action rifles. The ladies of the Auxiliary would accompany the color guard to these grave sites and sing patriotic hymns a cappella. Then, having sufficiently honored the dead, all would descend on the American Legion building in nearby Natoma for a hearty meal of beef and noodles, graciously and tirelessly served by the ladies.

We made our way to the Immanuel Lutheran Cemetery just a mile away. A steady wind stirred the smattering of weathered cedar trees. I stood quietly among the crowd of nearly fifty, glancing at the graves of my ancestors. Morning dew provided a bluish gray tint to the green carpet upon which we stood. The air was still cool but the sun signaled the heat that was to come as the hours wore on.

As we waited with quiet reverence, one of the Auxiliary women, nearly seventy and wearing blue slacks, a white blouse, and a red, white, and blue vest, spoke into a microphone connected to a portable speaker.

My grandma stood behind her with ten of her compatriots, all similarly adorned in patriotic business casual attire. They looked like a living American flag.

I strained to hear over the wind as the woman in front solemnly read off names from a list of twenty veterans buried at the Immanuel Lutheran Cemetery, veterans of every war our country had fought since the Civil War. After each name, a young girl pulled a red paper poppy out of a basket and dropped it onto the ground. Each time, the persistent Kansas breeze pushed the poppy a few inches off target and ultimately to a stopping place in the thick, damp buffalo grass.

When all the names had been read, the Auxiliary ladies sang two verses of "God Bless America." A two-man color guard presented the American flag. Then seven men, Grandpa Luhman among them, marched into view. They were all dressed as Grandpa was. Each carried a bolt-action rifle. Most were World War II veterans, but one had served in Korea and one in Vietnam. The commander of this detail was dressed the same as the others save for the addition of a holstered .45-caliber pistol. He soon broke the silence.

"Detail, attention! Present arms!"

The rifles were now held forward.

"Ready, aim, fire!"

The seven rifles erupted as I flinched, shocked at how loud even blanks could be. Seven empty brass casings were flung to the ground as the bolts were pulled back and a new round was placed in the chamber of each rifle.

"Ready, aim, fire!"

I covered my ears this time. The report from the rifles was still deafening.

"Ready, aim, fire!"

The final volley echoed and rolled across the plains into ultimate silence.

The silence was broken by a lone trumpeter, standing behind us at the far edge of the cemetery. The somber tones of taps bathed the audience in a wave of emotion.

Once taps had concluded, the color guard marched away, and the kids, myself included, ran to the place they had just stood to gather the spent shell casings from the blank rounds.

I admired the cylinders of brass, proof of Grandpa's service, symbols of a glorious past and a bright and shining future.

The ceremony was part of a national celebration, but it had personal significance. My great-grandpa Carl Luhman, who had served in World War I, was buried there. His name had just been read, and one of the poppies resting on the grass was dropped in his honor. My great-uncle Vic Luhman, Grandpa's only brother and a Korean War vet, would be buried here as would Grandpa himself.

That night, as Grandpa unwound from a day of honoring the war dead at the local cemeteries, I peppered him with questions.

"Why did you join, Grandpa?"

He considered the question before responding. "Well, I suppose I would have been drafted, but I just didn't want to wait for that. I knew that I needed to serve. Hitler was taking over Europe, the Japanese had attacked us, you know? It was just something we had to do, fight them people, so I volunteered. I had flat feet, though, so they put me in the field artillery. Otherwise I probably would have been in the infantry."

"Did you ever have to shoot anybody?"

"No, we were a long way from the front lines," he said with almost a sense of boredom. "I only had to fire my carbine a few times. We fired a lot of shells, though. A lot of shells," he admitted.

"How big were they?"

"Oh, about ninety-five pounds."

"Wow! And you loaded them all by yourself?"

"Well, when I had to. Sometimes we didn't have enough men, so I'd have to load the gun and fire it myself. I was one of the bigger guys and was used to the work from being on the farm. Some of the guys got to calling me 'Horse' as kind of a nickname." He said this plainly with no hint of boasting.

"Did you ever get shot at?" I sensed I was getting somewhere.

"Oh, well, you know, not really. I mean, we did get strafed by German aircraft a few times earlier in the war, but they didn't have much. By the time we got past the Po Valley in the north, we could see all they had were carts to pull their supplies. They didn't even have trucks or tanks no more. The Italians had surrendered. By that time, the Germans were surrendering more and more, and a lot of them were just kids. There was always a Nazi, you know, one of the SS officers, with a unit, but the rest of 'em were just kids like us and a lot of 'em even younger. I couldn't believe it. They's just the people, you know? If I lived over there, I might have been in the German army too. They was just the people. Hard to believe," he said slowly shaking his head.

I was close to something but would get no closer. He answered my childish questions politely with no desire to offer deception or glorification regarding the act of war in which he'd engaged.

★

Our family was Christian. All four of my grandparents attended the same small Lutheran church in nearby Natoma, Kansas. I was baptized as an infant in the Lutheran Church, but my mom, Cindy, soon left that denomination in favor of a more open and demonstrative version of her Christian faith. She and my dad, Mark, divorced shortly after I was born, and she would say it was during that time that she found the Lord and became a follower of Jesus. Prior to that, she had a sense of religion but no relationship with God.

At the age of four, while driving in the car with Mom, I made an announcement. "I want to follow Jesus," I told her, having done so with no pressure or suggestion.

"Well, why don't you tell him that?" she said simply, staring ahead as she drove, and I did.

Mom never remarried, and I had no other siblings. Grandma and Grandpa Luhman were always close by, offering all manner of support to their daughter, the youngest of three, who would raise me on her own.

Grandpa and I spent a lot of time together. I was his "helper" on projects big and small. I rode in the combine with him as he cut wheat, the smell of diesel and dirt marking the joy of the harvest he so dearly loved. I gardened with him. His favorite pastime was to simply watch things grow. He was a man of the land in the truest sense, but his life as a farmer stood on the youthful pedestal of his military service. Somehow that seemed the starting point, and as a very young child, I thought that's what I would do: to fight, to serve and be like Grandpa.

As childhood turned into adolescence, I harbored no thought or ambition toward military service. I greatly admired those who had served but couldn't see myself traveling down that road. My childish rehearsals of combat were nothing but a game that many boys played.

I was a good student, bookish and quiet, and as my high school years progressed, I found myself more interested in a career in law. Perhaps I had read one too many John Grisham novels, but the idea of fighting for those who otherwise couldn't fight for themselves, to be the good guy helping the underdog, seemed to speak to me. I didn't know exactly what shape that would take, but I knew that if I continued to be a good student, I could do well for myself and reach a place where I could help others in seeing the truth win out and justice prevail.

When I graduated from high school in 1999, I chose to attend Oral Roberts University (ORU), a small Christian college in Tulsa, Oklahoma. ORU's mission is to educate the "whole person"—spirit, mind, and body—which resonated with me.

In the fall of 2001 I began my junior year at ORU. I was studying business and working as an intern with a financial planning firm. The practicality of a business degree and the flexibility that offered was appealing, though I didn't know exactly what I wanted to do with it. That fall semester, I didn't have any morning classes on Tuesdays or Thursdays, so on that particular 11th day of September in 2001 I was fast asleep in my dorm well into the late morning.

A friend woke me up.

"Hey Steve," he said, "you might want to get up and see what's going on."

The message couldn't have been delivered with greater understatement.

I stumbled to a television and was horrified to see news footage of people leaping from burning windows to their deaths and two of the tallest buildings in America crumbling to the ground. It was beyond belief. Beyond comprehension. Despite the thirteen hundred miles between New York and Tulsa, the horror unleashed on 9/11 felt personal.

The images were searing. The implications were sobering. Everything changed that morning. Everything.

As the school year progressed, I began to reflect on conversations I'd had with Grandpa in which he suggested that "it wouldn't hurt to talk to a military recruiter" just to see what my options would be. He was never heavy-handed in these suggestions, but I had always dismissed them. Now, in the wake of 9/11, the question of military service persisted.

With the invasion of Afghanistan well underway, it soon became evident that the newly declared "War on Terror" would not be won quickly. We were now a nation at war, not simply a nation conducting a military strike in Afghanistan.

I completed my junior year at ORU and went home to Kansas for a break before heading back to campus for summer school. I had a few courses I wanted to knock out to make my senior year more manageable. I spent some of that time at the home place with Grandma and Grandpa. After an afternoon working in the garden, Grandpa and I sat on the front porch and talked as we often did.

"What made you want to join?" I asked as conversation meandered to the war.

"Well, I just felt like I had to, I guess. I felt like if I didn't, I'd always be sorry. The Japanese attacked us and Hitler declared war against us. I knew I had to serve."

"How long were you in?"

"Let's see, I's in training for about a year in California and Oregon, and then we shipped out for North Africa at the end of '43. We landed in Italy right after Anzio and was there until the armistice. I guess about two and a half years."

"Wow. Were you ever homesick?"

"Oh man, yeah. Gosh, I felt like I was a million miles away, you know? Didn't really know when we'd come home."

"What was that like? Coming home, I mean."

"It was somethin' else. After taking the ship back to Alabama and the train to Salina just an hour and a half away, the bus dropped me off at Alton about twelve miles north of here in the middle of the night. The folks didn't have a phone, and I didn't want to wait 'til morning, so I just walked."

"You walked the last twelve miles?" I asked, smiling.

"Well, I'd walk a bit and run a bit. I's wearin' a suit and had a suit-case. I didn't mind too much. The folks sure got a shock when I knocked on the door," he said as he savored the taste of that memory—the memory of his final walk to the porch where we now sat.

I returned to ORU unsettled. I soon knew that between me and whatever else life had in store was military service. I couldn't shake that sense, that drawing. Part of me was angry. We had been attacked on our soil in a magnitude that had not been seen since Pearl Harbor. This was my generation's call to arms. I too felt that I would regret looking back and not having served during this time. I didn't think poorly of anyone else who chose not to serve; I just knew I would regret it myself, as if I had chickened out somehow. I couldn't shake it. I couldn't shake this challenge that I knew I couldn't refuse. But most of all, and this I can only somewhat understand in hindsight, I loved Grandpa. In loving someone, there can be a desire to share a common experience and love them more. He never asked me to serve, never pushed or prodded. But he was a man, and I wanted to be like him. Part of that, I came to know, would mean choosing to serve.

As summer school started and my decision to join became more and more real, I did what I was good at: I researched and read books. I went to bookstores and pored over every book on the military I could find. I was especially attracted to those works dealing with the world of special operations, particularly the Rangers and Green Berets.

I then contacted my dad's cousin Bob, a retired full-bird colonel who had spent his career as a member of Special Forces (the Green Berets) and was now living in California. He was a Vietnam vet. I was trying to understand the distinctions of the various communities and where I might best find my place. He provided clarity, particularly as it related to distinctions between Rangers and Special Forces, the former being much more of a shock infantry unit and the latter focusing more on training and force multiplication, though also possessing a combat function. One thing was clear to me: I wanted to fight. Like Grandpa, I wanted to serve in combat, seeing what I was made of and fulfilling my own self-imposed rite of passage in the process. A desk job was out of the question. Our country was at war, and I sensed a duty to participate and serve in my generation's fight.

For the next few weeks the wheels were constantly spinning, and I found myself pulling up to the nearest army recruiting station situated in one of Tulsa's many strip malls. There I met Sergeant Jackson.

Sergeant Jackson looked and sounded exactly the part of an army recruiter. Stocky with blond hair cut neatly into a high and tight and with green eyes to match the uniform, he wore his mint green class B dress shirt tucked neatly into his perfectly creased dark green slacks. His voice betrayed the life of a smoker, and it was after a long draw on a Marlboro that he greeted me as he stood outside the door of the office.

"Hello, young man. Can I help you?"

I briefly froze, realizing I was taking a step from the theoretical to the real, and for all my analysis and thought, I found myself slightly embarrassed as I spoke the words: "I want to see about enlisting in the army and joining the Rangers."

I felt stupid as I said it. Sure, join the Rangers. Me and every other guy who had watched *Black Hawk Down* one too many times. *I just want to drop off my application for one of the most elite infantry units the world has ever known. I'm great with spreadsheets and ratio analysis. You'll be lucky to have me.* Who was I kidding? I felt like a fool.

I expected him to immediately berate me, but after taking a final drag on his cigarette, he said, "Well, you're in the right place. Come on in, and let's talk it over."

As I sat across the desk from Sergeant Jackson, it quickly became apparent that this was not a normal conversation for him.

"So let me get this straight. You're a year out from graduating near the top of your class with a business degree, and you want to go in enlisted, not as an officer, and try to join the Rangers."

It still sounded like a dumb idea when he said it but slightly less dumb than when I had uttered that thought a few minutes before. Perhaps if I heard it spoken out loud often enough, I'd begin to embrace the reality that I was pursuing a dangerous profession and one that would require more of me than I could ever imagine.

"Yes. I want to be at the tip of the spear"—I had just learned that phrase and used it whenever I could—"and I don't want to spend a bunch of time becoming an officer."

He pondered this and then explained the steps: basic training, infantry school, airborne, and then finally RIP, the Ranger Indoctrination Program that served as the selection phase for entry into the Ranger regiment.

I soon took my Armed Services Vocational Aptitude Battery test (ASVAB), which the military uses to determine what jobs you're qualified for. I scored in the 99th percentile on the ASVAB as a whole and got a 134 on the GT score, an additional measure of aptitude, which meant I could basically do anything I wanted. The military especially needed intelligence analysts and linguists, both requiring high aptitude scores and both desk jobs.

Again, Sergeant Jackson challenged me. "You know, a lot of folks would kill to get a linguist job. You'll spend a couple years at the

Defense Language Institute in Monterey, California, and you can pretty much write your own ticket from there."

"No thanks," I said. "I don't want to be stuck in a schoolhouse no matter where it is."

"Well, you're in luck, I suppose, because the required ASVAB score to be an infantryman is 50 and the minimum GT is 108. That makes you overqualified."

"Great. Where do I sign?" I said dryly and directly. The question I kept pondering was, *Am I overthinking or underthinking this?* I tried not to think about it.

By August I had completed all the paperwork to go to the final stage of my enlistment, MEPS, the Military Entrance Processing Station in Oklahoma City, where I was poked and prodded by all manner of doctors to ensure I was fit for service. Sergeant Jackson drove me from Tulsa and waited for me all day as I jumped through one bureaucratic hoop after another.

At the end of it all, I and the other recruits who had passed muster stood in an elegant room with royal blue carpeting from wall to wall and the American flag hanging gracefully in the front. We were called to attention and instructed to raise our right hands, and then we took the oath of enlistment.

This final step was real but not real because I was enlisting as part of the Delayed Entry Program, which basically meant I was enlisted but my start date was delayed so I could finish school. I was eager to join, but it never occurred to me to not graduate. That was a commitment I had to complete before moving on to whatever was next.

I climbed in the back of Sergeant Jackson's Dodge Stratus and promptly fell asleep as the afternoon sun beat down through the window.

That night I hung out with Evan Essenburg, a guy who was quickly becoming my best friend. Evan was a year older than I was and had finished his undergrad in psychology the year before. He was now in his first year as a master of divinity student at ORU's School of Theology.

Evan and I met through ORU missions training and discovered we had mutual friends and a common background. He too was the only son of a single mom, his dad having died unexpectedly when he was very young. He too was from the Midwest, hailing from Fort Wayne, Indiana. And he too was unsure what his future would hold and was seeking his own path beyond his schooling. We both loved the outdoors and had climbed Pike's Peak together with another friend, Dan Russell. The three of us were always plotting our next adventure.

After a quick shower at the dorm, I hopped in my car and drove over to Evan's apartment, and we grabbed a bite at Taco Cabana next door to ORU. Besides my summer school roommate, Evan was the only other person at ORU I'd told about my decision, which was now a reality.

Evan was and is one of the best listeners on the planet, so his attention to my words was not unusual, but I could tell he was strangely focused as I recounted my deliberations, conversations, and ultimate action to enlist.

"So, I'm officially enlisted as an 11X, which is basically an infantryman with a Ranger option. It means that if I can complete basic, airborne school, and RIP, then I can go to one of the three Ranger battalions. I'm hoping for Second Batt up in Washington. I can't imagine I'd want to live in Georgia, where First and Third Batt are."

"What did your mom say?" Evan asked with no small measure of curiosity and concern.

"She told me what she's always told me, that if that's what I feel God has for me, then I should do it. I can tell she doesn't like it, though. My grandpa was shocked and proud. He didn't think I'd ever join the military."

He took a deep breath and looked out the window into the parking lot, staring at nothing in particular but seeming to be thinking a great deal.

"I'm proud of you, man," he finally said. I knew he meant it.

A couple of weeks later I dropped by Evan's apartment, knocked briefly, and let myself in to his one-room flat befitting a first-year theology student.

"Come in!" he hollered from the bathroom.

"I already did!" I hollered back.

Upon stepping into his living room, I was immediately struck by a two-foot pile of books stacked next to his recliner. It appeared that Evan went to the nearest public library and checked out every book he could find in the "military" section. There seemed to be a particular emphasis on special operations in general and Rangers in particular. I was beyond curious and couldn't help myself.

"Whatcha' readin'?" I asked.

As he entered the room, he looked at me sheepishly, and immediately I knew that he wasn't just thinking about enlisting but that his heart was already there while his brain was playing catch-up. Evan was nothing if not methodical in his decision making, and this level of research clearly indicated that his wheels were spinning big time.

Before he could say a word, I said, "You're going to enlist, aren't you?"

"Well, I don't know. I just—well, I'm sort of just thinking about it, you know?"

"Really?" I said skeptically. "Seems like you're immersing yourself pretty deep in the literature to just be thinking about it."

"Yeah, I went and talked to Sergeant Jackson too. I'll be taking my ASVAB soon and, well, we'll see. I dunno."

"What, you think you'll fail the ASVAB?" I chided him. "That sort of sounds like you've already moved beyond the 'just thinking about it' stage. When were you going to tell me, when we bumped into each other in Afghanistan?" I was shocked and overjoyed at the same time. From that moment forward, we were no longer just good friends; we were brothers. I had someone with the same heart and same vision to walk alongside me as I prepared for what was to come.

Before long, Evan had completed MEPS, and he, too, had a Ranger contract with the goal of serving at Second Batt. Evan had an uncle who lived in Seattle whom he had visited as a kid, and he had always loved the Pacific Northwest. Serving there as opposed to Georgia was a no-brainer for him, as it was for me. His enlistment would begin a few months after mine as he wanted one final summer as a civilian before starting basic.

For the remainder of my senior year until I graduated on May 3, 2003, Evan and I became virtually inseparable, training together six days a week. I was built for the soccer pitch and Evan for the football field. He was a solid six feet tall and was a standout lineman on his high school football team and one of the more athletic guys around campus. He pushed me in the weight room, and I pushed him as we ran the hills of South Tulsa, five and six miles at a time. Never knowing if we'd measure up. Never knowing if it would be enough. Never knowing if we could do it but taking comfort in the fact that we could share these hopes of success and fears of failure with each other.

Writing school papers on contemporary English literature seemed abstract. Completing projects for strategic management class seemed pointless. Studying US foreign policy seemed purely academic as I was preparing to be a tool of that very policy. As I completed my classes that year, it was all I could do not to focus only on what lay ahead. The prospect of combat, of war, made my studies feel so much less consequential.

The war I joined for in the fall of 2002, to destroy those who had brought the terror of 9/11, would evolve before I would begin my enlistment and include not just the Taliban in Afghanistan but Saddam Hussein in Iraq. As 2003 began and it was evident that the United States would invade Iraq with or without the support of the international community, I became somewhat confused.

I understood Saddam was anything but a benevolent dictator, but I didn't understand his tie to the terror attacks of 9/11. Why would we go to Iraq? Ultimately, it was the testimony of Colin Powell before the United Nations that put my mind at ease.

I had read his biography and greatly admired Secretary of State Powell's military service and leadership. As an infantry platoon leader wounded in Vietnam, he more than anyone understood the dangers and devastation of engaging in ill-conceived and unnecessary wars. He wouldn't be making the case for an Iraq invasion on the world's stage if he felt there were any other options.

I acquiesced both to the judgment of a leader who had fought in Vietnam and to my own eventual place in the Department of Defense, which would be far from the level of policy makers. To even consider or debate such things began to feel odd and unnecessary. I could only hope and pray that those in authority knew what they were doing.

After graduation, I returned to Kansas, to the home place, to await the beginning of my enlistment just eighteen days later on May 21. It was a long three weeks as I attempted to quell my ever-present anxiety regarding what was to come. I just wanted to get the training over with, but the prospect and pain of leaving home was setting in.

I wasn't much of a morning person at the time, and the days were hot, so I reserved the later afternoon/early evening for my workout routines. I'd jog down the driveway, through the white, metal arch that simply said "Luhman," and turn right along the white rock road toward the cemetery. Each intersection was exactly a mile apart. The land within that square mile constituted a "section" in farm speak, or six hundred and forty acres.

Halfway through one of my four-mile section runs, I passed the black archway of the cemetery, glancing briefly at the old church bell as I wiped sweat from my brow. In the state of meditation that came during a long, steady run, I considered the land around me, the openness and light in which I was enveloped. I considered the stories of war I had heard Grandpa tell whenever I had pressed him for details as a young boy.

After sprinting back, I stretched and sat on the porch to watch the sunset, the light softening as the shadows lengthened.

As I lay in bed that night, I stared at Grandpa's picture on the dresser. The night-light was off, and his face was invisible in the darkness. All I could see was the rectangular silhouette of the frame. There I lay, between waking and sleeping, a shadow lingering. A sadness growing.

What will it be like to be a Ranger? Can I do it? Am I good enough? What will it mean to kill? Will I have to? If I go to war and come home, what stories will I have to tell?

2

ON MY WAY

We find after years of struggle
that we do not take a trip; a trip takes us.
JOHN STEINBECK

Drill sergeants. To accurately describe the professional nature of these people would require the use of language not fit for polite company. Simply imagine every stereotype of a sharp-witted, foul-mouthed soldier with a Smokey the Bear hat, and you pretty much have it. The drill sergeants at the Infantry Training Brigade at Fort Benning, Georgia, were certainly no exception and faithfully played their role in all its profane cruelty.

In fairness to drill sergeants and trainers from all branches of the service, new recruits, generally speaking, are stupid. Not intellectually necessarily, although that is sometimes true, but stupid in the sense that they are completely ignorant regarding the new culture and way of life being thrust upon them. They don't know how to behave, and their exposure to the military via Hollywood offers little practical help in transitioning from being civilians to being members of the armed forces. As such, in the simple attempt to get large groups of people to accomplish a common task, drill sergeants are tough, demanding, and simply mean, fulfilling every cliché regarding their language and intensity that one would expect.

In truth the hardness and even meanness of the drill sergeants and other training cadre are a form of kindness. Drill sergeants are mean and the training is difficult because the job is ugly and hard. It would be unkind to be any other way with young men preparing for the profession of war.

That was certainly my experience upon arriving at Fort Benning at 11 p.m. that Saturday night. I left a civilian world tripping over itself to thank me for my decision to serve. I came to Fort Benning and met professional soldiers who cared nothing for who I had been and whose only job was to help me become someone else—in my case, an airborne infantryman and hopefully a Ranger in the United States Army.

This leg of my journey at Fort Benning began at a place called Reception Battalion. I couldn't imagine any aspect of the army less aptly named. Reception is where the army's newbies are given crew cuts and uniforms and stuck with multiple needles offering inoculation to diseases I'd hardly ever heard of. It's also where we stood in the heat and humidity, hour after hour, day after day, simply waiting for our turn to begin basic training. It felt like prison. Within the first week, I saw guys who couldn't handle the culture shock and the rigidity of the environment. Some broke out of our confines just to visit a convenience store. Another purposely wet his bed every night. He was eventually declared medically unfit to serve and discharged under a Section 8.

I'd already figured out that part of the secret to making it through the next six months was to become anonymous. Drill sergeants were like sharks in the water, sniffing for blood and any scent of weakness. The moment you made a mistake was the moment someone was in your face, screaming and cursing and reinforcing the fact that mistakes in war cost lives—yours or someone else's. In the training environment, the cadre couldn't kill us to prove their point, so they resorted to shaming, physical punishment, and verbal abuse.

It wasn't advisable to do well, either. Then they knew your name for a different reason and watched you all the more intently. My goal was simply to blend in and come out on the other side.

Unfortunately, only three days after my arrival at Fort Benning, I began to feel sick. Horribly sick. I was achy, feverish, and coughing up unspeakable abominations of phlegm. I assumed I had simply caught a bad cold and didn't go to sick call to report it. My turn to start basic was coming soon. I didn't want anything to delay my exit from Reception.

At 3:59 a.m. on May 27, I was asleep in my metal bunk in the huge barracks jammed wall to wall with recruits. A minute later, the fire guard—the platoon member charged with staying up on watch all night—shook my bunk and announced, "First call!" I coughed painfully, my abs sore from hacking for a few days, and hustled to put on the standard physical training (PT) uniform of black trunks and gray T-shirt displaying the single word "Army." By 4:30 I found myself standing on asphalt in formation with at least eighty other young men, all with the same bad haircut. It was still dark outside as we awaited the day under the yellowish-purple fluorescent lights. The thick Georgia air was already eighty degrees.

I stood in the front row at parade rest, a modified position of attention with feet apart and hands placed neatly in the small of my back. There was nothing restful about it. For the next fifteen minutes we waited in silence. I was certainly still sick and relatively miserable but no more so than the night before and felt like I could manage.

There was no warning. One moment I was standing at parade rest; the next I realized I was horizontal and people were carrying me into a doctor's office. I had passed out, which is definitely on the list of things not to do in order to remain anonymous. My blood pressure had dropped dramatically, which caused the blackout. After a few tests, a physician's assistant told me I had a 103-degree fever. "You've got a pretty bad case of bronchitis," she said. "You need an antibiotic."

That sounded logical.

"But you need to know," she continued, "that if I prescribe an antibiotic, you'll need to remain under my care while you're taking it, which will be about three weeks. I can't start you on an antibiotic regimen and then pass you off to another doc."

I frowned. "So, you're telling me that if I start taking an antibiotic, I have to stay in Reception Battalion for the next three weeks? No thanks. I'll be fine. I'll just let this run its course."

"Fine," of course, is a relative term. I could still run and do push-ups. But I felt absolutely awful. As the seemingly endless days of standing and waiting passed, the biggest toll was mental. I had far too much time for reflection and couldn't help thinking I'd made a mistake. Joining the army, I began to think, was a terrible idea. *If I can't manage to make it through Reception Battalion, maybe I'm not cut out for the rest of it.*

The mental clouds began to part a few days later when I was finally transferred out of Reception Battalion. I was one of 240 recruits who were now members of Charlie Company. I began a fourteen-week combination of basic and infantry training, which consisted of daily physical training, classroom instruction, and education on the army's assault rifle of choice, the M16. Once we got to our actual infantry assignments, we'd be wielding the slightly smaller carbine M4 assault rifle, but while in training, we were still using older models that had not yet been fully retired. The bronchitis wasn't any better, but I was able to endure it well enough to escape the wrath and attention of the new batch of drill sergeants.

Less fortunate was a fellow recruit named Landry. On the morning of our first day in basic, I was standing in the middle of our formation until we failed to accomplish some objective or meet some time hack and then found ourselves doing the army's favorite exercise—the push-up. Truly a classic, and an exercise I would become quite accustomed to. We sounded off as always: "One, two, three, one! One, two, three, two!" As we continued to exercise and sound off, I noticed two drill sergeants purposefully move from the front of the formation to the back. I soon heard yelling, though I could not make out the words.

Finally, we were ordered to halt and recover to the position of attention. Though I wasn't supposed to, I sneaked a glance at the back corner of the formation. Immediately I understood what had caught the drill sergeants' attention. We were all winded, our chests heaving as we attempted to "relax" while standing at attention, but the recruit in the back corner was gasping for air. He was about five foot eight, at least 230 pounds, and clearly not in any kind of shape for basic. A drill sergeant was screaming in his left ear.

Landry was crying.

Why are you here? I thought. I couldn't imagine him surviving the next fourteen minutes, let alone the fourteen-week course. *How did he pass the PT test to even get into the army?* His presence in our formation made no sense to me and clearly made even less sense to our drill sergeants.

It didn't help that the man in Landry's left ear was Drill Sergeant Shane. Shane was six feet tall, bald, and trim, and his pale blue eyes looked out from behind black-framed goggles held in place by a black strap that wrapped around the top back of his skull. The effect of the military-issue goggles was that he appeared slightly insane. This added to his already intimidating persona. He didn't appear completely insane, mind you. He looked just insane enough to make you question whether his look was accidental or calculated. My bet was on the latter.

I quickly discovered that Shane was far from crazy. He was highly intelligent, a true artist in the medium of verbal insults, and just plain mean. I came to believe he actually hated us. I later learned he might have had some reason to. After spending most of his army career stationed in Savannah, Georgia, as a member of First Ranger Battalion, Shane was transferred to drill sergeant duty just before First Batt was sent into combat in Afghanistan. He'd trained for years to do battle as a Ranger only to miss the action and babysit recruits like me—and worse, recruits like Landry. To the extent he was bitter, he was more than happy to take out his bitterness on us, training young men who would see combat before he ever did.

In our platoon, the obvious initial target was Landry. I soon learned that Landry was the son of a retired sergeant major, which may have explained why someone looked the other way regarding the physical requirements for enlistment. He couldn't even do three push-ups. Landry continued to cry as the berating continued.

This was the first of many such encounters. Each time, the drill sergeants became less and less venomous as they realized their prey was in no position to respond to their attacks. Landry was not worth the trouble, and it was quickly accepted that he was beyond motivation. Steps were taken to remove him from this environment for which he was so ill-equipped. Each time his weakness was highlighted, I found whatever pity I might have had overwhelmed by the irritation of having someone in our midst who was so very weak. We all just wanted him to leave.

Leave he would, but not before he threatened to kill himself. Our chain of command was forced to place Landry on a twenty-four-hour suicide watch as they awaited the final paperwork to send him on his way. The responsibility for this would fall to Landry's platoon mates, including me, who shared this job in rotating one-hour shifts, every hour of the day.

I drew my first one-hour shift at 2 a.m., being shaken awake by Farrar, my bunkmate who had just completed his hour of obligation. Landry was still alive, and it was my turn to watch him for the next sixty minutes.

Few things will create more instant resentment than being awoken in the dead of night to do anything, let alone watch someone else sleep. That resentment only deepened as I sat next to Landry in a metal folding chair, watching his ample chest rise and fall in seemingly restful slumber—sleep that I envied and of which I was being robbed because of his weakness. But then a measure of compassion rose up in the darkened barracks as I observed what were the only moments of peace for Landry in this place. I didn't want him to hurt; I didn't want him to die. I just wanted him to leave. I wanted to not be burdened by his weakness that I didn't understand and to not be reminded of such weakness in anyone. As I hacked up phlegm in the darkness, I swore I'd never be the burden that Landry had become.

I was still really sick, but at least I was keeping it together. Compassion can be far more fragile and fleeting and certainly less immediately satisfying than self-righteous indignation. I didn't know what Landry deserved. I didn't know whose fault it was that he was there. All I knew was that all of those decisions and deficiencies made him my burden for sixty minutes. A burden I didn't want. I just wanted to sleep.

My bronchitis was getting worse. I consistently ran a fever and was constantly hacking my guts out. Standing at attention in formation without a coughing fit was all I could do. What energy reserves I still possessed were slowly draining away.

At the end of the second week, we took our first PT test in the army, which consisted of a two-mile run, two minutes of push-ups, and two minutes of sit-ups. Each component offered up to 100 points with 300 points constituting a max score.

I gave it everything I had that morning and managed to be one of the few who achieved a max score on the test. As one of the drill sergeants was congratulating me on my score, I almost passed out. That proved to be the last gasp of my efforts.

Two days later, I found myself sitting on my bunk, wearing my PT gear and barely able to stand. As we prepared for the day's training, Farrar wasn't having it. "You have to go to the infirmary. This is ridiculous. You're really sick. People get sick. You can get meds and then get better."

"I don't know, man. What if I miss something in training and then get recycled? I don't want that, and I don't want to be singled out. I just need to get through this on my own."

"How's that workin' out for ya?" Farrar said flatly with an eyebrow slightly raised.

He was right.

"Okay, I'll see if I can get on sick call. Maybe I can spend some quality time with Landry if he's still around," I joked feebly.

Farrar rolled his eyes and chuckled. "Just get to the drill sergeants' office and get better. I'm sure we'll still be here when you get back."

I felt like a dead man walking as I plodded along the length of our platoon's barracks. When I reached the end, I saw our drill sergeants' office ahead and hoped that when I knocked, it would be one of the two drill sergeants assigned to our platoon whose last name wasn't "Shane."

I knocked and waited.

"Enter," responded the low gruff voice belonging to Drill Sergeant Shane.

I opened the door to behold Shane sitting behind his desk, in neatly pressed camouflage battle dress uniform (BDU). His Smokey the Bear drill sergeant hat rested on the naked desktop. He stared at me intently behind the thick lenses of his insanity goggles.

"What?" he asked flatly.

"Drill Sergeant," I said, "I'm really sick. I think I need to go on sick call."

He stared at me for an uncomfortable few seconds, letting me dangle before replying, "Well, there's only two reasons why people get sick. You either got weak genes, or you're a p—. So, which is it?"

There was of course no arguing with the choices I'd been given. "I've got weak genes, Drill Sergeant."

Apparently satisfied, Shane said, "Okay," as if now he could mark the "weak genes" box on the sick call form.

That morning I reported to the infirmary and was again diagnosed with acute bronchitis. I was sent to another large but mostly empty barracks and was given a bunk and a face mask. As campers go, I was not of the happy variety, nor were my pathetic, mask-wearing, mouth-breathing infirmary mates. Some of them were malingerers, simply trying to avoid training; others, like me, were genuinely sick. I didn't want to catch what any of them had, whether a physical ailment or laziness. There was nothing to do but watch a VHS tape of *Hamburger Hill*, a Vietnam-era flick about a platoon assaulting a meaningless position where most of the men were killed. This nihilistic narrative was the only distraction from staring at the rectangular pattern of bedsprings on the bunk above me.

My temperature, which registered a solid 103 when I arrived at the infirmary, had to be consistently at or below 99 in order to be released. Our only activities were having our vitals taken in the morning and at night and of course shuffling ourselves to the chow hall for food we had no appetite for.

Doubts lingered as I found myself out of commission before even getting close to the most difficult component of training, Ranger selection, which wouldn't begin for another four months. I hoped and prayed I would have the strength to perform. I couldn't imagine failing, yet it felt like that was exactly what I was doing. I wanted to fight the Taliban, but I was stuck in the infirmary with a bacterial infection. *Pathetic*, I thought.

After three days, my temperature finally dropped to an acceptable range, and with a bottle of antibiotics in hand, I headed back to the platoon and picked up where I left off. I wasn't 100 percent, but I was in far better shape than I had been.

A couple of months later, on a sultry August evening, I was standing in the chow line when another drill sergeant holding a clipboard announced that six of us needed to report to battalion flag detail at 2000 hours. He rattled off the names, and mine was among the six.

I was annoyed. What little free time I had would be eaten up with some quality drill-sergeant time lowering the American flag that was flying above our battalion headquarters.

At the appointed hour, the six of us practiced our flag detail duties with another noncommissioned officer (NCO) in the open-air space directly below our barracks, which served as our company formation area. We rehearsed where to stand, how to properly lower the flag, and how to transition it from a flat, taut piece of fabric to a tightly folded triangle with only stars on a blue field visible.

Our rehearsal went fine, but I was not entirely confident we'd come through when we would have to perform this ritual for real. If anyone blew it, we'd all suffer, as was the army way.

We stood around for a while, and I wondered who the staff duty NCO would be.

At a few minutes before 2100 hours I sat on the concrete floor, my back against the brick wall of our barracks, my BDU cap tilted back on my bald and sweaty head when the answer to my question was revealed. It was Drill Sergeant Shane.

Great.

Upon seeing Shane, someone shouted, "At ease!" which is the call to jump to the position of parade rest and easily qualifies as the military's most profound oxymoron.

As usual, Shane was all business. "Detail, fall in!" he ordered, and we immediately jumped to our positions, forming two parallel three-person lines. "Right face! Forward march!" he said.

We stepped in unison until we reached the thirty-foot flagpole. "Detail, halt! Center face!"

Each line of men turned toward the other. I was one of the two farthest from the flagpole, which meant that I and the soldier immediately across from me would be responsible for completing the final folds of the flag and presenting it to Drill Sergeant Shane.

We waited at attention, facing each other and yet trying not to make eye contact. It wasn't clear how long we'd be forced to stand here until we were ordered to begin our task. After a few moments, a loudspeaker burst to life and the unmistakable notes of taps began to play.

The emotion I felt was unexpected. It was a potent combination: pride in what I was doing and what I may one day soon be fighting for. Honor for the fallen. Memories of a far-off cemetery on the plains and a recognition that I was no longer standing on the sidelines waiting to pick up a few brass shells but was now joining those who had served and who continued to serve our nation in uniform. Joy at somehow, for a moment, finding myself by being lost in something much bigger than me.

As the song concluded, the sound of pulleys squeaking was all that could be heard as the flag was otherwise silently lowered, and we responded to each command given that takes the flag from its place at the top of the pole to its folded, triangular form.

We performed the maneuver flawlessly, feeling a measure of transcendence as we collectively partook of a ritual of honor. I handed the tightly folded flag to Shane as he stared at me with great intensity, goggles firmly in place.

He showed no visible reaction, and we waited for some indication of how he viewed our work. After holding the flag for a few moments and scanning each of our faces, he uttered words that were a revelation. "Men," he said, "that was one of the most squared-away things I have ever seen."

To be called men in this context meant the world, especially from Shane. Normally, we were "s—birds." Sometimes "a— clowns," and occasionally, when his anger with our collective ineptitude was so great to not even be honored with profanity, we were simply "you people." Never "men."

It was as if the clouds had parted and offered a glimpse of daylight, the daylight of purpose and of becoming something more significant together than we could ever be on our own. The sense of unity and satisfaction in that moment was palpable. I was proud of the sweat-stained BDUs we were wearing that bore both our names and the words "US Army." I was proud to take another step toward becoming an American soldier.

After fourteen weeks of basic and infantry training, I was ready to graduate and officially become an infantryman in the United States Army.

On a clear, warm September day, we stood in our formation area wearing our class B uniforms—mint green shirts, open at the neck, and dark green slacks. To the side of the formation were family and friends we had not seen for months. In the crowd I was happily able to pick out three familiar faces: Mom, Grandma, and Grandpa.

Mom came forward when the order was given to place the blue infantry cord on my uniform. This signified my completion of this training and my place in the infantry community. Any fear she had with respect to my chosen profession seemed to be overcome by her joy at just seeing me and knowing I was okay.

Grandpa was enlivened. He was reliving his own days as a young man entering the army, and as we ate dinner later that evening in nearby Columbus, Georgia, he told stories I'd never heard before. He peppered me with questions, intensely curious about the nature of my training.

Turns out, drill sergeants were drill sergeants back in the 1940s, too. It was nice to discover that some things don't change.

"Man, them guys put us through the paces," Grandpa said. "But they made us tougher. Made us ready for the job we had to do."

As the evening wore on and our conversation continued, it was clear we were becoming closer as we shared a common experience separated by sixty years. He felt a connection to his youth; I felt a connection to the brotherhood of men. Our joy met in the middle.

The next step in the process of becoming a Ranger was the three-week airborne school, located on the other side of Fort Benning. The four of us walked around the jump towers after I got checked in for school, which would start immediately that Monday.

Grandpa was in awe of what I was embarking on. He didn't care for heights, and the thought of willfully jumping out of an airplane was completely inconceivable to him. As for the Rangers, he was impressed.

"Them's a tough bunch of guys. That's not gonna be easy," he said. He wasn't doubting my abilities but rather was proud I would take on the challenge. Grandpa's respect for the road I was walking was life-giving to me.

After a wonderful couple of days between infantry school and airborne, Mom, Grandma, and Grandpa headed home and I began three weeks of jump school. Those weeks were largely uneventful—that is, as uneventful as jumping out of airplanes can be. I successfully completed the course, logged my five required jumps, and felt that now my life in the army was finally ready to begin. Everything else up to this point had been a prelude. I was there to be a Ranger, and the gateway to that community was about to be opened. But the gatekeepers were in a class all their own.

★

On a crisp October morning, the Ranger Indoctrination Program (RIP) began. About 160 of us, mostly infantrymen and all jump-qualified, stood nervously in formation with our single green duffel bags lying next to us. Two large white school buses pulled up. As they hissed to a halt, two men wearing starched BDUs, glossy black boots, and tan berets emerged. Their lips bulged with chewing tobacco as they approached our formation and cast their eyes distastefully on our appearance. So it began.

Our initial interaction with our new cadre was innocuous enough as their job was simply to transport us from the airborne school barracks down the road to the Ranger Training Detachment, which would be our home for the next month, or the next day, or the next few hours. It was up to us. There was nothing compelling any of us to partake in this process. It was all completely voluntary. At any point, we could say, "Thanks, but no thanks," and we'd immediately be assigned to an airborne infantry unit. But we'd also never be able to wear that tan beret and never be part of the Ranger community.

We came to learn that our Ranger cadre were as tough as they come. They were proven combat leaders who were serving for a time in the selection course while they awaited new assignments in the special operations community. These men had all served in combat, some fighting in the 2002 Battle of Takur Ghar in Afghanistan, where seven Americans lost their lives. Some had a coveted gold star sewn onto their jump wings, indicating they had successfully completed airborne jumps in combat. All of them were intensely protective of the Ranger scroll affixed to their left shoulder, the unit patch and symbol worn by no more than a couple of thousand men at any given time. These were the gatekeepers.

As the buses arrived at our new barracks, we were given three minutes to disembark and stand in formation with our gear placed neatly beside us. This was the first of countless time hacks we would fail to meet. As the seconds were counted down, I prepared myself for the inevitable punishment that would follow.

We scrambled to complete the command on the pitch-black asphalt that would serve as our formation area and place of frequent pain. Perched a few feet above us on the steps that led into the World War II–era barracks was Sergeant First Class Nash, the six-foot-three, black-haired leader of the Ranger training cadre. Time had expired, and he let us hang for a moment with no expression. I could see

patches on his uniform I didn't even recognize, indicating his completion of schools and training well beyond our skill and comprehension. The gold star on his jump wings flashed back at us.

He glanced casually at his wristwatch, dropped his arm, and
simply turned his head, offering a subtle nod to the Ranger standing to his left. Immediately this man exploded. "Get the f— down!"
he shouted at us. "Push!" For the next half hour, we performed a
smorgasbord of calisthenics: push-ups of course, flutter kicks, and
finally mountain climbers. In the army, it's called "getting smoked"—
vigorously enhanced physical activity given at the direction of one's
superiors as a result of being individually or collectively inadequate
in performing the task at hand. In other words, "You f— up, and it will
hurt until we, the enforcers, get tired of punishing you."

Finally, the command was given to recover, at which point we all
pulled ourselves off the ground and returned to the position of attention as our hearts raced and sweat dripped from our faces.

"What?! What?!" one of the cadre cried. "Oh, I get it! F— the
Airborne Ranger in the Sky! Get the f— down!"

The Airborne Ranger in the Sky? No one had told us about him.
Fortunately for us, our cadre was kind enough to educate us as we
did more push-ups.

"Check it out, s—heads! The Airborne Ranger in the Sky is the
fallen. The Rangers that have died. Every time you do an exercise
and are told to recover, you will do one additional repetition of that
exercise and sound off, 'One for the Airborne Ranger in the Sky!' You
will do this every time, or you will pay!"

I was at muscle failure. I arched my back for a second or two
before attempting another push-up.

"Let's try this again, shall we?" the cadre continued. "Recover!"

The formation erupted as we all struggled to do one last push-up.
"One for the Airborne Ranger in the Sky!"

Next, we were instructed to sit on the blacktop, consume a full
MRE (meal ready to eat), and return to the position of attention in
formation within twelve minutes. Everything had to be eaten, and not
a scrap of trash would be tolerated. A single MRE is more than twelve

hundred calories. Once again someone missed the deadline, and we got smoked. Our cadre shouted "encouragement" as they sized up the new class of "Rippies" they'd been presented with.

After another hour or so of these antics, it was time for another MRE. Now I understood—this wasn't about our sustenance but was merely another tool to try to break us. It was the same rules, with the same result. My body failed to keep pace with the demands to simultaneously fuel the work of exercise and digest that fuel, and intense cramping began. *It could be worse.* The sounds and smells of vomit filled the air, which only angered the cadre even more. "How dare you waste food provided to you by the taxpayers!" And "Who do you think you are to foul the formation area?" Simply more reasons to smoke us.

Finally, we were again ordered to recover and assigned to our barracks. Our PT test would be the following morning.

Welcome to RIP.

Over the next few days, our class size shrank almost by the hour as guys either failed to meet physical standards or tired of the cadre's abuse. The 120 or so who were left, myself included, were taken out to a dreaded location at Fort Benning—Cole Range, a remote grassy field surrounded on all sides by Georgia pines. This was where Sergeant Nash and his cohorts would spend the next ninety-six hours doing whatever they could to make us quit. We got maybe two hours of sleep per night. I was told it was not uncommon for half the class to quit at Cole Range.

I quickly learned that, while there are certainly physical standards that had to be met, this was largely a mental game. The easiest way to lose was to start telling yourself what you were willing to deal with. It was the uncertainty of the duration of pain that could be maddening. Knowing you're not in control. Knowing that if you're going to make it, you have to put up with it as long as someone else wants you to. The more I let myself go, knowing that I would do whatever was asked of me regardless of what I thought my limits were, the easier it was. The more I sought to take control in my mind, the more impossible and frustrating it all became.

Day one of Cole Range was replete with all manner of tactics designed to frustrate and exhaust. The culminating event was a six-hour land navigation course, three hours in the daylight and three in darkness. I completed the course but didn't excel, barely meeting the time hack only to discover I had missed a point. That counted as failure. One more of those and I'd be out.

That night the fun continued as the cold set in. The cadre warmed themselves by the fire with the rest of us shivering in formation.

"Oh, I'm sorry. You ladies cold? I forgot to tell you—hit the wood line!" That was the first of many commands to sprint to the tree line behind us about two hundred yards away. It was kind of them to allow us to warm ourselves with our own body heat only to become colder than we had been as sweat turned to vapor while we stood in formation. Eventually, they allowed us to lie down for a while. About thirty guys quit that night. Strangely, seeing others' weakness provided additional strength from the worst possible source: pride. *I'm better than they are,* I thought. *I can do this.*

Starting at four the next morning, we began a ruck march, which meant walking quickly, normally at a fifteen-minute-per-mile pace, in single-file line with a load of about thirty-five pounds on our backs. It was pitch black; the only light we saw came from the flickering headlamps of the cadre who were driving us onward. We weren't told how far or for how long we'd march on the asphalt and gravel range roads. We just knew that falling behind wasn't an option.

As the pace was established, I found myself running to keep my spot in the formation, not allowing too much space between myself and the man in front of me. I expected the pace to slacken but it never did. We were running, not walking, and the pace was much faster than what any of us were used to. The rhythm I could normally find when engaged in long-duration cardio exercise never came. I was just sucking wind with no end in sight.

The minutes and miles piled on. I was keeping up, but there was nothing pretty about it. If I'd had to stop on a dime and fight the Taliban, they could've whipped me with a wet noodle. I had already

failed an event and couldn't afford to fail another one, so I kept pushing, hoping it would end before I did.

The cadre were enforcing very tight intervals between us. Anyone
who was just a couple of yards behind the man in front of him was
pulled out of line and put in the slower, failure formation.

After about forty-five minutes, I noticed that our formation had
shrunk significantly. I glanced behind me and was shocked to see I
was the last guy in line, with a Ranger cadre right on my tail giving
me a dirty look. There was no margin for error.

That continued for another hour and fifteen minutes. Two hours
covering about ten miles at a full 25 percent faster than the standard
infantry pace. Only forty of us finished in the "passing" group. The
other sixty or so guys were in the failure formation.

We were given the order to take off our rucks, and we joyfully
placed them on the ground at our feet. We stood there heaving,
watching the steam roll off our sweat-soaked BDUs in the cool fall
morning. Nothing I did in the army offered more satisfaction. I had
done it. I had kept up with a Ranger combat veteran on a ruck run
designed to make people quit, and I didn't quit. The trepidation and
doubt that had accompanied me up to this point were gone. I knew
at that moment I had the strength to do this. On my own, I possessed
the strength and endurance to succeed. For the first time I allowed
myself to believe it and could see myself becoming a member of the
Ranger community.

After a month of physical fitness testing, marksmanship training,
small unit tactics, medical proficiency training, and Ranger history
education, it was over. I had made it, one of sixty-three graduates of
the RIP class of November 2003.

On November 13, our class stood on the blacktop where our
RIP journey had begun and awaited our battalion assignments. The
Seventy-Fifth Ranger Regiment is composed of three battalions: First
Batt in Savannah; Third Batt at Fort Benning, right next door to where
we stood; and Second Batt at Fort Lewis in Washington State. My
heart was clearly set on heading west to Second Batt, but the regiment had little regard for what any of us wanted. I had stated my

preference when asked and assumed naively that it would be considered. My adrenaline spiked and my heart sank when I saw the arbitrary process for battalion assignments that began to unfold. Our superior simply called off each battalion and how many men they would send to each post. It was a random, first come, first served affair. I began to visually chart the path I would take to bolt through the formation and make it to the Second Batt line in time.

A cadre raised his hand and yelled, "Second Batt!" I busted through my place in the formation and managed not to knock anyone over but not by much. I stood at the rigid position of attention as the third man in line. I made it. Others who didn't were ultimately assigned to Third Batt, which meant they would stay at Fort Benning. I saw a couple of guys cry with frustration at the prospect.

Also joining me in the Second Batt line were my good friends Dustin Broek and Josey Boatright. We had been together since day one. Now we'd be fulfilling our own version of Manifest Destiny as we headed to the West Coast to continue the adventure. Evan, who was finishing basic at the time, would join us at Fort Lewis a couple of months later after completing his own RIP course.

The next day was graduation. Mom and her sister Susan drove all the way from Kansas for the event. Grandma and Grandpa would have loved to have been there, but it was too much of a trip for them to take again. It was so good to see family, especially at that moment. To feel, see, and hear some semblance of home in the form of those you love intersect with a place that exists to train men for war was truly refreshing.

"It's so good to see you guys!" I exclaimed, giving them both big hugs.

Mom was especially excited. "You look great! How are you feeling?"

"Terrific! I'll be on a plane for Seattle tonight and reporting to Second Batt next week. I might even get some Christmas leave, so hopefully we can spend more time together then."

I could tell that though both Mom and Susan were smiling and clearly happy for me, they harbored more apprehension regarding my future than I did. In my mind, I had made it; the hard part was over. Now I would get to go do my job and really begin my career—a career whose chief hallmark was danger and violence. They understood this much better than I did.

"I love you," Mom said, "and I'm so proud of you. I'm just not so sure if I'm okay with all of this." She offered the final sentence with a smile, but the words had an obvious note of concern. I knew at that moment that this was perhaps just as hard for her but in a different way than it was for me.

"Oh, Mom, it'll be fine," I said with the unflinching confidence reserved for those who have largely experienced nothing but success and have reached the age of twenty-two.

"Form up!" The command was given so the ceremony could begin. We stood in the center of the Ranger Memorial on Main Post at Fort Benning. It's a granite courtyard, the entrance to which is framed by its own imposing stone archway with the word "Ranger" emblazoned across the top. Having passed through that arch, I stood at attention as the ceremony began.

Soon we were told to "don berets," at which point we retrieved our brand-new tan berets from our cargo pockets and happily replaced our camouflage BDU caps with this new, distinctive headgear.

Then family and friends were invited into the formation to pin our battalion scrolls to our shoulders. Mom somewhat nervously came forward, thrilled to be participating but certainly out of place in the military setting.

I handed her my Second Batt scroll, which had a safety pin attached. She affixed it to my left shoulder indicating that I had a unit. I had a new home.

She hugged me briefly but firmly. "I love you," she said quickly, as if to conclude her words before a greater swell of emotion took hold.

"I love you too, Mom. Thank you."

The ceremony concluded with the graduates reciting the Ranger Creed in unison. Wearing my own tan beret, I proudly joined my fellow newly minted Ranger brethren. The creed had been drilled into us both in word and in spirit for the past month, and it read in part,

Recognizing that I volunteered as a Ranger, fully knowing the hazards of my chosen profession, I will always endeavor to uphold the prestige, honor, and high esprit de corps of my Ranger Regiment.

Acknowledging the fact that a Ranger is a more elite Soldier who arrives at the cutting edge of battle by land, sea, or air, I accept the fact that as a Ranger my country expects me to move further, faster and fight harder than any other Soldier.

Never shall I fail my comrades . . .

Our recitation of the Ranger Creed ended as it always did, with a loud and forceful, "Rangers lead the way!"

As those words echoed into silence, my pride swelled.

I did it.

3

KILL OR CAPTURE

War and drink are the two things man
is never too poor to buy.
WILLIAM FAULKNER

Fort Lewis lies thirty-three miles south of Seattle in Washington State, its eighty thousand acres sprawled over both sides of the heavily traveled Interstate 5. The army post can be scenic in summer, its streets lined with green fir trees, the landscape dominated by the snowcapped volcano Mount Rainier. But the post is dreary at best in winter, smothered by gray skies from which rain falls incessantly.

A little more than a week earlier, I was one of fifteen new Rangers sent to Fort Lewis to join Second Ranger Battalion. Shortly after reciting the Ranger Creed at Fort Benning and bidding my mom and my aunt farewell, I was on a plane bound for Seattle. To sit on an airplane and have someone serve me anything, even ice water and a comically small bag of peanuts, was a tremendous luxury after spending the last six months at Benning. The flight west was a giant exhale. I could feel the relief wash over me as I sat in the opulence of a coach-class window seat. Opulence because there was no drill sergeant or Ranger cadre in sight. I would have been just as happy tucked in the baggage compartment. Free of the strain and intense scrutiny of military training, I relaxed.

The sanguine feeling of relief wore off. I had spent virtually all of my energy up to that point focused on completing the training to get a job. Now on the flight I had the space to consider the job that lay before me. I thought back to the first day of RIP. In between the yelling and smokings, our class was addressed for a few moments by the command sergeant major of the Ranger Training Detachment. I remember it being a welcome break from the day's activities because he was not there to test us but simply to ensure that we were aware of what it was we were volunteering for.

Standing at parade rest in a semicircle around the sergeant major, we listened intently as he told us plainly what our job would be as Rangers. "As a member of the regiment, your job will be to kill people on behalf of the United States government. If that's not what you want to do, then there's no use wasting your time here. You can leave, and there's no shame in that."

It's strange how sometimes a warning or simply the statement of a fact can be heard as a dare. In that moment, I thought I heard a question: "Are you man enough to kill in combat?" The sergeant major's statement didn't dissuade anyone from participating in the selection process, though many would eventually quit or be kicked out.

As the plane broke below the clouds and circled the Seattle skyline, I pondered what it might mean to kill someone. I wondered if I could do it. I wondered, albeit briefly, what it might do to me. It became clear that everything up to that point had been a game. The real business of preparing for war, of preparing to kill, was just beginning.

Five of us newbies were assigned to Alpha Company, one of the four companies at Second Batt. I use the word *assigned* loosely. A Co.—in fact, the entire battalion—was on deployment in Afghanistan. Until they got back, we wouldn't get our platoon and squad assignments, which meant we didn't have beds of our own. We were told we could sleep in any bunk that seemed open while we waited for the battalion to return. The last thing I wanted, however, was to wake up to an angry Ranger fresh from deployment. Josey Boatright took his chances and slept in the barracks, trying to select a room and bunk that seemed least likely to have an owner. Dustin Broek and I chose to sleep in his car. We shivered through five damp nights but were slightly warmed knowing we wouldn't be encroaching on anyone's turf.

The handful of Rangers not on deployment were waiting to leave. Some were near the end of their enlistments and were out-processing from the army. Others had screwed up in one way or another and were in the process of being kicked out of the regiment. And still others were too banged up to serve and were in some stage of rehab and recovery.

One of the latter was Specialist Moore, a veteran of Iraq and Afghanistan. I didn't know what his medical issues were, but I was keenly aware of the chasm between his experience and my greenness. He could have easily used his status to put me and the other new guys in our place—plenty of others had already done so—but for some reason he felt responsible for us. In between stories of his deployments, he passed on wisdom on a range of topics: finances ("Save 20 percent of your check every month"), women ("Don't get married—army marriages don't last, and most girls just want your paycheck"), discretion with sensitive military information ("Don't tell anybody anything; I know guys who got kicked out because somebody was listening to their conversations. Operational Security is serious business"), and drinking ("If you're going to drink, do it on post. Don't get a DUI. If you do, you'll be gone. Don't even think about smoking weed. They give random drug tests all the time, and you'll get caught"). The stories and evenings spent listening to them sometimes dragged on, but I appreciated his advice and the spirit with which he gave it.

One particular evening, six of us were gathered in an A Co. barracks room: Moore and two other veterans, me, Broek, and Boatright.

The barracks itself was old, having been built in the sixties. Blue tile floors and white cinder block walls lit with endless banks of fluorescent lights created a sterile, almost hospital vibe. The decorative motif was typical of Ranger barracks, best described as prisoner with a *Playboy* subscription. The colorless walls were unadorned with the exception of the occasional centerfold taped haphazardly to the surface. We sat in a rough circle in worn, oak-framed chairs covered in faded blue vinyl. A wall-length radiator hissed while a stereo blasted Metallica—Black Album, of course.

Each of the veterans had two brown bottles, one filled with beer and the other on its way to being filled with chewing tobacco and saliva. Broek, Boatright, and I had neither. I didn't drink anyway. I had no interest in consuming something that would dull my senses or make training even more difficult. But it wasn't just that. Somehow it wouldn't have felt right to drink with these guys. They had earned the right to cut loose and party a bit. We had earned nothing.

I sat with my back against a wooden wall cabinet. Moore sat three feet to my right. He was thin and had close-cropped brown hair. He was dressed plainly in a gray jacket, baseball cap, blue jeans, and hiking boots. It wasn't his appearance that made me listen with rapt attention. It was his intensity. His tone wasn't loud, but his words were concise, measured. Each syllable felt imbued with purpose. Nothing was wasted.

"You guys need to understand the difference between line dogs and maggots," Moore said, pausing to fire a stream of spit and chew into his bottle. "Line dogs are the guys who actually kick down doors and assault the objective. Maggots are the machine gun teams. Their job is to provide support by fire for the line dogs."

Moore fixed each of us with a look to make sure we were paying attention. Then he continued: "A lot of you may get assigned to the maggots. But if you do well there, you can get a slot in one of the line squads. That's what you want to do if you hope to advance here at battalion."

As he spoke, Moore took off his cap to scratch his head. He kept talking, but I couldn't listen. I had never seen him without his hat on.

Now I knew why. The back-left quadrant of his head was caved in. You could store a grapefruit in that divot.

Later, one of the new guys got the story from one of the veterans. During a nighttime training jump, Moore burned in—that is, his parachute didn't open properly, and he came down way too fast. No one knows for sure what happened. They just found him on the drop zone unconscious and bleeding out. He should have died. Instead, despite a massive head injury, he survived. Now he was in between reconstructive surgeries and hoped to become a helicopter pilot.

Moore talked and I stared. Then I realized I was staring. I forced my eyes away and glanced at Boatright to my left. Our eyes locked for an instant in recognition.

Moore put his cap back on and continued, either not noticing or ignoring our reaction. But the image of his crushed cranium was impossible to forget. This wasn't a training environment anymore. This was real. This was dangerous. There was no guarantee I wouldn't get seriously hurt or killed.

I had always known it, intellectually anyway, but somehow in the moment the reality of my new life sank in. As they continued to drink, I was increasingly sobered by that reality.

For me and the rest of the new guys, waiting for our platoon assignments was its own form of purgatory. We were there but not quite, not until we got to our platoons and our respective squads. Since we didn't "belong" to anyone yet, we were fair game. Anyone who outranked us—which was basically everyone at battalion—could order us to do whatever they thought might provide the most entertainment. Usually that meant thirty push-ups, with feet elevated on a curb or a chair. I did close to three hundred push-ups some days, very few of my own volition. Other times it meant running and climbing training ropes. All of it was part of the initiation, the more experienced guys "sharing" their experience with us. Inflicting a measure of pain was part of welcoming us to the family.

After nearly a week of this, the battalion finally returned from what was a short but harsh winter deployment to Afghanistan. A couple of days later, the five of us assigned to Alpha Company were told to report to the first sergeant's office to get our platoon assignments. We waited tensely at parade rest at the end of the company headquarters hallway just outside the first sergeant's open door. The place was like Grand Central Station. Everyone was scurrying to finish paperwork, turn in weapons, and account for sensitive equipment so they could get out of there and start a well-deserved long weekend. None of these guys would have an ounce of patience for a bunch of newbies waiting to find a home. I avoided eye contact at all costs and tried to melt into the wall as they rushed back and forth.

Perpendicular to the first sergeant's office was the charge of quarters station, a space cut into the wall similar to a receptionist's window. Sitting at the desk was one of the most physically imposing soldiers I had ever seen. Being a Ranger requires both strength and the ability to endure long periods of intense aerobic stress. As a result, most Rangers looked more like me—five feet nine inches and 185 pounds, muscular but not big, built more for soccer than for football. This guy, however, had to have been over two hundred pounds of pure muscle. The badges on his uniform indicated he had already been to combat. With his square jaw and dark brow furrowed as he read a book, this guy looked just plain mean.

I hoped he wouldn't look up at us. He clearly had nothing else to do but read, and I'd rather not navigate another conversation that had the possibility of turning into a smoke session.

While still trying to avoid eye contact with everyone in the vicinity, I couldn't help but sneak a closer look at this guy. I was surprised to see on the desk in front of him a copy of the global weekly news magazine *The Economist*—I had read this in business school, and it hardly qualifies as typical Ranger literature. But I nearly chuckled in surprised confusion when I scanned the title of the book in his hands: *Tuesdays with Morrie*, the poignant story of a dying professor and the life lessons he passes on to a former student, a book described by reviewers as "sweet," "moving," and "nourishing." Hardly Ranger reading material.

The Ranger glanced up and caught me observing him. Without hesitation he pushed back his chair and stood.

Great, I thought. *Here we go.*

But he surprised me again. A smile broke out on his face. Then he extended his hand. I was highly suspicious, but I took his hand and shook it, instantly enveloped in his firm and friendly grip.

"Hey, I'm Pat," he said. "Welcome! You guys did so good getting here! Congratulations on making it!" I noticed the name "Tillman" stitched on his uniform. It rang a bell, but I couldn't recall from where.

Pat shook hands with the rest of the new guys. I was flabbergasted. And he wasn't finished. "Do you have your platoon assignments?" he asked.

"Not yet," I said. "That's why we're here, waiting for the first sergeant to tell us where to go."

At that moment, another Ranger, slightly smaller than Pat but with strikingly similar features, appeared in the stairwell next to us. "Hey, Kev!" Pat called. "These guys are new to the company, and they're waiting to get their platoon assignments. Can you help me get them squared away?"

"Sure!" he replied. It was as if we had just stumbled into their living room and our new hosts wanted us to be both welcomed and comfortable. It was beyond weird.

"How you fellas doin'? Puttin' up with the bulls— okay?" Kev asked.

There wasn't time to reply, but I noticed the same name, "Tillman," on Kev's uniform as well.

He and Pat quickly disappeared into the first sergeant's office and were informed that Boatright and I were to be assigned to Second Platoon, known as the Black Sheep, which was also the platoon of our new friends, Pat and Kev (whose full name I correctly guessed was Kevin). Soon Kevin was leading Boatright and me upstairs to the Second Platoon sergeant's office.

Only later did I realize why the pair seemed familiar. Pat Tillman was the twenty-seven-year-old NFL star who had walked away from a multimillion-dollar contract to join the Rangers in 2002. Kevin was his twenty-five-year-old brother, a former minor league baseball player who enlisted at the same time as Pat. I hadn't watched Pat play—I liked football but didn't have cable at ORU—and I hadn't followed his life closely, but I'd heard the story. Their willingness to serve was admirable, and they sure seemed like good guys.

Kevin took us as far as he could—the hallway outside Sergeant Eric Godec's office.

"You're on your own, boys," he said with a grin and a wink. "Glad you're here."

"Thanks, Specialist," Boatright and I replied in unison and somewhat robotically.

We found ourselves standing again at parade rest, this time waiting for our squad assignments.

After fifteen minutes or so, two men emerged from the office. The first was Sergeant Godec, the Black Sheep platoon sergeant. His salt-and-pepper hair and weathered face seemed strangely aged when paired with his trim, athletic frame.

The second, a slightly shorter and no less fit Ranger, was my new squad leader, Staff Sergeant Jonathan Owens. His brownish blond hair was cropped neatly into the prescribed high and tight, the regimental standard at the time. His dark brown eyes looked at me with angry suspicion as his boss, Sergeant Godec, made the introduction.

"Elliott, you're heading to weapons squad," Godec said. "You'll be one of the maggots. Sergeant Owens here is the weapons squad leader and also from Kansas, which is why I thought you two might get along." Godec acted as though all us Kansas folk already knew one another. Owens seemed less thrilled with our shared geography.

Owens looked me up and down, his attitude much more similar to my RIP cadre's than to that of our Alpha Company concierges, Pat and Kevin. His lower lip bulged with chewing tobacco. He raised a soda can to his lips and spat.

"Follow me," he said flatly, moving down the hall at a fast clip and not looking back. We turned a corner and passed the heart of Second Platoon. I saw Clyde, our taxidermy black sheep who hung on the wall.

I passed by a large glass case containing all manner of memorabilia. Pictures and mementos from the platoon's exploits in Panama,

Grenada, Iraq, and Afghanistan. Memorials to those who had served with the Black Sheep and offered the ultimate sacrifice.

This is my home now, I told myself. *This is my home.*

I followed Owens into a room at the very end of the Second Platoon area of operations (AO), past a large black, white, and red mural painted on the otherwise plain white wall with the word "Maggots" writ large.

Owens pointed to a chair and said, "Sit," as he himself took a seat. We were in a barracks room.

"You will sit at the rigid position of attention," he commanded with irritation.

I almost laughed at how odd that sounded but managed to keep a straight face. *How do I sit at the position of attention?* I wondered. I just sat up straight and tried my best to show him I was uncomfortable, since I thought that's what he was going for.

"Where in Kansas are you from?"

"Hays, Sarn't. Out west on I-70."

"Hays?" he said with mild disdain. "That's way the f— out there. I'm from Shawnee Mission," he said, shaking his head and chuckling. "Hays, huh?"

"Roger, Sarn't."

Clearly our Kansas connection meant little. He was from eastern Kansas right next to Kansas City, which, not to split hairs, is a world away from the sparsely populated western plains of Hays.

"You know what the maggots are, Elliott?"

"Roger, Sarn't. They're the machine gun teams. That's where the acronyms come from: MGT."

"Yeah, but what do they do?"

"Support by fire, Sarn't. Line squads assault an objective, and the maggots suppress the objective to support the assault."

He seemed satisfied with the answer and continued his inquisition.

"Do you know how the squad and gun teams are set up?"

"No, not really, Sarn't."

"All right. Here's the deal. There's three guns in the squad, three 240B belt-feed machine guns. Each gun has a gunner and an assistant gunner at minimum. If we have more than six guys, then some guns might have an ammo bearer. The gunner is in charge of the gun team and operates the gun. The AG reports to the gunner, carries ammo for the gun, and spots targets. The AG's job is to make sure that weapon is well fed with rounds and that the gunner has targets to engage. You're going to be an AG working with Specialist Ashpole. Think you can handle that?"

"Roger, Sarn't," I said.

"Yeah, we'll see," he said, spitting in his Pepsi can again.

"You'll live next door. That's also the squad room, so beginning at work call and until close of business, it's where we conduct our squad business, so make sure it's cleaned up. I'll go get Ashpole, and you guys can start training together on the gun until we're done here today."

"Roger, Sarn't."

"I don't give a s— what you do when you're not working, but when you're here, you're training. Do you understand?"

"Roger, Sarn't."

"All right. Find an open bunk and wall locker next door. Unless otherwise instructed, you're to be reading the Ranger Handbook. Is that clear?"

"Roger, Sarn't," I said, continuing to sit uncomfortably.

"Well, get the f— outta here," he said.

I hopped up, grabbed my bags, and went next door. The squad room was divided in two sections separated by a long, green couch that was no less than forty years old and formed the "living room" complete with a TV. To the right of the door were two sets of bunks separated by large wardrobes or wall lockers. I threw my stuff in an empty one and sat on the couch, Ranger Handbook in hand.

I began to study "Battle Drill 1A: Squad Attack" when I was interrupted.

A dark-haired, uniformed stranger came into the room. He was wearing the all-black Ranger PT uniform—black running shorts and black T-shirt, with the Second Battalion scroll diminutively placed on each garment. Given his uniform, I couldn't tell who he was or his rank. As such, I immediately dropped my book and stood at parade rest just to be safe. I assumed it was Ashpole and we were going to get to work.

"Who are you?" he fired off.

"Elliott, Sergeant," I said. "I'm a maggot and new to the squad."

"I'm not a sergeant. You'll call me Specialist. What the f— you doin' in here?"

"Well, I'm a maggot, Specialist, and this is our squad room."

"No s—. I'm not talkin' about that. Didn't they tell you? The newest maggot is responsible for volcano watch, so get out there."

"I'm sorry, Specialist. No one told me about that. What is it?"

"Don't play dumb with me, Elliott! You get out on the deck outside the company bar, and you stand at parade rest facing Mount Rainier! You're our first line of defense if that mountain blows!"

I tried to take him seriously, but I couldn't bring myself to immediately comply.

"Volcano watch, Specialist?" I asked skeptically. *That can't possibly be a thing,* I thought.

He took a long step closer, his face a few inches from mine. "You deaf? Get your a— out there!"

"Roger, Specialist." I bolted out of the room, down the hall, through the company bar, which was just a few feet from my room, and out onto the flat roof that served as an unofficial deck. It was late on that December afternoon and was nearly dark. Mount Rainier was nowhere in sight given the clouds that provided a steady drizzle, so I oriented myself as best I could and stood at parade rest, staring off into the distance for any sign of volcanic activity.

This is ridiculous, I thought. *Do I leave and disobey this guy's order? Will I get points for going back inside?* Stay or go, it felt like I couldn't win.

After twenty minutes or so, I heard Sergeant Owens's familiar voice. The warmth of his words was a welcome relief to the cold, wet, winter darkness.

"Hey dumba—, get in here!" he barked.

I happily and sheepishly complied.

I was home.

Second Platoon was my new family but more specifically the weapons squad, of which Owens was the leader. Most of our training would happen at the squad level. Also part of weapons squad was Kevin Tillman. He was one of the M240B gunners along with Ashpole (my gunner) and Jean Claude Suhl. They were the senior guys in the squad and reported directly to Owens.

I met the squad that afternoon while I was drying off from volcano watch. As I followed Owens back inside and entered the squad room, I quickly realized that the guy who sent me outside was not present, which meant he was just some random Ranger in the platoon who wanted to mess with me.

A lanky, dark-haired guy with an easy smile stood up and shook my hand. "I'm Ashpole," he said. "We'll be working together. What the h— were you doing out there?"

"Someone told me I had volcano watch, Specialist."

He shook his head and laughed. "Look, that was Specialist Tafoya from first squad. He used to be in weapons squad and likes messing with the new guys. You don't have to listen to him or anyone else. You take orders from us, you understand? Nobody else can f— with you now. If they do, you tell us."

"Roger, Specialist."

"Work call tomorrow will be 0600. Uniform is PTs, and we'll form up as a company downstairs. We've still got work to do, so go easy if you're gonna party. We'll be doing a five-mile squad run in the morning, so if you can't keep up, there will be no mercy," he said, his intensity rising as he made his point. He had a difficult task: maintaining focus and discipline after these guys had just been to war and right before they'd have some time off.

"All right. We're done. Get outta here."

The rest of the guys introduced themselves. In addition to Kevin, Ashpole, and Suhl, there was Ping (who worked with Suhl), Bailey (who worked with Kevin), and finally my roommates, McCoy and Schrader.

As guys scattered, Owens called me into the hall for a quick chat before going home.

"Listen, Schrader is getting RFSd. He can't pass his PT test to go to Ranger School. He's failed it three times. Do not hang out with him, you understand me? He can't meet the standard. You are not to associate with him. Is that clear?"

"Roger, Sarn't." It was clear that my place in the family had always been and would always be conditional on my performance and strict adherence to the cultural norms. The thought of getting RFSd, which simply meant "released for standards," was horrifying after going through all I had put up with to get here. Being at regiment was a privilege and not a right. They could kick you out for anything. There was no trial. No appeal. If they didn't like you, they'd RFS you, and you'd go on to be an airborne infantryman in the big army.

In Schrader's case, he couldn't pass the PT test for Ranger School, which meant he had no future at regiment. Ranger School was the next step in the process, one that everyone had to complete in order to solidify their career in the regiment. It was a two-month leadership course back at Fort Benning. To be clear, we were all Rangers by virtue of completing RIP. But a Ranger could only hold a leadership position in the regiment by completing Ranger School and earning the coveted black-and-gold Ranger tab that would accompany the black, red, and white Ranger scroll on the uniform.

Schrader's presence and Sergeant Owens's instructions were a clear indicator of how temporal this all was, how truly fragile our place in this family could be.

With those final instructions given, I was on my own for the evening, left to settle into my new abode with my new roommates. Schrader was gone before I had the chance to avoid him.

McCoy was in the room, hip-hop music blasting. He, too, had yet to earn his Ranger tab, making us both "privates" in regimental shorthand. He had a slot in Ranger School, however, and would be heading there in the next month or so.

Before coming to regiment, McCoy was part of the Old Guard, the unit in Washington, DC, responsible for guarding the Tomb of the Unknown Soldier and performing all manner of highly skilled ceremonial functions. He was a lean six feet and Korean American, born and raised in Baltimore.

"Hey, Steve, it's great to have you here!" he said. "Don't let Owens get to you. He was my squad leader in Iraq. He knows his s—. This is our room when it's not duty hours. We might party in here a little tonight. Is that okay? If it's not, just tell me."

"Sure, whatever. Thanks, man. I might hang around for a while and then go out."

It didn't take long for the party to get started. Within an hour, drunks began wandering in and out of our room, which was directly adjacent to the company bar. Somehow Metallica was always playing from somewhere. I wanted to meet the people with whom I'd be going to war but found myself out of step. As Dorothy Gale once said, "We're not in Kansas anymore."

"What do you like to do, Steve?" McCoy asked as he chugged a beer and we sat on the couch, watching *Family Guy*.

"I like to read," I said lamely.

"No s—, that's awesome," McCoy said. "You like music? I prefer hip-hop mostly. Is that okay with you? I hate this place sometimes. It can really get to you. I do art to relax. You can check out my work if you want," he said somewhat manically as he pointed to a large black three-ring binder next to the couch.

Taking his cue, I opened it and thumbed through page after page of colorfully crafted, miniaturized graffiti tags, words and images you'd expect to see on a warehouse wall or train car. McCoy was a gifted artist. Next to the binder was a duffel bag.

"That's full of spray paint," McCoy said with a smile. "My work can't stay contained on the page. I have to share it with the world." He laughed. "I'll head out later tonight to do some tagging in downtown Tacoma. I'll try to be quiet when I come back."

"Cool," I said, not entirely sure how to respond.

We continued to chat, and as guys from around the company stumbled into our room, McCoy was quick to offer an introduction, clearly wanting me to feel at home. I wanted to ask him about their deployment, what it was like and all, but I was held back by not wanting to seem too eager and not knowing how he and the other guys felt about it.

Before long, I found out more than I wanted to. A guy from First Platoon staggered in, a good friend of McCoy's who had gone to basic with him. He was hammered. He managed to plop down on our couch.

"Hey, man! Good to meet you, good to meet you!" he said with inebriated eagerness, which quickly turned to anger.

"F—ing IED! Moving in the daylight. We all knew it was bulls—, and the battalion commander had us moving in the daylight anyway. Blew out that truck. Jay was in pieces. Blown to pieces," he said as his breathing quickened and jaw muscles flexed. He chugged what was left of his beer, got up, and left.

"Sorry about that, Steve," McCoy said, still fairly sober, but the alcohol was beginning to lower inhibitions and loosen his tongue. "He's having a hard time. He was really close to Jay."

"Who?" I asked, somewhat ashamed I didn't know who he was talking about.

"Oh man, yeah, you probably don't know. Jay Blessing got killed over there. Last month. He was the arms room NCO and a super good dude. Our convoy got hit with an IED while we were moving in the daytime, which was stupid. He's the first guy to die at Second Batt since 9/11."

"Wow. That sucks. I'm sorry."

"Yeah, f—in' war, right?"

"Yeah, f—in' war," I said, having no idea what I was talking about but knowing that's what I was supposed to say.

★

I passed the weekend thankful I had a car and spent as little time as I could at the barracks. I went to church in Tacoma on Sunday, a megachurch that the woman who sewed new patches on my uniforms invited me to attend. When I returned to base on Sunday afternoon, I found guys attempting to recover from forty-eight hours of straight partying. Some had even self-administered saline drip IVs to speed the process. Work hard, play hard was putting it mildly.

Monday morning, Sergeant Owens flicked on our lights and greeted us with a "get up, f—ers," thus announcing our work week had begun. After a grueling run and a series of rope climbs, we grabbed a hearty breakfast at the chow hall and went back to the barracks to train on the 240 and prep for the week's training cycle.

A typical week in garrison for a Ranger company began at 6 a.m. with squad PT. PT could consist of running, ruck marches, or jujitsu training. We would often hit the weight room in the afternoon, then prepare for the week's field exercise. Tuesday, Wednesday, and Thursday might involve training to assault an objective or to practice clearing rooms. For an assault, my role as a maggot was to provide overwatch and support by fire, which simply meant firing on the objective while the other squads bounded up to it and ultimately assaulted it. We performed each training iteration no less than four times: once in daylight with blank rounds; once in daylight with live rounds; once at night, using night vision and blank rounds; and the ultimate test, at night with night vision, using live rounds. Friday was usually our easiest day. We might go to the range to zero (align) our weapons, fire a few rounds, and mostly recover ourselves and our equipment from the week's activities.

A constant in all of the training was shooting. Every training event included firing large numbers of rounds, most of this on the 240, as we were weapons squad, but the AGs (myself included) also carried an M4 carbine and an M9 Beretta pistol, which meant we had to be proficient with all three weapons systems. When I first arrived at battalion, the thought of being able to fire thousands of rounds through these weapons sounded like fun. It quickly turned into work. As a gun team, Ashpole and I could easily go through five thousand rounds over the course of a training exercise or day at the range, all of them fired at human silhouette pop-up targets. Constantly seeing a target, orienting the gun, engaging with a burst of three to five rounds, and repeating the cycle over and over and over again. It was exhausting. The fun would wear off as we muscled the 27.6-pound machine gun, having to apply consistent pressure to keep the gun steady and accurate.

As the first full training week came to a close, I was waiting in the squad room for the rest of the guys and Sergeant Owens's end-of-week briefing.

"Elliott, get the rest of the squad. Let's get this over with," Owens said.

I went to get the other guys and found Kevin next door. He was still in uniform, sitting on a couch, legs crossed at the ankles, reading Plato's *Republic*.

"Hey," I said. "Sergeant Owens wants us."

"Right, okay." Kevin tossed the book aside and stood.

I couldn't help myself. "What are you reading?"

"Aw, it's just this bulls—," he said, pointing to the book. It's clear he wasn't knocking one of the great works of Western literature; it was his way of saying that, even though he was reading one of the greatest philosophical and political treatises of all time, that didn't make him better than anyone else. He didn't want to be seen as some snobby intellectual. He was a real twenty-first-century person who just happened to be reading Plato.

"You read that kind of stuff often?" I asked.

"Well, I kind of like it. I studied philosophy in school. I read different stuff."

I was intrigued. I could sit and fire off questions for hours, hungry for bookish conversation that didn't involve work.

"That's great," I said. "What else are you reading?"

"Larry McMurtry. Western stuff."

"The guy who wrote *Lonesome Dove*? I love his books."

Owens bellowed for us from down the hall, cutting our talk short.

Kevin and I ran out of the room, but I was looking forward to more conversations with him.

Kevin, Pat, and I were the only ones in the platoon besides the PL with bachelor's degrees, which created a strange dynamic at times, having a civilian diploma that qualified all of us to be officers yet serving under NCOs who had less education but all the power. I followed the Tillmans' lead, quickly realizing that my education meant nothing here and could in fact be intimidating to some. Most guys who had joined the Rangers had little else in the way of civilian experience. For people like Owens and Ashpole and the like, battalion was their first taste of adult life, the place where they "grew up." Some were pursuing a dream to serve in special operations; others were fleeing broken families and broken lives. Everyone was committed to the unit, and as such who you were before you joined didn't really matter. For a lot of guys, that clean slate was a gift.

Pat of course had the most well-known pre-army life of all of us, although I never heard him speak a word of it. He had attended Arizona State on a football scholarship and was named Pac-10 Defensive Player of the Year as a linebacker in 1997. He was also the rare student athlete who excelled academically. He earned a marketing degree in three and a half years, graduating with a 3.84 GPA. Pat won a number of college academic honors, including the Honda Scholar-Athlete of the Year award in 1997. He then gained national fame playing in the NFL for the Arizona Cardinals.

Pat was in a different squad in Second Platoon, where my friend Boatright was assigned. I didn't see Pat all that much, but he often wandered down the maggot hallway looking for Kevin, as they both lived in the same house off-post along with Pat's wife, Marie.

Rain or shine, Pat was wearing flip-flops along with his jeans and T-shirt, more appropriately dressed for the beach than a western Washington winter. One day I heard the flip-flopping of his footwear as he entered the maggot squad room. I was changing after the workday, and Pat was looking for Kevin so they could head home.

"Hey, Steve, how's it goin'?" he asked. When sergeants weren't around, I was always "Steve" to Pat. "Is Kevin here?"

"I think he's next door getting changed. We just got off work a couple minutes ago," I said.

"Cool. How are you doin'? How are things goin' for you?"

"I'm surviving," I said.

"Well, it's f—in' great that you're here. Kevin mentioned you went to school—where'd you go?"

"Oral Roberts. I studied business there."

"Oh, that's awesome! I'd love to hear more about that."

Pat and I chatted for a few more minutes until Kevin showed up. His interest in our conversation was clearly genuine. It didn't feel as though he was using me to kill time. Pat and Kevin helped make this strange place feel a bit more familiar. A bit more like home.

The third member of the Tillman household was Pat's wife, Marie. I didn't know her story at the time, but Pat and Marie met while on competing soccer teams in California. They were each four years old. Their first date wasn't until they were high school seniors, and they quickly became a couple and had been together ever since. They were married on May 4, 2002.

When I met Marie, it was a year and a half after their wedding at an ugly sweater Christmas party. I didn't think Rangers had Christmas parties, and hanging out with superiors was the last thing I wanted to do on a Friday night. McCoy wasn't jazzed about the idea either, but he told me we had to go, at least for a while. I borrowed a knitted puke-green sweater for the occasion.

When we arrived, folks were polite, but no one went out of their way to welcome me. Then I spotted Pat, Kevin, and an attractive blonde woman sitting at the dining room table surrounded by a few other folks. They were laughing and clearly having a great time. When Pat saw me, he called out, "Hey, Elliott!" Several folks in the room, Sergeant Owens included, outranked me, so I was Elliott this time. "I want you to meet Marie."

He and Marie stood. They were wearing two of the most garish holiday sweaters I had ever seen. Kevin's was even worse. They were really going for it.

Pat introduced me, telling Marie I went to college and studied business. "Well, welcome," she said to me with a sincere smile. "It's good to meet you."

While Pat turned back to his prior conversation, Marie and I chatted about our backgrounds.

"How do you like living in Washington?" I asked.

"We like it a lot. We have a great place overlooking the Puget Sound in Tacoma. It's really beautiful but, being from California, the rain takes some getting used to." We laughed.

There was nothing profound about our brief exchange, but it was refreshing to have a "normal" conversation outside the bounds of Ranger life, especially with people who were down to earth.

Second Battalion began to feel a lot more like home when Evan showed up. Having made it through RIP, he not only managed to get assigned to Second Batt but also to A Co. He became a member of First Platoon, and his room was right down the hall from mine. Soon he and I were spending most of our off-duty time together, swapping stories as we continued our journey.

By March of 2004, Evan and I had been frequenting the church in Tacoma I'd been going to before he arrived. We quickly connected with folks in the young adult group and were only too happy to find some community outside the bounds of the regiment. Were it not for the social element of that church, I'm not sure I would have continued going, as I felt little connection to the leadership of the congregation or the culture. All that mattered was that I was meeting people, and those people were civilians offering a welcome reprieve from the intensity of the regiment.

One Friday night in early March, Evan, Boatright, and I went to a gathering at Mike's apartment. Mike was part of the young adult crowd, and we became fast friends. Evan and I found ourselves increasingly distant from the Christian culture we had previously been so accustomed to, but the young adults at the church were good folks and we had fun hanging out. Boatright would often tag along. He couldn't care less about church, which was fine; he just didn't want to be stuck on post, and since I had a car, he'd come along whenever he could. He was becoming a good friend.

On this particular Friday night, a new character came on the stage, one who would change my life in ways I could scarcely imagine. That night I met a girl named Brook.

I would later come to learn that this was a difficult time for her. She was a single mom of a two-year-old daughter, Gracie. She had moved back in with her folks a year prior after splitting up with Gracie's dad. That move took her from hip Seattle to suburban Puyallup and away from many of her friends and her community. She was going to community college and working at the YMCA as she worked to establish herself and her future.

She wasn't dating anyone and was actually praying regularly for God to bring her the person she was supposed to be with. She didn't want to waste time, and as a full-time student and full-time mom, she had very little time to waste. Brook, like me, was looking for community and for the time being found that with this group, which Evan, Josey, and I were now part of.

Brook was sitting quietly on the couch when we entered Mike's apartment. Mike introduced us to everyone, and I found myself politely shaking her slender hand while she looked at me with blue eyes framed by straight red hair. Betraying nothing beyond polite directness, she said simply, "Hi, I'm Brook," to which I profoundly replied, "Hi, I'm Steve." A new journey began as our handshake ended.

The journey began inauspiciously enough as we all played a game called Mafia. Mafia is essentially a game where a member of the group is "killed" and everyone else is trying to figure out who the killer is. Brook was the victim, which meant she didn't really have anything to do but watch everyone else play. She was visibly annoyed. I was the cop, charged with finding the guilty party. For the next forty-five minutes I conducted my investigation while the victim watched, arms crossed, in silent, agitated boredom. The killer was found, the game ended, and we left soon afterward.

The whole evening was kind of awkward. To the rest of the group, Evan, Josey, and I were like creatures from another planet. Everyone was super nice but there was a gap somehow. We didn't quite fit in with this crowd, and they didn't know quite how to treat us. It was nice but weird.

I had no interest in dating. I was open to meeting someone but had no sense that now was the time to meet my soul mate. Yet I do remember wanting to get to know Brook. She exuded a quiet albeit annoyed confidence that, to me, was uncommon. She looked like a slightly angry version of Kirsten Dunst from the Spiderman movies. A quiet conversation with her would have been nice, but my mind was largely elsewhere.

A few days after I met Brook at the party, our squad had just finished our morning PT when we were told to report to the company
formation area outside. After the rest of Alpha Company was formed
up, we marched down Division Street to a movie theater that must
have been fifty years old if it was a day. We crowded into rows of
creaky wooden chairs and faced the stage. The whole battalion was
there, all five hundred of us.

I wonder what's up, I thought.

My question was soon answered as a major in BDUs walked on
stage. The blank white screen behind him came to life with the words
"Operation Mountain Storm" in plain black text. This major was a
battalion intelligence officer, and judging by the PowerPoint slide, we
were about to be briefed.

The raucous audience eventually quieted down, and the major
got to the point.

"Men, you're going back to war," he said, knowing the effect that
statement would produce.

The crowd erupted.

He continued, obviously pleased with the energy that had been
unleashed. "You'll be part of Operation Mountain Storm on the
Afghanistan/Pakistan border. This will be a spring surge to counter
Taliban activity. Your mission"—he paused for effect—"is to kill or
capture UBL."

The cheering erupted again. UBL was the military acronym for
public enemy number one, Osama bin Laden.

Finally! I thought. *This is why I'm here. This is why I joined. It's
happening.*

The presentation continued. We would operate on the border
with Pakistan in Khost Province to disrupt the Haqqani network,
the insurgent force aligned with al-Qaeda and bin Laden. There was
more information about overarching objectives, but we weren't paying much attention. He had us at "kill or capture." We were going to
war. My adrenaline surged at the thought. Sergeant Blessing came to
mind, and that adrenaline was tempered with fear. I hadn't come this

far to fail. I hadn't come this far to not do my job. I certainly hadn't come this far to die, as if that were up to me.

A week later I was offered the chance to take my Ranger School PT test. Sergeant Owens felt I was ready and wanted to get me to Ranger School to "get my s—" (my Ranger tab) as soon as possible. I was nervous and relieved. Honestly, I felt sick at the thought of having to go back to Benning for one of the worst courses the military had to offer but excited that my career was progressing more quickly than planned and that I'd have a chance to get my Ranger tab and cement my place in the community. Since arriving at Second Batt, I kept an actual Ranger tab in my wallet, a reminder of the next task to be completed.

I maxed the test and was offered a slot in the next Ranger School class. There was one problem: if I went to Ranger School now, I wouldn't go on deployment. I'd get my Ranger tab, proving I was qualified to be a leader in regiment before actually serving in combat. That didn't sit well with me.

Sergeant Owens helped talk me through it. His demeanor toward me had softened somewhat as I had proved myself over the last few months.

"It's up to you, Elliott," he said. "You can go get your s— or go on deployment, but right now you can't do both."

"Sarn't, Ranger School isn't going anywhere," I replied. "I've been training to go with the squad, and that's what I need to do. I'm going with you guys. I'll get my tab later."

It was a little funny how pleased Owens was with the answer. It felt great to have the option, and it felt even better to have chosen deployment over school. I couldn't stand the thought of letting Owens, Ashpole, and the rest of the squad down. I was going to Afghanistan.

Ten days later, at roughly 2100 hours on April 5, I was in the squad room with the rest of the guys, getting ready to deploy. In a few minutes we'd haul our weapons and gear onto buses for the short ride to the McChord Air Force Base flight line and catch a cargo plane to Afghanistan. We wore our desert camo BDUs for the first time, a dead giveaway that we weren't headed to the woods of Fort Lewis for a routine training cycle. We all just wanted to go, but the military axiom of "hurry up and wait" was in full effect. We were actually supposed to leave a couple of hours earlier but were delayed for some reason that no one bothered to explain. I had nowhere to go, so I just waited in the squad room with my new roommate, Marc Denton. McCoy was in Ranger School and Marc had just arrived. Marc was a sharp-witted New Englander from Rhode Island. He was only eighteen, but you could see the makings of a good Ranger. We counted the minutes until our departure, hoping no other delays would drag it out.

Others had left post to get the most out of their final hours in the States. Pat and Kevin were part of that group and had just returned. Kevin plopped down in the squad room, a to-go coffee cup in hand. I could hear Pat out in the hallway with Marie.

Marie poked her head in. "Hi, guys," she said with a warm smile. "Good luck and be careful, okay?"

"Thanks!" Marc and I replied.

Kevin just offered a half smile as she looked at him and then turned away to say her final good-byes to Pat.

I wondered what Mom was doing right at that moment. What Grandma and Grandpa were doing. Part of me wanted desperately to call them. I worked to kill the thought, to kill the emotion that longed for a few simple words with the ones who knew and loved me best. I couldn't allow such sentimentality a place in my mind. I wasn't strong enough for that.

Finally, and thankfully, the order came to load up. We happily complied and were a strange sight, armed to the teeth and loading school buses. After a short ride in the dark, we arrived at the flight line and piled into a large, open hangar. The smell of jet fuel filled the air. We waited a few minutes and then began filing across the tarmac to the open jaws of a Boeing C-17, one of the largest transport planes in the world. The night was black but thankfully dry.

We're going. We're actually going, I thought.

The interior of the plane was outfitted with four parallel rows of orange cargo-net seating. The rows in the middle had their backs to each other, and each faced a row of seats along the skin of the aircraft. I grabbed a seat in one of the middle rows near the center of the plane, between Sergeant Owens and Denton. Pat and Kevin sat in the row facing us. The flight crew began passing out earplugs and Ambien, which was the closest to in-flight service we'd get on this transcontinental journey.

I glanced at Pat, Kevin, and some of the other more seasoned guys in the platoon, seeking to gauge their reaction to this moment and respond accordingly. They all looked far more relaxed than I felt. There was very little chatter. A couple of guys had taken their Ambien already and were playing a game to see who could stay awake the longest, but most everyone was quiet. It was difficult to hear with the engines blaring, and conversation took extra effort.

I stared out the back of the aircraft onto the open ramp I had just walked up, wondering what the world would look like on the other side. Suddenly, the ramp began to close, sealing us tightly in the large metal tube. With the metallic assurance that the plane was secure, I felt my heart grow slightly colder. There was no going back now. On the path between where I sat and the safety of home was war. I felt the chill of death, though at the time I didn't know its name.

This is what I wanted. To be here in this place that was the "tip of the spear." Fear turned to doubt and doubt to a cold determination.

I'll do my job and I'll come home, I thought. *We all will.*

As the aircraft sped down the runway and began to lift, my heart sank lower as I considered the work that lay ahead.

I leaned in to the cold void and focused on the task ahead. I was preparing for war. I was preparing to kill.

4

WAR

Never think that war, no matter how necessary,
nor how justified, is not a crime.
ERNEST HEMINGWAY

After nearly twenty hours of flight time, not including a stop in Germany, we arrived at Bagram, the massive installation thirty-seven miles north of Kabul that served as the chief base of operations for the United States and its allies in Afghanistan. Guys were waking up, chatting, cracking jokes, and just happy to know we'd be off the plane soon. There were no "fasten seat belt" signs, no warm introductions from the pilot regarding the weather at our destination. No tray tables to close, no seats to return to their full upright and locked positions. No warning of any kind. We just started dropping like a rock.

Initially, the rapidity of our descent caused concern of some aircraft malfunction. Owens, almost reading my mind, was quick to reassure me, leaning over and motioning for me to take out my ear protection. "They corkscrew the plane down to the airstrip," he yelled. "Makes it harder for hajji to take a shot at us."

Comforted that this was a "normal" descent, I focused every ounce of energy on not throwing up. Airsickness seemed decidedly un-Ranger-like, and I shuddered at the thought of being the "vomit guy" as we rode into war. I was clearly not alone. Virtually every face I spotted in our platoon had turned some shade of green. Before long we felt the wheels of the C-17 scrape the runway, and the world thankfully ceased to spin as we were jolted back to earth.

After taxiing for a few moments, the plane came to a stop, and the sound of hydraulic arms loosening their grip on the ramp was accompanied by the bright light of an Afghan day.

"Second Platoon, get your s— on and get outta here!" Sergeant Godec yelled above the still persistent whine of jet engines. We were already dressed for combat; the only thing missing was ammunition. Wearing my full battle kit, my M9 pistol holstered on my right thigh, and my M4 slung over my chest, I threw on my ruck and shouldered my large green duffel bag. As I ferried my load down the long silver ramp, I felt the heat of the sun's rays strike me. The intensity of a blue sky set the backdrop for a jagged and menacing mountain range. The Hindu Kush. The towering peaks reached twenty-five thousand feet at their highest point and dominated the otherwise barren horizon. These mountains seemed somehow defiant, daring us to come to them. My aunt Susan would sometimes joke that "if you've seen one mountain, you've seen 'em all." As I gazed at these snow-peaked crags, I found myself differing from that assessment. I'd never seen anything like the Hindu Kush.

Bagram was a zoo. It was home to several thousand US troops, international forces, and private contractors. Although a few permanent structures dotted the airfield on the edge of the installation, most of the landscape was dominated by tents and row after row of makeshift concrete bunkers and plywood huts. We loaded onto what appeared to be old city buses and were taken from the airfield to our home for the next week. Pat's squad leader, Staff Sergeant Matt Weeks, stared out the window in awe. He had deployed here early in the war and couldn't believe how it had changed. "Man, when I was here two years ago, Bagram was nothing more than two privates, taking a knee pulling security. Now look at all this!" One empire supplanted another. As our presence and infrastructure was being established, we were reminded of other world powers that had fared poorly in this region. Rusting carcasses of Soviet aircraft lined the runway, a reminder that whatever order was imposed today could easily be left to rot in the Afghan sun.

We finally arrived at our plywood huts, known affectionately as "hooches." Alpha Company would spend a week there, drawing ammo and prepping for our mission on the border. As a member of Second Platoon's weapons squad, my job was to work with Ashpole to draw the ammo we needed for our weapons, prep our kits, and ensure every weapon system was in full working order. These were monotonous days with the only breaks coming in the form of eating and working out. We broke bread three times a day at the Bagram chow hall and worked out twice a day, once before breakfast and once after lunch. Evan and a couple of other guys in the company were experimenting with and promoting a strange, new kind of workout called "CrossFit," but Owens wasn't having it. We'd run and hit the weights as we always had, forced however to listen to the one CD they had in the makeshift weight room adjacent to our hooch.

"I'm going to Wichita . . ." Jack White belted out on the first track of the album. I must have heard that song at least a dozen times in just a few days. No other music was available. It underscored the *Groundhog Day* feeling that accompanied deployment. No rhythm of home. No Saturday-morning joy as the weekend began. No Monday-morning dread as the workweek started. Each day exactly the same as the last.

After working out, Ashpole and I headed back to the hooch to go over our gear, weapons, and packing list yet again. We'd been issued our ammo, grenades, and flares. Our kits were now ready to go. I cleaned my weapons until my cleaning seemed to make them dirtier and experimented with ways to more effectively and less painfully carry the six full mags of M4 ammo and one thousand rounds of

240 ammo I was expected to have on my person. The 240 ammo alone weighed seventy-five pounds. The term "light infantry" that was used to describe the Rangers struck me as ridiculous in that moment.

"F—!" Ashpole exclaimed as he sat on his green folding cot, staring down the scope of the 240. "You're kidding me."

"What's up, Specialist?" I asked, happily distracted from considering the weight of my combat kit.

"This f—ing scope is fogging up all of a sudden. It's got moisture on the inside of the lens, and I can't see." Ashpole was rattled. Ultimately, he was responsible for the gun, and I could sense his fear for the responsibility he'd carry if every aspect of that weapon wasn't in full working order. Ashpole was both meticulous and lazy, but lazy in the most complimentary sense of the word. It seemed his singular goal in life was to "chill," and in order to achieve that goal, he worked hard and was one of the most efficient and prepared guys in the platoon.

"I gotta go see if I can get a replacement," he said. "That thing is useless."

Each 240 in the squad was fitted with a scope called an Elcan that offered a powerful level of magnification that enabled us to accurately engage targets up to a whole kilometer away in the daytime. All of our training with the gun had been with that sight. At nighttime, we'd rely on night vision and the infrared lasers affixed to the gun that, if properly zeroed, made us far more accurate at night than even with the best sight in the daytime. The concern now was for our daytime effectiveness. If we didn't have a scope, we'd be forced to rely on old-fashioned iron sights and have no magnification of the battlefield whatsoever.

"All right, Specialist. I'll be here."

As the afternoon wore on, I felt the intensity of the heat beginning to bake the west wall of the hooch. Ashpole crashed in through the door and plopped down on his cot, covered in sweat.

"I've been to every supply NCO I could find. Nothing. I talked to guys rotating out and begged them to let me use their scope. They wouldn't help."

Owens came in a moment later to check on us and quickly observed that all was not well.

"What's goin' on?" he said as his gaze sharpened.

"Our scope is fogged up on the inside, Sarn't," Ashpole said defeatedly. "I don't know how it happened. The gun didn't get dropped. I can't see through it, and I can't find a replacement."

Without a word, Owens began to examine the gun and the scope. Satisfied with the accuracy of Ashpole's assessment, he said, "Okay. I'll figure it out. Just hang tight." Our problem was his problem now. The rank on Owens's collar meant that it was his job to fix it, and if it wasn't fixed, it would be his blame to bear. He marched off, and you could see the tension in Ashpole's face dissolve. I felt sorry for the people who would have to deal with Sergeant Owens.

An hour or so later, right before dinner chow, the scene was repeated.

We could hear Owens cursing even before he entered the hooch. "Those supply room rats are worthless! How the f— do we deploy to Southwest Asia without so much as one extra Elcan in the whole battalion?!"

Ashpole and I took the hint and surmised that there would be no replacement scope.

Owens, having gotten that out of his system, apologized, clearly bearing the failure of not having appropriate optics for the gun. "I'm sorry, guys. You're just going to have to make do with iron sights."

"Elliott," he said, "please tell me the ACOG on your M4 is still working." The advanced combat optical gunsight was the type of scope affixed to my carbine and would be the only magnification we as a gun team would possess. "In the daytime, you're going to have to be that much more on it spotting targets for Ashpole. Beyond a couple hundred meters, you're going to be his eyes. You understand that?"

"Roger that, Sarn't," I replied.

At the time, it never occurred to me that Ashpole would only man the 240 if we were dismounted. If we were on vehicles, Ashpole would cover down on the much more powerful .50-caliber machine gun mounted in the vehicle's center turret, which meant that manning the sightless 240 would fall to me.

As that day came to a close, I happily crawled into my sleeping bag on my green cot. The hooch's bright fluorescent lights still burned brightly, but I was exhausted and couldn't wait to sleep. Some guys read, others messed around with their newly purchased iPods. As I lay down, I heard a familiar voice from a visitor.

"Hey, guys!" Pat called out as he came in the other side of the hooch. I looked over my shoulder and saw him plop down next to Kevin. Soon they were telling stories—some about their past deployment in Iraq but mostly about Ranger School, from which they had both recently graduated, earning them their black and gold Ranger tabs. Ranger School was always good for stories because you have men chronically deprived of food and sleep who, as a result, do strange things in their borderline delirium.

The stories were of little consequence, and I could tell that Pat and Kevin had shared them with each other before. That didn't seem to matter. They just wanted to be together, and Pat just needed to soak up the conversation and the laughs that accompanied it. I drifted to sleep, my back to them, listening to two brothers who found their home in the company of one another.

★

On April 13, as we were about to leave Bagram for our base of operations at Forward Operating Base (FOB) Salerno, Owens barged into the hooch from the back door.

"Elliott, Denton!" Owens yelled. This was an attempt to see what he'd find us doing if his arrival were sudden and unannounced. Denton and I were doing the right thing, prepping our gear and thus avoiding any wrath that might have otherwise befallen us.

"Roger, Sarn't!" we replied in unison, snapping to parade rest.

"Get out here!" Owens beckoned as he walked back outside. Both Denton and I wondered what was up, shooting each other a glance. We figured we'd screwed up and were going to get smoked. I racked my brain to think of anything I might have done wrong or left undone.

Denton and I stood next to each other at parade rest on the thick gravel that surrounded the hooch facing the afternoon sun. We wore our tan boots, black running shorts, and brown tucked-in T-shirts. Owens, dressed the same as us, was slightly backlit, the features of his face clear but somewhat shrouded as he spoke.

"Listen," he said, "I know we're going into the s—. You guys—you're squared away, okay? Just watch your team leaders, and you do what we do, you understand? You're gonna do good. You're gonna be fine," he said earnestly, betraying a knowledge of the danger we faced that was beyond our own and betraying a care for us that was all too often expressed through his incessantly demanding and abrasive leadership style. He was hard on us because he cared for us. The greatest affection he could show was doing all he could to prepare us for the harshness of our job.

Denton and I went from the fear of being smoked to the closest we'd ever come to a heart-to-heart with our squad leader. I wanted to put my hand on his shoulder and respond in kind, to tell him I understood and appreciated his leadership and his confidence in us. That sort of response, however, would have brought the smoke session we dreaded, so we simply replied, as always, "Roger, Sarn't."

"All right," Owens said. Relieved that this moment had passed and with his former swagger in full effect, he said, "Get the f— outta here," with the faintest of grins.

Just as the C-17 had spiraled down to the runway, we seemed to be spiraling closer to war—a war that was begun two and a half years earlier by President George W. Bush in response to the 9/11 attacks. Bush demanded that the Taliban turn over Osama bin Laden, believed to be the mastermind of 9/11 and founder of al-Qaeda, the Islamic extremist organization thought to be responsible for numerous terrorist acts around the world. The Taliban—Islamic fundamentalists who rejected anything tainted by Western influence—had taken power in Afghanistan in 1996 and had a close alliance with bin Laden and al-Qaeda. In October 2001, when the Taliban did not comply with the president's demand, the United States and its allies invaded Afghanistan.

Neither al-Qaeda nor the Taliban were as well armed as we were. Their primary weapons had been unchanged for years: Soviet-designed Kalashnikov, or AK-47, assault rifles; rocket-propelled grenade launchers (RPGs); mortars; and improvised explosive devices (IEDs) buried in roads and trails. They didn't possess night-vision optics and had no air support whatsoever. But many of them had fought in this country and these mountains for decades, possessing an innate understanding and command of the landscape. And they were ruthless—they had no qualms about using women or children as human shields.

I invested little energy in assessing our enemies' motivations. To me it was simple: they attacked our nation in a brutal fashion, and we were responding to that attack. My attitude was detached and cool in its animosity. The enemy was known as "hajji," the only moniker we would use. For Muslims, *hajji* is a term of respect for someone who has completed a pilgrimage to Mecca. For us, it was derogatory shorthand, similar to "gook" during the Vietnam War or "Jap" during World War II. They weren't humans; they were the enemy. They were "f—ing hajji," and we were there to kill them if we could.

★

Alpha Company, approximately 150 men, flew out of Bagram at about 0200 aboard CH-47 Chinook helicopters. I shuffled onto the outstretched ramp of the Chinook, fighting the rotor wash that whipped at me more harshly than any Kansas wind. A crew chief welcomed us energetically as we sat on the floor, knees tucked into our chests, happy to have some reprieve from hauling our full battle kits. In addition to my weapons and ammo as well as rounds for the gun, I hauled the 240's tripod and two extra barrels, another thirty pounds of dead weight. A famous and long-held joke among infantry machine gun teams comes in the form of a question: "What's the maximum effective range of the tripod?"

"As far as you can throw it" is the appropriate reply. I would have happily chucked that piece of steel rather than carry it on top of the rest of my kit.

As we sat in the red glow of the Chinook, Ashpole, seated in front of me, craned his neck sideways as far as he could and asked, "You okay?"

"Roger, Specialist. I'm good."

"Just so you know," he continued, "once we clear the airfield, the crew chief will test-fire the bird's weapons systems." Those systems included a 240 mounted on one side and a minigun, capable of releasing hundreds of rounds in just a couple of seconds, on the other. "We're not being engaged, so don't worry about it."

"Roger, Specialist," I yelled back and promptly forgot the warning.

The bird's already blaring engines somehow became even louder as we lifted off and began the hour-long commute to the FOB. I could see the black and blue-gray landscape through a circular window on the left. My mind was slowly lulled to a state of numb distraction by the rhythm of the rotors, themselves engaged in a war with gravity to keep us airborne.

Suddenly, a 240 cackled to life behind me.

I glanced back to see the crew chief blasting a few bursts of the weapon and remembered Ashpole's warning. He then moved to the other side of the plane to fire the minigun. It sounded like a buzz saw, the auditory signature of which was far more benign than the reality of the death it could unleash.

Before long, the bird descended and came to rest on the dusty airstrip of FOB Salerno, named for the beachhead of Salerno, Italy, captured by the 505th Parachute Infantry Regiment on September 14, 1943, right after Grandpa had himself landed on Italian soil with the 91st Division. I thought of him as I pondered the name. He arrived at the battlefield after weeks on a transport ship across the Atlantic. We arrived after mere hours on modern aircraft.

FOB Salerno, nicknamed "Rocket City" for the frequency of attacks it endured, was a mini version of Bagram, though I could see little of it in the predawn hours. Salerno was isolated from the rest of the country by the mountains, accessible only through the treacherous Khost-Gardez Pass. This post sat near the border with Pakistan and was just thirty miles south of Tora Bora, the cave complex where bin Laden and al-Qaeda fighters hid from a massive coalition bombing campaign in December 2001 and from where bin Laden had escaped into Pakistan.

As the ramp of the Chinook dropped, we beheld nothing but a dusty darkness before us. The crew chief yelled, "Everybody off! Everybody off! Move it!"

Inciting an inverse domino effect, the crew chief pulled up the first man in each seated column, laden with a "light" infantryman's load, who in turn pulled up the Ranger behind him, and so on until we were all standing. Blood struggled to provide strength to my numb legs, and I shuffled off the bird behind Ashpole and the rest of the maggots.

We were ushered into large, dark, empty tents with plywood floors. These would be transformed into our own hooches on our return to the FOB, but for now they served as a resting place for the gear we would leave behind.

"Dump your gear and get to the motor pool!" ordered Owens.

We did so and arrived at our Humvees about a hundred yards away.

"Ashpole and Elliott, you'll be attached to Sergeant Baker's vehicle." We were going on a mounted patrol, and the gun teams would be split up among the platoon, tasked with manning the heavy weapons, the .50 cals and Mk 19 grenade launchers, and of course ensuring the firepower for the 240s could be brought to bear.

"Roger, Sarn't!" Ashpole and I yelled back as we jogged over to Baker's vehicle. We were somewhat relieved. Baker was a much more easygoing but no less competent squad leader than Sergeant Owens. He made everything look easy and loved every minute of being a Ranger. Back at Fort Lewis, if the weather was remotely cooperative, he'd ride his bike twenty miles to work and joyfully complete the rigors of a Ranger training day before pedaling back home. It would have surprised no one if Baker went on to selection for Delta Force, the army's most elite ground force on par with SEAL Team Six.

"Hey, boys!" he said with a smile and a chuckle. "Looks like we got us some guns now."

"Roger, Sarn't," we said. While we were on mounted patrol, this stripped-down Humvee would be home and Baker the man who would command the mobile arsenal. One of his team leaders, Kellett Sayre, would drive while Baker commanded the vehicle from the front passenger seat. Specialists Chad Johnson and Trevor Alders would sit in the backseat as "waist gunners," Johnson with his M4 carbine amped up with a 203 grenade launcher and Alders manning the SAW (squad automatic weapon), a belt-fed, shoulder-fired machine gun, smaller than the 240 but equally potent.

"Here you go, Elliott," Ashpole said with a hint of pride as he handed me the 240. "The gun's yours now, man. I'll cover down on the .50 cal in the turret."

"Roger, Specialist," I said as I took the 240, one hand wrapped around the buttstock behind the trigger well, the other under the barrel. I climbed into the open bed of the Humvee and found the double-hinged swing arm that was welded to the back right of the vehicle's frame. I pulled out the two pins on the mount and slid the 240 in place, securing the gun tightly as I pushed the pins back in. I then took stock of the ammo in the back for both the .50 cal and the 240.

"Would you hand me one of those cans of .50 cal?" Ashpole asked as he got comfortable in the turret.

"Roger, Specialist," I said as I heaved a heavy green can laden with six-inch-long .50-cal rounds. The .50 cal had been in use since World War II, its primary function as an antiaircraft weapon. The size and power of its rounds could take out an engine block or cut a man in half, making it one of the infantry's deadlier weapons.

In addition to the thousand 240 rounds I had on my kit, I had another thousand in ammo cans in the back of the Humvee. I pulled out a can and placed it in the mount next to the feeder tray of the gun.

"Get ready to lock and load, men!" Baker announced. "We're leaving the wire in two minutes!"

I opened the can and pulled a belt of 7.62 mm rounds out and into the slowly approaching morning light. The brass glinted faintly, contrasting with the black links that held these rounds together. The actual bullet that would detach from the brass casing when fired was a copper color, with every fifth round in the belt possessing a red painted tip, indicating that it was a tracer round and would be visible as a bright red streak of light when fired in order to help see where rounds were landing, thereby enhancing the accuracy of the gunner.

I laid the belt of rounds in the feeder tray of the 240 and slapped it shut. I would wait to charge the weapon until given the order but still ensured the weapon's safety was engaged.

I unholstered my M9 pistol to ensure there wasn't a round in the chamber and that it was also on safe. It was an unneeded liability to have a round in the chamber of my pistol given the great unlikelihood that it would be put to use. If need be, a quick pull of the M9's upper receiver would make it ready to fire. I replaced the pistol in my leg drop holster and fastened it in place.

"Hey, Elliott, give me your M4, would you? I'd feel a little better having it up here in case I need to engage a target too close for the .50 cal," Ashpole asked.

"Sure, Specialist. I'm happy not to have to keep track of it," I said as I pulled back the charging handle of the M4 to ensure there was no round in the chamber, checked that the safety was engaged, and handed him the carbine, buttstock first.

The sun was just beginning to peek over the eastern horizon. At that moment, Specialist Russell Baer walked up to our vehicle. Baer had grown up in Livermore, California, and had also spent time in college though he had not yet graduated. He too was a bookworm and was friends with Pat and Kevin.

With his SAW sitting at a forty-five-degree angle to his torso, Baer came up and shook me on the leg as I sat in the back of the Humvee, my hand on the 240. "You ready for this?" he said with an intense smile. "You're gonna do great, Elliott." Baer's brief encouragement mirrored the mood of the growing dawn.

Sergeant Sayre fired up the Humvee's engine and we lurched forward toward the dirt-filled Hesco walls that formed the perimeter of the FOB. As we passed through the barriers, guard posts on our right and left, Baker yelled out, "Lock and load!" which caused a chorus of metallic sliding and clacking. In Afghanistan, outside the wire, rounds in the chamber. We were finally at war, the tip of the spear searching for worthy flesh to pierce.

Nothing happened.

As the engine droned on and we scanned the largely empty land-scape for threats, our adrenaline wore off. We bounced around the landscape driving on "roads." We passed the random earthen home, saw the occasional patch of wheat, green and yet to be harvested, which served as a faint reminder of the home place that somehow made Kansas seem so distant.

After some hours, by the early and increasingly hot afternoon, we reached our objective: a small village tucked neatly within the walls of brown cliffs. This village comprised a smattering of huts con-structed of mud and sun-dried bricks of sand and clay. A group of half a dozen bearded men sat in front of them betraying nothing in their countenance, seeming as though they had been seated there since the day the mountains sprang into existence. Each man wore the traditional Afghan garb—a long, loose shirt and pajama-like trousers (known as a *salwar kameez*) and a wool hat with a kind of double-pancake appearance (the *pakol*).

Sergeant Godec directed the placement of our vehicles so as to maximize our fields of fire and security. We were parked about fifteen meters from the front of the village in a blocking position, charged with ensuring that nothing got in or out from the objective. As the rest of our vehicle dismounted, Ashpole and I settled in, dividing our field of fire and continually scanning for potential targets. The line dogs would sweep the village, hoping to gather intel and looking for anything beyond the allowable household weapons.

The mission was conducted without incident or the acquisition of meaningful intelligence. As was the next and the next and the next.

This is war, I thought as I waited and waited and fought to maintain my focus on the rough and barren landscape, looking for anything that would qualify as a threat. Anything that would qualify as "the enemy."

★

Four days into this clearing operation, we had pulled in for the night, and after ensuring our platoon's security had been put in place, Ashpole and I sat in the back of the Humvee with our kits off and began to tear hungrily into our MREs. I had just finished my main course, beef stew, and was preparing one of my favorite desserts: spiced apples mixed with crushed saltine crackers and peanut butter heated to the point that it became a molten liquid. The three together almost reminded me of a caramel apple strudel. Almost. As I drizzled the peanut butter that had been brought to temperature by the heater contained within the MRE, Sergeant Baker ran up to the truck and began to put on his kit.

"Get up," he said. "We're movin'."

Ashpole and I hopped to our feet and began throwing on our body armor and helmets.

"Go ahead and mount your NODs on your helmet," Ashpole instructed. "It'll be dark soon, and we want to be ready."

"Roger, Specialist," I dutifully replied.

Our night optical devices (NODs) were essentially monocular night vision lenses, four-inch-long black cylinders that we stored in our kits during the day and affixed to the hinge on the front of our helmets for nighttime operations. My lens would descend over my left eye and provide a bright green hue to an otherwise dark world, leaving my right eye free to scan the landscape in the darkness.

Baker continued as the rest of the vehicle's residents assembled and began the prep for movement. "Intelligence has spotted a company-sized element moving from Pakistan toward an Afghan Military Force outpost on the border. They want us to head up there, dig in, and reinforce their position if they get hit. I guess them guys up there get rocketed all the time, so be ready for a fight."

Game on. Here we go.

Dusk was upon us as we reached the top of the ridgeline. As we crested, we could see the tribal plains of Pakistan spread before us to the east.

Ashpole consulted his handheld GPS and announced, "We're in Pakistan! Don't tell anyone!"

We all chuckled. The border between Afghanistan and Pakistan was somewhat of a geographic suggestion in certain parts of the mountains, and depending on whose map or Garmin you consulted, you could find yourself in either country. Augmenting an Afghan

Military Force (AMF) outpost was clearly within our rules of engagement (ROE), but much more beyond that was not. We were forbidden from venturing into Pakistan unless we made contact with an enemy element in Afghanistan and maintained that contact if they then fled into Pakistan. Otherwise, we could just sit tight and watch, waiting to get shot so we could shoot back.

Our Humvee was positioned parallel with the ridgeline, offering Ashpole and his .50 cal a clear 180 degrees of visibility. I dismounted along with the 240 and placed the gun on its more stable tripod at the edge of the ridge and with a clear line of sight to the valley below. I linked a two-hundred-round belt into the gun and lay down behind it to get comfortable as it appeared this would be my bed for the night.

Fortunately, I'd have some company. Will Aker, a newbie even newer than me, came over. Will was an M4 rifleman in Sergeant Weeks's squad, serving alongside Pat, O'Neal, and Boatright. Aker was one of the taller Rangers you'd find, a lanky six foot three. "What's up, Elliott?" he said kindly.

"Not much, man. What are you doin' over here?" I asked.

"Sergeant Godec told me to be your AG on the 240. We're supposed to switch off every hour so one of us can sleep."

"Sweet. Happy to have the company. You fired the 240 lately?" I asked.

"No, not since basic," Will admitted. There would have been no reason for him to as a member of a line squad.

"Well, let me check you out on the weapon to make sure you're comfortable with it. There's no Elcan, but that won't matter at night."

I walked him through the weapon system, and he quickly reoriented himself with the gun and was ready to shoot bad guys if need be.

"You guys okay?" Baker asked as he inspected the various firing positions along the ridgeline. "There's nothing friendly out there, you understand?" he said, pointing to the wide, flat landscape that spread before us. "You see muzzle flashes and you see us engage, you do the same, got it? Pay attention to me, Ashpole, all right? I'll check on you boys after a bit."

He was calm and focused. You could see he was even more at ease as the threat of violence increased.

Will and I sat on the rocky ground behind the 240, scanning the horizon and chatting a bit.

"How are things going in your squad, Will?" I asked.

"Okay, I guess. Weeks is a good teacher. Boatright's a good dude, but he doesn't say much. I never know what that guy's thinking. You can tell Weeks likes Josey, but he messes with him a lot. Calls him 'Boatramp' and 'Boatdock' all the time. It's funny 'cause all you see is Josey's ears turn red when he gets mad." Will laughed and so did I. I'd seen Josey's ears turn red many times.

"How's the other guy that came with you, Bryan O'Neal? How's he doin'?"

"Oh, he's good. Man, that guy can run. Better than me, that's for sure. O'Neal's in Pat's fire team, and Pat's really taken him under his wing. He's great, you know, Pat is. You'd never know he was some famous guy. I feel real lucky to be with those guys. What's it like workin' for Owens? I'm glad I'm not in his squad."

"He's not that bad," I replied. "Once he knows you're committed and giving your best, he gets off your back. Hey, why don't you catch some rack, Will? I just ate, sort of, and I'm plenty awake, so I'll take the first hour."

"You sure? All right, yeah, that sounds fine." He adjusted his lengthy frame, complete with kit, helmet, and weapon, to find the most comfortable reclined position on the Afghan/Pakistani rocks. I thought about the hot peanut butter that had now undoubtedly hardened back into a strange-looking goo, especially when mixed with the apples and crackers. *So much for dessert,* I thought, staring through my NODs. *These guys better show up.*

We proceeded to wait and wait and wait. Every hour, Will and I changed off our watch as we shivered in the chill of the mountain air.

At dawn, everyone was awake, prepared for an attack. Dusk and dawn are the most common time frames for an engagement. It's the time when we are most vulnerable—the advantage of our night vision is negated with just enough light to make that technology useless but not so much as to provide visual clarity. There was nothing to see in the east but the sun. No attack came.

We spent the day with the AMF soldiers, which marked our first interaction with our Afghan allies. They were a rough-looking bunch, seeming to have come to life from the rocky crags they inhabited. The translator assigned to our platoon offered a verbal history of some of these men. Almost all the older ones had fought the Soviets. All of them had been fighting the Taliban for years. The look in their eyes betrayed a life far more comfortable with war than peace. They were impressed and fascinated by us, though, and wanted to see our weapons in action and to show off their armaments as well.

After breakfast chow and with security in place, the platoon gathered for a little cultural exchange, us firing our big guns and them firing theirs. Suhl and Ashpole were the designated representatives of our platoon. Suhl fired a half dozen rounds from the Mk 19, the hollow thud of each explosive round ending in a brief plume of smoke on the adjacent hillside as the projectile exploded. Ashpole did likewise with the .50 cal, the steady weight of the gun evident as a dozen rounds, including a few tracers, poured forth in a satisfying arc. The AMF soldiers loved it. The joy of guns seemed to transcend language and culture.

It was now their turn to demonstrate two of their own weapons systems, both left over from their Soviet occupiers. The first was a large antiaircraft gun called a DShK. The gun itself was attached to a giant turret, and the gunner would sit in that turret as he oriented and fired the gun. A few rounds later, one of the Afghans came forward with a small arms classic, the RPG (rocket-propelled grenade).

He loaded the projectile in the front of the tube, placed it on his shoulder, and faced the valley below. I watched as his finger depressed the weapon's trigger. Nothing happened but a hollow *click*. He stood motionless as we all wondered what was going on.

"Sometimes the grenade takes a few seconds to arm and fire," our interpreter explained. "He's waiting to see if it will catch."

Tension rose as we waited and hoped for the weapon to fire. The trigger was pulled again with the same result and the man stood there patiently.

He then took the RPG off his shoulder and placed it on the ground with the projectile pointing toward his face. Without being commanded, we all found cover. The Afghan fighter calmly examined the projectile, placed his hand upon it, and removed it from the firing mechanism. We were horrified. He then took the projectile and coolly tossed it down the side of the mountain.

"That one was a dud," the translator explained. "Very old ordnance and very unpredictable."

We all relaxed and were grateful he hadn't blown his head off. The incident seemed to reveal an ease with violence and war that we did not quite possess. For all our training and the thousands of rounds we'd fired at targets shaped like people, most of us had never shot at actual people. For us twenty-first-century Americans, violence was the exception to the rule of peace and prosperity. For them, peace was the exception in a landscape that had changed little since the British retreated nearly a century before. We stood in a high-elevation time capsule. War had kept the hands of the clock from advancing, and these men had no idea that time was violently standing still.

As fascinated as the AMF guys were with our weapons, they were even more taken with Pat. His build was certainly unique among his Ranger peers, but he was like a different species compared to the scrawny AMF soldiers.

Later that afternoon, as I was cleaning weapons, Ashpole hollered at me, "Hey, Elliott, check this out." I noticed a crowd was forming in a clearing on the Afghan side of the ridge. A couple of the AMF guys had boldly challenged Pat to a rock-throwing contest. Judging by their build, the "contest" appeared to be a pretext simply to see how far this American Hercules could heave a rock. The rocks themselves were about twenty pounds and perhaps the size of a large cantaloupe, so they were throwing them shot-put style.

I walked over and stood next to Sergeant Owens. Pat was a good sport about it, but you could tell he was uncomfortable being the center of attention. The cues from our chain of command indicated that Pat was clear to proceed and that this minor spectacle was embraced as a welcome bit of fun amid work that was decidedly monotonous.

Pat's reluctant smile vanished into ferocity as he heaved the rock off his shoulder and past his face, far outdistancing his Afghan competitor. With a yell, the vanquished challenger embraced Pat. Their speculation as to Pat's strength had been proved. The weakness of their own effort only served to further accentuate Pat's strength and therefore added to the sense that these men were in the presence of greatness. Pat happily melted back into the crowd as the contest died down and we returned to whatever work was waiting for us.

When we weren't working or sleeping, there was time to read. I had been ill prepared for that fact, but I managed to procure a few Stephen King paperbacks from Bagram at the last minute. Kevin had brought his Larry McMurtry with him and happily buried himself in its pages whenever time permitted.

A couple of days later, we had moved to augment another AMF position in danger of an imminent attack that never came. Kevin and I took up residence next to each other on the ground under a scraggly tree. As the morning turned to afternoon, we both tired of our books and chatted for a while.

"What was it like to go to a Christian college?" Kevin asked. "ORU's a Christian school, right?"

"Well, it was certainly interesting," I said. "There were good things and not so good things about it. Having a group of people with the same worldview offers its advantages but also provides a bubble that shields you from other perspectives. I made some amazing friends and learned a lot. It's not a perfect place for sure, but I'm glad I went there."

"That's really great," Kevin said. It was clear that he meant it.

I knew that Kevin wasn't a man of faith. He assumed correctly that I was. "So, what's it like for you?" I said. "How do you respond to somebody like me who believes in God and the Bible?"

"I don't have a problem with it," he said. "I mean, you're a good kid. I just don't believe in it. To me, a lot of it seems like a crutch. A lot of what I've read seems contrived or invented by men. And so much damage has been done by people who have abused the power of faith and religion. It flies in the face of what's reasonable and good for people. No offense," Kevin added with a sheepish grin.

"None taken. I agree with some of what you just said, especially about people abusing others."

We were just getting started when Sergeant Owens's voice called, "Tillman, Elliott, get over here!"

Kevin and I jumped to our feet and joined the rest of the maggots. All of them, including Sergeant Owens, were standing at parade rest, which was odd until we noticed a new face among the crowd. His name tape read "Bailey," and the rank on his collar was a black oak leaf cluster. His salt-and-pepper hair cropped tight showed a man of greater age than any of us. This was Lieutenant Colonel Jeff Bailey, the commander of Second Ranger Battalion, known simply as the "BC" among the ranks.

Kevin and I both saluted as we approached. "Rangers lead the way, sir," we chimed.

"All the way" was the BC's reply along with a quick return salute.

We joined the others at parade rest.

"Relax, relax," the BC said. When a Ranger officer tells you to relax, you ignore it as the test that it is, sort of like when your wife tells you that you don't have to get her anything for Christmas. You never fall for it, and the position of parade rest would be as relaxed as you would find any member of Second Platoon's maggots, Owens included. Seeing our leader at parade rest, same as us, served as a reminder that we all work for somebody.

"What's the word, men?" the BC asked as he spooned the contents of an MRE into his mouth.

"Ready to shoot some hajji, sir," Kevin replied.

"Roger that, Tillman," the BC replied, taking strength from the aggressiveness of one of his men. "We'll get 'em. Be patient and we'll get 'em."

Kevin continued in reply, unsatisfied with the nonresponse he'd just received and genuinely curious to probe as to whether there was a method to our mission. In half jest he said, "You know, sir, maybe we should cross that border and shake things up. Dress us up like hajji, put us in the back of one of those jinga trucks, and send us across."

We all laughed, as did the BC. It was a ridiculous suggestion, and

Kevin knew it, but behind the joke was a question: "Why are we just sitting here? We see the bad guys moving without obstruction across the border. Why are we just waiting to get shot at so we can shoot back?"

We never got a satisfactory answer, and the BC quickly moved on to mingle with the rest of the platoon. His visit, meant to inspire confidence and bolster morale, did just the opposite. It confirmed our fears. We were bait, waiting for the enemy to conform to the ROE.

The next day we got word that we'd be taking a more active role on the border along with our AMF brethren helping to secure and operate checkpoints for incoming traffic. It still seemed a far cry from the role we had been trained to play, but at least we'd be doing something besides waiting for an attack that never seemed to come.

Ashpole and I were to be paired with Pat's fire team running one of the checkpoints. Minutes after Sergeant Baker told us this, Pat appeared out of nowhere.

"Hey, Elliott! How's it goin', man? Say, looks like we'll be running this checkpoint, and I wanted to go over some of these Pashtun phrases to make sure I'm gettin' 'em right."

"Sure, Specialist. Just give me a second."

Back at Fort Lewis, each platoon in the battalion had sent an individual for a week's worth of Pashtun language training. Sergeant Godec picked me for the job, which meant I got to spend a week in a dry, warm Fort Lewis classroom while the rest of the platoon spent four of the wettest days you could imagine in the field. Our teacher was an Afghan expat, a former doctor who exuded a quiet dignity befitting his position in the professional ranks of society. On the Friday of that week, as the rest of the platoon was cleaning gear and weapons, Godec called us together in the platoon AO under the watchful gaze of Clyde the Sheep to get a language lesson from the platoon "expert," me. As they say, in the land of the blind, the one-eyed man is king, and while I was anything but an Afghan linguist, I had four more days of language training than anyone else in the platoon.

I had printed out and laminated a quick reference card of useful phrases for each of the guys. Useful within our context, that is. Things like "hands up," "where are the weapons," "on the ground," and so on.

I'd stood awkwardly in the spotlight among my platoon mates, trying to get the "class" over with as soon as possible. "Shut up, Sheep, and let Elliott teach us some Pashtun" was Godec's awkward and highly effective command. I passed out the cards, reviewed a couple of key phrases, and said to talk to me if they had any questions. Class dismissed. Everyone scattered that day except for Pat. For him, the lesson was just getting started, and he followed me back to my room with a notepad, asking great questions about tone and accent that I largely couldn't answer.

Now we were in the hinterlands of the Afghan wilderness, and my pupil was back. I knew he wanted to go over more language stuff, which was great. I just wished that, for his sake, I wasn't so ill equipped. Class was back in session.

"What's up, Specialist?"

"Yeah, I wanted to go over some of these phrases and make sure I had the accent right. Can you help me?"

"Maybe, Specialist," I said with a laugh. "I'm happy to go over it with you and help you as best I can, but I'm far from a native speaker."

"I know, I know," he said smiling. "I really appreciate it. I just want to get it right."

"Stop is *wadrega*, right?" he asked.

"Yes, just put a little more emphasis on the first syllable," I replied.

"*Wa*drega, *wa*drega," he practiced.

We worked through all the phrases likely to be used in running a checkpoint. We talked through who would stand where and do what. His appetite for detail was insatiable.

I happily rehearsed with him while harboring doubts that any of this would matter. That we'd actually need our feeble language skills. That bad guys bent on harming the innocent would be dumb enough to pass through a checkpoint run by US soldiers. That Pat's ability to say "stop" would make any difference.

5

AMBUSH

April is the cruelest month.
T. S. ELIOT

"What's he doing, Specialist?"

"Looks like he's diggin' through the burn pile," Alders replied. "Hungry, I guess."

The burn pile was in the middle of the AMF post. It sat at the bottom of a shallow pit perhaps twenty yards wide. That was where we piled our garbage, mostly MRE packaging, to be burned.

Suddenly, the figure sifting through our platoon's trash yelled victoriously while he held up his prize.

"Whatcha got, Tillman?" Baker yelled with a laugh.

"Unopened chocolate brownie, Sarn't!" was Pat's joyful reply.

"Good for him," I said with a weak laugh, made weaker as I prepared to open our newly delivered cold-weather MREs.

Normal MREs had "normal" things. They were still filled with lab-created franken-food, but normal MREs had water in them. Beef stew that was actually stew and just needed to be heated. Chili mac that was actually chili mac. Cold-weather MREs were completely freeze-dried meals without an ounce of moisture so they couldn't freeze and be destroyed. Somehow cold-weather breakfast MREs had made their way into our supply chain even though the Afghan winter was behind us. We had a mountain of freeze-dried eggs that would require hot water to bring them to some semblance of palatability. We had no hot water.

Our regular MRE supply having been exhausted, our platoon paid for an Afghan meal from the AMF guys the day before. They fixed a nice spread of roasted goat and watermelon, but we couldn't eat much of the meat and a few guys got sick on it.

So there I sat on the back of our vehicle and poured cold water into the army's freeze-dried version of a Denver omelet. I ate as much as I could, fighting my gag reflex until it just wasn't worth it anymore. I was hungry but not that hungry. Not yet.

Maybe I should dig in the trash too. At least we got the fuel pump. At least we won't be stuck here much longer, I thought.

Along with the cases of winter MREs that had come that morning via helicopter, we had also received a much-needed Humvee part—a fuel pump that, when properly installed, would get our platoon's broken Humvee fixed and get us back on the move.

As dawn turned to morning and morning to afternoon, we waited anxiously for word that our Humvee was fixed. Guys were constantly "casually" checking out our mechanic's progress. I felt for the guy. For reasons beyond his control, his work was now the thing our platoon's future depended on.

The moment came, and the Humvee's starter was engaged. It wouldn't turn over. It wouldn't start. And now neither would we. Anyone with an inkling of mechanical know-how was consulted. Our capable mechanic was out of answers.

"Can't we just sling load this thing out of here?" I asked Sergeant Baker that afternoon. "Why are we all stuck because of one bad vehicle?"

"I don't know, Elliott. Higher wants us to get it fixed and for us to get it outta here. That's just what they want," Baker replied.

The day dragged on. Cold freeze-dried eggs both beckoned and taunted. I took a few more bites that evening and tried to sleep as the mountain chill set in. I shivered slightly, waiting for my body to warm my sleeping bag.

I awoke on April 22 in a sweat. Disoriented, I groped to find my way out of my bedding, and as I unzipped my sleeping bag, the bright light of another Afghan day slapped me in the face. I was a camouflaged version of Punxsutawney Phil, peeking out of my hole to see what light and shadow might portend for the future.

I'm still here, I thought, having come out of a deep and dreamless sleep. This Groundhog Day would be repeated seemingly without end.

I walked back over to our vehicle to see what was going on. "What's up, sleepyhead? I was about to get you up," Ashpole said as he was cleaning the .50 cal. "We're moving out in a few, so get ready."

"Really, Specialist? They fixed the Humvee?"

"No. We've been ordered to tow it out," he said skeptically.

"Tow it out? On these roads? You're kidding, Specialist."

"Nope. That's the word. We gotta get it back to Hardball Road so a wrecker can come and get it. Should be a solid eight-hour drive from here."

Hardball Road was the partially paved Khost-Gardez Highway and was the only hope for getting our Humvee towed back to base. The "roads" near our position were virtually impassable to all but the most rugged vehicles, like our Humvees and local "jinga trucks," diesel rigs that are common in Southeast Asia.

Great. Now we're a wrecking crew, I thought.

At 0700 we pulled out, useless Humvee in tow. Second Platoon was fifty-four men strong, including seven AMF soldiers and two Afghan interpreters. We were traveling in six functioning Humvees and four Toyota HiLux king cabs—and of course towing one inexplicably disabled Humvee.

The "road" we traveled was actually a wadi—a twisting, dry riverbed filled with boulders both large and small. As dry as the wadi appeared, a rainstorm could turn this pathway into a powerful river, with little vegetation on the surrounding mountains to stop a flash flood. We had learned this lesson a week prior, barely making it up the ridgeline as the wadi attempted to swallow our vehicles with freakish speed as a spring rain drove down upon us.

We moved at not much more than a walking pace due in part to the treachery of the terrain and because of the vehicle that was being towed. The tow bar that attached the broken metallic beast to its makeshift tow truck eventually snapped, unable to handle the strain of navigating the terrain.

Heavy-duty nylon ratchet straps were then applied. The front of the vehicle was moving but was now more exposed to the rocky terrain that was slowly chewing up the vehicle as a predator would feast upon felled prey. The scrapes and screeches of the metal echoed through the air.

There's no way that thing is making it back to Salerno in one piece, I thought. *We'll destroy it getting it to safety, and for what?* My frustration grew.

In the course of four hours we managed to cover only five miles. Finally, the broken Humvee's tie-rods snapped, so the wheels no longer turned in the same direction. At about 1130, we came to a halt in an open, flat wadi, fifty yards wide from one end to the other. A hundred yards to the south were gradually sloping hills that rose twenty feet above our position. One hillside contained a handful of mud-and-brick huts. We had arrived at the village of Magarah, which appeared deserted.

"All right, boys. Keep sharp," Baker said as he dismounted the vehicle to confer with the rest of the platoon's leadership. We sat tight in the vehicle, Ashpole continuing to man the .50 cal in his turret, I on the 240. Sayre directed the remaining occupants of our vehicle—Alders, Johnson, and Roberts—to higher positions near the vehicle to pull security. We waited.

Baker walked briskly back to us.

"PL's on the satellite radio with the FOB," he said. "We gotta wait to see what they want us to do."

The PL was our platoon leader, Lieutenant David Uthlaut, one of the few infantry officers I'd met who wasn't a jerk. He was captain of his West Point class and was given the honor of accompanying the newly elected president and first lady down Pennsylvania Avenue for the 2001 inauguration. The platoon trusted him implicitly. He commanded us but seemed like one of us.

The PL's constant companion, his "battle buddy," was the platoon's radio transmission officer, Specialist Jade Lane. Jade was a wiry Kansan himself, born and raised in Dodge City. His thankless job was to ensure that communications were up and running for the PL, and as such the two were hardly separated. It also meant that Lane knew all the good stuff. He always had the best gossip as there was no other lower enlisted person in the platoon as close to the source as he was.

We waited. Baker went back to confer with the PL, platoon sergeant, and other squad leaders. He came back. We waited.

"Come on, Sarn't," Ashpole said from his perch. "What are we doin' here?"

"I'll tell you what you need to know when you need to know it. Just keep pullin' security."

The task of pulling security took on greater importance as the seemingly deserted village came slowly to life. Small groups of Afghans, men and young boys, began to appear seemingly out of nowhere.

The men mostly squatted and stared from the other side of the wadi. Their expressions betrayed nothing. The young boys, however, gave in to curiosity and couldn't help but approach us. Three of them walked up to our vehicle, less afraid of us than we were of them, as it was impossible to tell the good from the bad.

They carried homemade slingshots, hand-carved wooden *Y*s with thick, orange strands of rubber fastened to them. We were then treated to yet another Afghan weapons demonstration, this one with far less firepower.

These young diplomats began to speak the ubiquitous language of boys of all ages—hitting stuff with rocks.

They nonchalantly picked up small stones, looked back at us to ensure they had our attention, and showed off their deadly accuracy on the nearby hillside.

"Nice shot, buddy!" Johnson called out as a projectile struck the dirt. We were happy for the distraction.

They came closer. They were more comfortable having received a friendly response, and we were now confident they possessed no lethal intent.

I made eye contact with one boy in a faded red T-shirt, shorts, and sandals. He was maybe seven or eight. He came closer, and as I held out a weathered US dollar bill, I motioned toward his slingshot to see if he'd trade. His eyes got wide as he understood my intent and nodded vigorously. I cared little for the slingshot but wanted to create goodwill. I used the tool most commonly used by my people to do so—cash.

He grasped the money excitedly and proudly presented me with his homemade weapon. He and his buddies ran off.

Baker returned from yet another leaders' meeting, his own patience wearing thin.

He leaned on the front of the vehicle as he took off his helmet and scratched his head. "They're arguin' right now. Captain Saunders at the TOC and the PL." Captain William Saunders was the commander of Alpha Company and was directing our movements from the Tactical Operations Center at FOB Salerno.

"CO says we gotta haul this thing back one way or the other. PL wants to sling load it or just pull off all the weapons and sensitive equipment and blow it up. We got more than enough C4 for that," Baker said.

"What the f—?" Ashpole said. Baker's body language indicated there would be no reprisal for questioning the wisdom of the TOC.

"TOC is saying a sling load mission with a Chinook would take a couple of days to line up, and he wants that vehicle back," Baker explained without conviction.

"Has he seen it, Sarn't?" Sayre said, referring to the rapidly deteriorating state of this precious and inoperable Humvee.

As if to underscore our mood, a Chinook appeared on the horizon, accompanied by two Marine Cobra attack helicopters. They flew almost directly over our position. We wondered if the gods of war had heard our lament and sent us an answer. Instead, the three birds flew on, never to be seen again, unwittingly taunting us with air assets that belonged to someone else.

We sat mostly in silence. Frustrations were voiced randomly.

"Stupid," Johnson muttered.

"Blow it up," Alders said with Texas-sized conviction.

By 1530—more than four hours after we arrived at Magarah—Baker began to lose his cool. He glanced over at the PL's vehicle, obviously considering yet another trip to try and get an update but thought better of it.

Our frustration was turning into concern as the crowd of Afghans grew. Nearly a hundred people had now gathered to watch the spectacle, most of them just sitting and staring. A feeling of claustrophobia washed over me. Our glances became more nervous. Our position was exposed for hours in the broad daylight, and we were unable to move. The hillsides full of people seemed to be getting closer.

We need to get out of here, I thought.

At 1730, as the afternoon light began to take on the shape of evening, Baker was again summoned to the PL's vehicle via his radio. He jogged over, and after five minutes or so, he returned with news.

"All right, boys, check it out. The platoon is hiring a jinga truck from the village to tow the busted-up vehicle. The platoon will be split into two elements, Serial One and Serial Two. Serial One will be commanded by the PL and is going to clear an objective tonight. We're assigned to Serial Two. Our job is to escort the jinga truck and Humvee back to Hardball Road."

Baker delivered the message as plainly as he could, but his dissatisfaction was clear.

"You're kidding, right, Sarn't?" Ashpole said. "We split the platoon to get a busted-up vehicle to the Hardball? What's at the objective, Sarn't?"

"Nothing in particular. No intel on it. We were supposed to clear it days ago, and the TOC is upset. They want it cleared."

Alders unleashed. "Our combat effectiveness will be cut in half so some of us can get to a meaningless objective and the rest of us can get that piece of s— to the highway? What's goin' on?"

"We're paying someone we don't know to haul this thing?" Sayre asked with rhetorical incredulity.

Roberts and I were the junior guys on the vehicle; this was our first deployment. We took our cues from everyone else and largely echoed what we'd already heard, now feeling safe to offer our own disdain.

"When are we movin', Sarn't?" I asked.

"Any minute," he said. "Get ready, boys."

I felt a brush of cool from the coming evening as the shadows lengthened. We had less than an hour of daylight.

"We're moving at dusk? If we have to do this, can't we just wait another hour or two? We've been here all day already," Alders asked with a heightened level of exasperation.

Having articulated our frustration, acceptance set in, and the only weapon left in our arsenal to fight this ridiculous scenario was humor.

"What if we 'accidentally' pulled off all the sensitive equipment and blew up the vehicle?" Johnson quipped with a smile.

Baker chuckled, as did the rest of us. "Yeah, I don't think the CO would buy that, but I wish," Baker said.

The collective attitude of frustration pervaded as we prepared for movement across this darkening landscape.

At about 1800 hours, the six vehicles that composed Serial One passed our position and headed north along a dry riverbed. Uthlaut's Humvee was in the lead. The second vehicle in the procession was a white Toyota HiLux loaded with crates filled with our precious winter MREs. Perched on top of those crates, holding his SAW machine gun, was Pat. He looked ridiculous, frowning as he bounced in the back of the truck, a truck that looked even smaller with his sizable frame in the back.

The riverbed wound around the corner into more hills. Serial One was soon out of sight.

A few minutes later, Sergeant Sayre fired up our Humvee to lead out Serial Two. Behind us was the jinga truck towing the broken Humvee and the rest of the platoon that included Platoon Sergeant Godec, who was now in command of us. After nearly two miles of driving, we came to an open area that served as a fork in the riverbed. We took the right fork toward Hardball Road.

We were stopped, however, by yelling from the jinga truck driver. Sergeant Godec went to confer with him, as did Baker and the other squad leaders. Baker ran back a moment later. "We're following him the other way!" he hollered above the hum of the idling engine.

To my surprise, we allowed the jinga truck driver to take the lead with our vehicle immediately following. Behind us were two more of our platoon's Humvees as well as a Humvee that included Sergeant Godec and, in the turret of that vehicle manning the Mk 19 grenade launcher, Kevin Tillman.

I had no idea what route Serial One had taken. I had no idea that, in taking the left fork, we were following right behind them.

"Can't raise Serial One," Baker announced with frustration. "F—ing mountains! Ain't got no signal! We got no comms with them!"

The tension was as thick as the coming darkness, its descent accelerated by the sheer cliffs that now surrounded us in shadow and bathed our world in muddled shades of gray. We continued to follow the jinga truck. The wadi narrowed dramatically. I pulled my gun in off the side of our Humvee; the vehicle itself was barely able to fit through this part of the canyon. A narrow strip of blue sky above us was quickly darkening, as was the rock that surrounded us.

It was too quiet among us as we drank in our surroundings and considered our situation. "Great place for an ambush," I said with a laugh. Alders was the only one who could hear me.

"Yeah," he said with a forced laugh. "It'd be so easy to take all of us out. So easy."

My pulse quickened. Each second felt like a minute. Each minute like an hour. We couldn't get out of here fast enough. The pace at which we moved, a pace set by the jinga truck and broken vehicle in front of us, was agonizingly slow. This was a kill zone, and we were crawling.

At 1830, we were winding north in a counterclockwise curve, the canyon having widened somewhat but not by much. The landscape was now a deathly gray as night approached. Our vehicles were about twenty yards apart. From where I sat, I observed the Humvee immediately behind us as they came around the curve we had just navigated.

An incandescent white flash erupted on the cliff forty feet above that vehicle. A billow of smoke pushed skyward by the explosive force. The sound of the explosion quickly followed the light and echoed violently through the canyon.

A boulder as tall as a man was dislodged. The explosion had occurred at its base. Gravity claimed its prize, and the boulder descended down the wall of the canyon, rocks crunching to dust under its terrible, rapidly falling weight.

My eyes traced a line from the falling rock to my comrades below, attempting to discern where the boulder would land. A Ranger in the Humvee behind us dismounted and stood, crouched at the ready with M4 pointed toward the rock above. His posture, ready to unleash death, was both appropriate and useless as the boulder paid no heed.

Adrenaline rushed. Fear pervaded.

The boulder found its new home between the two Humvees behind us, thankfully harming no one.

Relief quickly dissolved into the reality that we were under attack. When in a kill zone, the goal is to move through it as quickly as possible. I saw the jinga truck driver leap out of the truck. The canyon was too narrow to maneuver around the vehicle. We were stuck.

"Dismount!" Baker yelled as the men on our vehicle sought to find cover.

I took a step off the back of the vehicle, driven both by Baker's command and by my own fear. I wanted to crawl under the earth and hide.

I then realized my weapon was the 240 mounted on the vehicle.

I looked back at Ashpole, who sat frozen in the turret, his thumbs resting on the .50-cal trigger levers as he scanned for targets.

Ashpole's unwavering posture was all that kept me on the vehicle as I placed the 240 in my shoulder and turned the safety off. I felt as naked as a newborn standing on the back of that Humvee. I imagined what it would feel like to have rounds strike my exposed legs, thankful for the first time that I was wearing the burdensome body armor that covered my torso.

As I stared at the darkening cliff, waiting to fire, a thought washed over me. *I'm going to die here.* I believed this with as much certainty as the prospect of the setting sun. Having been led to this place at this time, how could there be any other outcome? We'd willingly walked into an obvious trap. *This is it, and for what? A Humvee?*

The pervasive fear of certain death morphed into confusion. *These people don't even know me,* I thought. *I'm a decent guy. Why would they want to kill me? They're strangers who've done nothing to me until now, and I'm going to have to try and kill them.*

The logic of war was undone in that moment. The politics were meaningless when reduced to humans trying to kill other humans.

Suddenly, muzzle flashes blazed from the cliffs above and the sound of gunfire quickly followed. The canyon erupted as the platoon returned fire. I focused down the barrel of the 240, taking aim at the place from which the muzzle flashed. The trigger pull felt heavier than ever. I was viscerally reluctant to fire at what I knew was not simply a target. *I just want my friends to be okay,* I thought. With that thought and justification, I squeezed the trigger, sending a five-round burst, watching the tracer round I unleashed as part of the volley impacted higher on the cliff than I had intended.

The sound of my weapon brought deafness as well as comfort. I had no ear protection and would continue to fire and be fired at without it, as would most of the platoon. Comfort at hearing the gun and seeing the rounds created the semblance of control. I had power. That power was my weapon. I had crossed a barrier. With the firing of those five rounds, the reluctance to kill was gone. Bloodlust grew as I felt the recoil of my weapon echo through my body. Hate burned brightly for the enemy on the cliffs, and that hate reached its apex in the form of searing, cold indifference.

F— 'em, I thought as my jaw clenched, pressing my shoulder in hard against my weapon, seeking the next target to engage.

By some standards I had become a man, now able and willing to kill. By others, I was losing my humanity.

More shots rang out and more muzzle flashes sparkled in the cliffs. Ashpole was on it. He opened up the .50 cal at the flashes and I did likewise, firing short bursts from the 240. As an enemy position was revealed, he and I alternated fire, "talking the guns" in an attempt to preserve ammo and also suppress whoever was behind or around that position. We were highly exposed and manning two of the most powerful weapons in the platoon. We wanted to not just kill the enemy but suppress the enemy and keep them from even taking a shot at us if we could.

Others who were dismounted were firing as well. My ears were nothing but one constant ring. I could barely hear the report of my own weapon.

I saw that Baker had run ahead, weapon raised and yelling at the jinga truck driver, obviously getting him to move so we could do likewise.

He ran back. "Mount up!" he yelled.

We were soon moving again, following the jinga truck for about forty yards when the convoy stopped again. More muzzle flashes erupted in front of and behind us. Johnson leaned through the back of the truck, firing his M4 directly to the left of me. Hot brass peppered my face. I glanced back at him angrily, and he moved to a different firing position.

The vehicle's occupants again dismounted, leaving Ashpole and me on the Humvee. More shooting erupted farther along the walls of the cliff. A rock outcropping kept us from engaging.

"Elliott! Move the truck!"

"Roger, Specialist!"

I hopped out and put the Humvee in gear, moving forward as quickly as the terrain would allow. Ashpole had his target, and the

.50 cal erupted as I came to a halt. Hot .50-cal brass rained down, burning the back of my neck as I moved out of the driver's seat and back to my position with the 240. I continued to trade bursts with Ashpole, seeing the muzzle flashes as well.

"Mount up!" Baker yelled again, and we moved forward in an increasingly dark yet open landscape. The faint breeze on my cheek indicated the speed of movement we had all been longing for. In another three-quarters of a mile the canyon opened dramatically. To our left was a high, sheer wall of rock that progressively fell away from the road. To our right was another canyon wall five feet high and thirty yards long that extended into the wadi and made a forty-five-degree turn to the right, following the path of the parched riverbed. Beyond the rock wall was a hillside filled with rocks and scrub brush that gradually sloped upward.

Hope sprang to life as adrenaline born of fear still coursed through my veins. *We haven't been hit,* I thought. *We're moving. We might be okay.*

We continued to scan the hillside, darkened and backlit by the setting sun. I saw a human silhouette on the ridgeline and honed my gaze, ready to fire. More muzzle flashes shone out from that position. Baker fired his M4 and the silhouette melted back into the rock.

Ashpole and Alders fired as well, keying off Baker's action, which indicated an enemy position. Still afraid but more hopeful of my survival, I hesitated but considered that we were the first vehicle through the canyon. We had extensive firepower. What if I failed to engage a position marked as the enemy's only to have men at that position hurt those behind us?

The ridgeline was the enemy's. No friendly could possibly be near, especially not on that ridgeline. Serial Two is alone.

I fired a short burst. Then another and another. The time from Baker's firing to mine was no more than ten seconds. Time strangely compressed as we continued to move forward.

As I fired a final burst to our vehicle's five o'clock we lurched to a sudden stop as an AMF soldier wearing tiger-striped BDUs frantically waved his hands in my face, having just run up to the back of the vehicle.

"Cease fire! Cease fire!" he yelled.

My eyes and mind zoomed out, no longer focusing narrowly on my field of fire searching for targets. Gears ground as I sought to orient myself. *It's over? We're okay? I thought all the AMF guys were with Serial One.*

Before I could consider much more, Sergeant Owens appeared. It was so good to see him ably running up to our vehicle, clearly unhurt.

"You guys all right?" he hollered. "Elliott, you okay?"

"Yeah, roger, Sarn't," I said with increasing relief.

"All right. Hang tight," he said as he jogged over to the vehicle coming to a stop behind us. I could see the dark shape of the Mk 19 in the turret and soon heard Kevin's voice as Owens checked on him.

"Tillman, you okay?" Owens yelled to Kevin.

"Roger, Sarn't," he yelled back. "But this thing is all f—ed up," he said, indicating the grenade launcher. "I couldn't get it to charge. Probably okay anyhow 'cause I don't think I could have fired it in the canyon. I got off a few rounds with my M9, though." Kevin said this with the sense of relief we all felt. Hearing his voice was a comfort.

Owens returned to our vehicle. "You guys sure you're okay?"

Am I okay? I wondered. My emotions were all over the place as I tried desperately to absorb and process the last fifteen minutes. I felt as though I were operating at multiple speeds simultaneously. Time was moving quickly and slowly. Things had changed but somehow seemed the same. So many voices competed for attention and melded into a mental static.

"Roger, Sarn't," I said. "I'm good."

"Good. I need you to pull security on our ten o'clock, so get the gun off the vehicle and redeploy over there. I'll give you a hand," Owens said.

I broke off the belt of rounds dangling from the 240, leaving a smaller belt of about twenty or so still inside the weapon. I had fired all the 240 rounds in my kit and searched to grab the most readily available can of ammo.

"Here, let me grab that," Owens said. "Just get the gun. How many rounds you want?" he asked.

Strangely, Sergeant Owens, my squad leader, became my assistant gunner. "One can is good, Sarn't."

"You got it," he said with confidence.

We walked over to face a long, open wadi, a road that fed into our position about forty yards from the vehicle.

"You think this is okay?" he asked.

"Roger, Sarn't. I've got a full field of fire. Should be good."

I set the gun down. The barrel was still hot.

"You good? I'll send Roberts over to AG for you in a minute."

"Roger, Sarn't. I'm good. Thank you," I said.

"You bet." He walked quickly back to the vehicles behind us.

I placed the gun on the floor of the rocky wadi, linked up a hundred-round belt, and replenished the two ammo pouches on my kit with the remaining rounds from the ammo can.

I took my helmet off and briefly scratched my sweaty head as I affixed my NODs to the front of my helmet. The dark landscape soon glowed in a bright green haze as I stared through my night vision. I tested the infrared laser on the 240 and, while lying prone, I settled the gun into the most comfortable firing position I could find. I lay there for a moment, feeling the empty safety of darkness.

After twenty minutes or so, Owens was back. I pushed myself up from the cold rocks.

He pulled a can of dip from his kit, packed it with two rapid snaps of his wrist, and filled his lower lip with Copenhagen.

"We got four casualties," he muttered through a mouthful of fresh tobacco.

I had no emotional response to that statement. I mentally registered concern and perversely felt more grown up in the way only a boy approaching death for the first time can feel.

"Who are they, Sarn't?"

The delivery was matter of fact, but even though we were standing alone, Owens lowered his voice: "The PL and Lane got hit, but I think they're going to be okay. Looks like one Afghan is KIA. And we had one KIA."

"Who is that, Sarn't?"

Riding on the exhale of a deeper-than-normal breath, the words "It was Pat" were pushed into the night.

I understood the words but they didn't compute. The adrenaline was draining from my system and exhaustion set in. The energy to emote was gone.

Pat is dead.

Kevin. Oh, God.

"You okay over here?" Owens asked again.

"Yeah, I'm good, Sarn't. I'm good."

"All right. Well, First Platoon is the quick reaction force, and they're on their way from Salerno. As soon as they show up, they'll take over security and you can get some rack."

"Sounds good, Sarn't." First Platoon. *Evan and Broek will be here.* I was comforted by the thought of friendly reinforcements.

Roberts eventually came over, and we debriefed our experiences in the kill zone. We quickly grew tired of talking and simply stood over the gun, staring down the alley of the empty wadi. My kit pressed heavily against my chest with no prospect of relief.

When First Platoon arrived, we were instructed to rack out. It felt like such a gift to have others pull security while we tried to sleep. I grabbed my sleeping bag from the Humvee and went over to join a familiar, shorter figure making his own bed in the darkness against the canyon wall. It was Boatright.

We awoke a few hours later, again baking in the Afghan sun, sweating as we greeted the day. I climbed out of my sleeping bag, fully dressed save for my kit and helmet, which were behind me. We talked briefly and tiredly as he crawled out of his sleeping bag as well.

I noticed a rust-colored stain on Boatright's BDU pants that had the unmistakable look of blood. He saw it as well, brushing at it a few times to no avail. It wouldn't go away.

We were quickly put to work cleaning the Humvee, limbs and hearts heavy. As I buried cold, empty cylinders of brass, I saved three of the spent 240 casings from my weapon as a memento of the day to make sure I wouldn't forget. I wondered how Lane and the PL were doing and how they were hit. I wrestled with the truth of Pat's death. He was gone. Just gone. How could that be?

At dusk, almost exactly one day after the firefight, we prepared to move out. The news then began to circulate. The cruel truth began to be spoken. Pat wasn't killed by the enemy. He was killed by friendly fire. By one of us.

Because .50-cal rounds were found lodged in the rock behind where he died, it was initially believed that Ashpole probably fired the rounds that caused his death. But several Rangers fired on that hillside. It could have been any one of us.

Including me.

6

BURDENS

Show me a hero and I will write you a tragedy.
F. SCOTT FITZGERALD

"Chow hall's closin' in ten minutes, maggots! Hurry up and get over there if you want some real food!" Sergeant Owens yelled to us, his words echoing through the latrine in which we were "freshening up." Having pulled into the FOB motor pool and dropped our weapons and kits at our tent, we were filthy and needed to knock off at least one layer of grime before getting some food.

I quickly turned on the faucet and threw warm water on my face. The dirt turned the water brown in the sink below. I washed until it was clear. As I lifted my gaze to the mirror in front of me, I greeted the face of a stranger. The lines and shape of the face were familiar, but the flesh and bone seemed animated by something unknown. A heaviness seemed to leak through my bloodshot eyes. I looked away, in no mood for self-reflection, and quickly jogged over to the chow hall.

Breakfast was underwhelming. Fruit medley and oatmeal were about all that were left. It didn't matter. I hardly tasted what I inhaled and would have eaten almost anything except cold, freeze-dried eggs.

With our hunger somewhat satisfied, we returned to our new home in the FOB, a large, green field tent with plywood floors. Weapons maintenance was the first order of business and included servicing the big guns, the .50 cal and Mk 19. After that work was completed, we were able to shower and put on a fresh set of BDUs.

As lunchtime approached, we weren't about to be late, and a much cleaner squad of maggots assembled outside the tent, waiting for Owens to march us over to the chow hall. I stood there along with Ashpole, Denton, Suhl, Ping, and Specialist Jason Bailey. Kevin was notably absent. He and Russell Baer were accompanying Pat's remains back to the States.

Even though I had just showered and put on clean clothes after almost two weeks in the field, I didn't feel as good as I should have. I slouched at the position of parade rest as we waited in silence. Ashpole stared straight at the ground. His eyes looked as though they were a moment away from tears.

Owens appeared from around the corner with his brisk, familiar step crunching the gravel. He took one look at us and let us have it.

"Parade f—ing rest, maggots!" His rhetoric seemed to awaken all of us to the fact that we were presenting a less-than-military appearance. We corrected our stance and with great effort stood fully upright.

Owens then took a breath, tempering his naked instinct to instill discipline at all costs. "Look, I know this is s—y, all right?" he said loudly, as if offering more decibels could erase the past. "This whole thing sucks. But it's not your fault, you understand? None of you gets to carry this by themselves. No single person here is at fault for what happened. Is that clear?" He addressed all of us but seemed to address Ashpole most of all.

"Roger, Sarn't," was our collective and feeble reply.

"Is that f—ing clear?" His tone nearly broke with intensity.

"Roger, Sarn't!" we yelled back with the same strained effort it took to stand.

As we walked quietly in single file toward the chow hall, I pondered his words.

Not our fault? How could that be? We fired. I fired. True, I didn't know there were friendlies there, but I fired. What's the penalty for that? What happens now?

Grief mixed with guilt until I couldn't tell the two apart.

Later that afternoon Sergeant Owens informed us we'd be able to call home if we wanted to but likewise reminded us of what we could and couldn't talk about. "You can call home and talk to whoever you want, but you are not to say anything about our operations or about what happened. Is that clear? You don't talk about it with anyone outside the platoon."

"Roger, Sarn't."

"No names of anyone. No nothin'. Some dumba— lieutenant from another company called home and said a bunch of s—, making it sound like he was out there with us. They're kicking him out and sending him home. They are listening to everything you say, so don't say anything. You got it?"

"Roger, Sarn't."

I waited in line at the FOB's Morale Welfare and Recreation tent to use the phone. For the first time since we deployed, I called home hoping to speak to Mom.

The phone rang until I heard a familiar "Hello?"

"Hey, it's me," I said.

"Oh, it is so good to hear from you," she said, clearly struck with emotion. Her voice carried more than just concern for her only son at war. She knew something. *What is on the news?* I wondered. *What does she know?*

"It's good to hear you too. Sorry it's taken me so long to call. We've been kind of busy."

"How are you doing?"

Her familiar voice evoked an emotion otherwise suppressed. "Not good," I said as my voice cracked. Had I spoken more, I would have broken down.

"I'm okay, though. I'm okay." I attempted to quell the concern that must have been growing in her heart and mind. "I have to go. I'm sorry. I have to go. We're fine. Nothing's happening now. I love you."

"I love you too," she said. "Please be careful."

"I will."

I hung up a failure. Unable to convince my mom that war was uneventful and that we were all having a great time. She knew. More than I did, she knew.

I went back to the tent and changed into boots, shorts, and a T-shirt so Ashpole and I could go to the gym. It felt good to work off some of the anxiety. We bench-pressed to exhaustion and did likewise with pull-ups. I felt better, but there was something inside me that the endorphins from a good lift just wouldn't touch. Something that would ebb and flow but never leave. Something that was now a part of me.

Later that evening, the maggots joined the rest of the platoon for a critical incident debrief. We were all there save for Kevin, Baer, Lane, and the PL. More than forty of us sat in folding chairs arranged in a circle lit dimly by two naked bulbs suspended from the roof of the tent.

I sat between Ashpole and Suhl. Sergeant Godec, now in full command of the platoon with the PL wounded, began. "Sheep, this is what's called a critical incident debrief. Anyone who wants to speak can speak freely. No one is recording or writing anything down. This is just a chance for everyone to talk about what they experienced and what they felt. We're not here to respond to what someone says but just to listen." His tone was calm, even soothing.

"Anything I missed, sir?" Godec asked of Captain Jeff Struecker, seated to his left. Struecker was the battalion chaplain and resident war god, having fought with Third Ranger Battalion at the Battle of Mogadishu in 1993.

Before Struecker could respond, we heard two successive explosions. Mortar rounds.

We all hit the deck, prostrating ourselves on the plywood and raising our heads as we took in our surroundings.

With no command, as if a school of fish were instinctively responding to a predator's strike, we got up and ran out of the tent, single file.

I followed Owens and the rest of the maggots as we ran the hundred meters to our tent. Still clad in our boots, shorts, and T-shirts, we proceeded to kit up.

I threw on my body armor and kit, placed my helmet on my head, and inserted a mag in my M4. I was ready to kill. The feeling was familiar; the switch flipped much more easily this time. I figured we'd naturally head out to our vehicles and hunt down whoever was firing on the FOB.

Owens placed a mag in his M4 and then paused, looking left and right. A spell began to break. "Hold on a second, Elliott."

He peeked his head outside our tent as I and the rest of the squad waited.

"You can take your s— off. It's okay. Just take it off, and let's head back to the debrief," he said, almost quietly.

"Roger, Sarn't," I replied as I took the mag out of my weapon and returned my gear to the foot of my cot. The rest of the maggots did likewise, Ashpole returning the 240 to its resting place on the floor.

The rest of the platoon had come to similar conclusions, and we piled out of our respective tents, leaving our battle gear behind. As we walked where we had just run, we noticed no one else had responded in kind. Other Rangers were casually talking, some were smoking, two continued their game of chess.

The Black Sheep reentered the debrief tent as sheepish as ever. Sergeant Godec and Captain Struecker sat unmoved where we had left them. A faint grin had spread across Godec's tan and weathered face.

The explosions we had heard were indeed mortars. *Our* mortars, firing flares into the landscape outside the FOB as part of the normal security routine—a routine we knew nothing about—meant to dissuade anyone from taking potshots from the nearby hillsides.

This was as good as any icebreaker you could come up with. With the shuffle of boots on wood and the creak of metal chairs, we again found our places in the circle.

"Anyone can speak," Godec restated. "You don't have to, but feel free to say what you need to say."

Pat's squad leader, Sergeant Matt Weeks, began with clear intensity, his words a horrific revelation. As he spoke, describing the gunfire and explosions they heard behind them in the canyon, their stopping, dismounting, and traversing up the ridgeline, pieces began falling into place.

Behind them, I thought. *We were behind them. They were in front of us. We were following them. F—.*

I listened as intently as I could. His words were like a blossoming flower, the bloom of which was just beginning to open and too hideous to stare at for long.

They had hoped to provide covering fire. Weeks and others in Serial One rushed to the high ground that overlooked the riverbed they'd traversed a few minutes prior. Everyone in Weeks's squad halted just short of the top of the ridge—everyone except for Pat, O'Neal, and AMF soldier Sayed Farhad, who was called Thani. The three of them continued over the ridgeline so that they had a clear view of the canyon floor. They received enemy fire from the opposite side of the canyon. Pat ran back to Weeks.

Weeks's voice cracked as he described approving Pat's plan and position to provide covering fire for Serial One. This was the last exchange Weeks and Pat would share. The guilt-laced words carried obvious implications: Weeks was blaming himself.

Sergeant Baker went next, his quiet monotone a departure from the emotion that Weeks had exhibited and largely squelched. But the emotion Baker harnessed was no less palpable. Baker recounted coming around the corner. Thani was firing over our heads at an enemy position on the other side of the canyon, and in doing so, he provided the muzzle flashes to which Baker responded. He told of putting six rounds into Thani and watching him fall, believing it was the enemy shooting at us. Baker seemed mildly dazed, a part of him broken, hollow.

He described us, the other occupants of his vehicle, following his lead. He almost emphasized that fact. We watched and listened as Baker impaled himself on his sergeant's chevrons. His words and tone echoed Weeks's: Baker was blaming himself.

Josey Boatright was next. He was part of Serial One, a member of Weeks's squad and squadmate of Pat and O'Neal.

There was no anger in his voice, his tone measured and empathetic. "We saw the canyon exploding behind us. Sergeant Weeks ordered us to dismount and take position to provide covering fire. I saw the first Humvee from Serial Two come around the bend. Their guns lit up. Rounds began kicking dirt all round me"—Josey raised his hands, whipping them toward himself to mimic the earth that was spitting at him—"and I felt trapped. Then a cease-fire was called."

The bud continued to open as we listened in horror. I didn't feel the relief of Boatright or the others' survival; I felt the weight of their death. How close that death had been. How close maybe I had come to killing them. I imagined all of Serial One gone, the circle that much smaller.

I reeled.

Josey went on to describe Pat's position after the cease-fire: "There was blood everywhere. Pat—he didn't really have a head. It was sort of caved in." He flinched faintly at the detail as his eyes moistened. "I helped get him prepped for medevac and helped carry him."

Others from Serial One seemed less grieved and more angry. Suhl recounted his actions and position as he looked at Ashpole and me. With a glance his feelings were clear: *Why were you firing at us?* He suppressed any direct accusation.

Will Aker was frank as he shared the horror of what we experienced. Getting shot at along with the rest of Serial One—shot at as they tried to help us. Seeing the bloody horrific mess that was once his friend, Pat. He didn't hesitate as he struggled to fight through his anger and confusion. "Why did you fire at us?"

Why were you on our flanks? I thought. *Why did you put us in this position?* My initial flare of anger became more measured. *How would*

I feel if I were them? Just as angry if not more so. Looking for someone to blame.

Still, I thought, *this needs to be over.*

Bryan O'Neal spoke next. He was with Pat when he was killed. Bryan was nineteen and, like me, on his first deployment.

Bryan sat almost directly across from me in the circle, twenty feet away. As he spoke, he more than anyone exhibited the thousand-yard stare, looking at nothing and yet seeing everything he was describing, living the moment all over again.

I struggled to focus. Each word he spoke felt like a knife plunging into me.

He described maneuvering up the ridgeline with Pat, positioning themselves to provide covering fire for us. O'Neal, following Pat's orders, said he maintained cover as Pat tried to mark their position with a smoke grenade. And then, "the rounds just kept coming in and coming in. I knew in that moment I was going to die. I prayed. Then I could hear pain in Pat's voice. I knew he'd been hit. He yelled out, 'Stop! I'm Pat f—ing Tillman! I'm Pat f—ing Tillman!'" O'Neal screamed Pat's final words into the dimly lit tent.

His cry was met with wretched silence.

The flower was in full bloom, its darkness displayed for all to see.

O'Neal's tone softened as he continued: "Then it went quiet, and all I could hear was the sound of water running. I couldn't figure out why I was wet. It was his blood."

Dear God.

Alders was next. With a tone of thinly veiled defiance, he described what he saw, what he remembered, why he fired. His apologetic fell flat when compared to the experience O'Neal had just shared.

Ashpole stared blankly at the floor. He quickly recounted his experience with no tone of defense. His demeanor dripped of guilt, practically imploring the executioner to proclaim the obvious and put him out of his misery.

I spoke only because Ashpole had. I couldn't break free from the hierarchy we were invited to briefly step outside of.

"I saw shapes, images moving on the hillside, and then I saw muzzle flashes. It was almost dark. It was hard to see. Sergeant Baker fired at those muzzle flashes. Everyone was firing there. It seemed like it was my job to fire too. I had no idea it was even possible for there to be friendlies on the ridgeline."

I was measured, exhibiting far more external detachment than I actually felt. It didn't seem safe to feel here. This was work. This was regiment.

I was wholly divided between two overwhelming emotions. The first was self-righteous anger. How dare they maneuver on our flanks with no comms and no way of us knowing they were there? But what would we have done in their position? Left the other half of the platoon to fight it out on their own? Of course not. We would have done the same.

The other feeling, a newer sensation fueled by the picture being painted by Serial One, was guilt-ridden horror. We caused this. The simple pull of triggers unleashed destruction and pain, the extent of which we had only just begun to understand. We caused this.

Others shared, their words always followed by a deafening silence. Finally, when it was clear everyone had spoken their piece, Captain Struecker brought things to a close.

"It was clearly an accident," Struecker said gently but directly. "You need not blame one another. In fact, in a way, it was everyone's fault."

Everyone's fault? I thought. *Where is the CO for our little debrief? He's conveniently missing. How can it be Boatright's fault? We were shooting at him. How can it be O'Neal's fault? He watched Pat get his head blown off. Maybe it's Pat's fault too? Or Lane? Or the PL?*

Who should carry the weight of remorse and responsibility? I couldn't say with certainty, but I knew I had my burden to shoulder as did our chain of command.

Struecker's words were the equivalent of approaching a gaping wound, with shrapnel lodged in the bulging and bleeding flesh, and neatly stitching it shut.

"There. All better," he might as well have said.

Bulls—.

The next morning after breakfast chow we were told we'd be having a company formation. This was the first and only such formation of the deployment, the purpose of which was unknown to me.

I stood at parade rest among the ranks of other BDU-wearing members of Alpha Company. I looked for Evan and couldn't find him. The sun beat down. The green tents of the FOB offered the only splash of color in a world filled with varying shades of brown.

"Company, attention!" called First Sergeant Thomas Fuller.

We immediately complied, bringing our right heel to meet our left and dropping our hands to our sides, head and eyes straight ahead.

The first sergeant began roll call. A name was called. Last name, first name, and then middle initial. Immediately and loudly the man who'd been named sounded off, "Here, First Sergeant!" Two more names were called with the same result.

Then the first sergeant called out, "Tillman, Patrick D.!"

Silence save for the breeze.

"Tillman, Patrick D.!"

Only the sound of stifled cries. He let the silence linger.

"Tillman, Patrick D.!"

Death had arrived in the form of silence where a voice should have been heard.

"Tillman, Patrick D., killed in action, 22 April 2004. Company, present arms!"

Alpha Company saluted.

A recording of taps began to play, drawing emotion from the otherwise silent formation. I fought back tears as the call of honor and remembrance I'd heard so many times played yet again.

The bugle stopped.

"Alpha Company, fall out!"

We went back to our tent, changed clothes, and worked out. We didn't say a word about the formation. We didn't say a word about any of it. We just wanted a distraction from the past that continued to unfold into the present.

That afternoon, Owens assembled the maggots and briefed us on what was to come. "All of us are going to have to give a statement to

Captain Scott. If you can't remember specifics, that's okay. Don't try to fill in blanks you don't know for sure. Just tell him what you know to the best of your memory. And whatever you do, don't lie. Just tell him the truth."

"Roger, Sarn't" was our reply.

Captain Richard Scott had been appointed to conduct an investigation according to Article 15-6 of the Uniform Code of Military Justice. Major David Hodne, a battalion team commander, made the appointment. Captain Scott was the commander of Headquarters Company, making him a direct peer of our Alpha Company commander, William Saunders, and a direct subordinate to the battalion commander, Lieutenant Colonel Jeff Bailey.

As the afternoon wore on, we waited for our turn to talk to Captain Scott. I lay on my cot in the darkened tent, reading Stephen King by the light of my headlamp.

"You're up, Steve," Denton said as he entered the tent having just come from talking with Scott.

"How was it?" I asked as Denton packed his Copenhagen and put in a dip.

"It was fine," he said. "There's a map in there so you can see where we were. I just told him what I could remember, and he seemed okay with it."

I felt a little better as I tossed the borrowed paperback on my cot and made my way to Captain Scott.

Scott's windowless tent was a makeshift office configured for meetings. Instead of cots, it contained a dozen six-foot-long wooden benches. It was the tent where chapel services were held. Today, however, the altar in this wartime church was a four-by-six topographical map of the April 22 operations area. The priest was a captain, his vestments were desert BDUs, and the elements of worship were a laptop, tape recorder, and pointer. The god we worshiped in this moment was named "What happened?" whose true character the priest sought to assemble from the broken fragments of our memories.

I was nervous. It was just the two of us. But Scott was friendly and professional.

"Specialist Elliott, sir," I said as I came to attention and saluted.

"Hey, Elliott. Have a seat," Scott said, politely returning my salute. "Relax. So, has anyone told you exactly what this is?"

"Not exactly, sir. I just know we're supposed to tell you what we can remember about what happened."

"That's correct. Specifically, this is an Article 15-6 investigation, which means we're just trying to find out what happened. You're not in trouble. This is not a criminal investigation. Do you understand?"

"Yes, sir."

"Do you have any questions of me before we get started?"

"No, sir."

"I'll be recording our conversation, if that's okay with you," he said, reaching for a small minicassette recorder.

"That's fine, sir."

"Okay. Why don't you start at the beginning? Tell me about 22 April."

I then described the day's events as I recalled them. He helped me orient myself to the area of operations. The large map was the first I'd seen of our AO. I told him what I saw. I told him where I thought I fired and why. He was attentive throughout. After about thirty minutes it was over.

"You're free to go, Elliott. Can you please have Specialist Ashpole come in next?"

"Yes, sir," I said as I stood to the position of attention.

"Rangers lead the way, sir," I said as I saluted.

"All the way" was the reply that accompanied his return salute.

Is that it? I thought as I left the tent. *Maybe that's it. Maybe that's the last time I'll have to talk about it.* I felt slightly relieved.

A routine was established as we moved beyond April 22. Eat, work out, train, read, work out, and sleep. Training was mostly Ashpole and me doing gun drills on the 240, practicing to get the gun ready to fire as quickly as possible. These drills took on a new intensity as Ashpole seemed to shift his grief and guilt into work. He shut down and focused and took me along with him. We never talked about what happened.

That night, as I was reading *It* on my cot, Ashpole, the 240 slung over his shoulder, said, "Come on. We're heading over to the motor pool."

"Roger, Specialist."

We started lying in the prone, he behind the gun, me beside it, linking and feeding rounds.

"Prepare to move," he said.

"Roger, Specialist." This was my cue to break off the belt feeding into the gun, leaving no more than a fifty-round belt still attached to the weapon. This enabled us to get up and bound to our next position.

"Pick it up," he said as we pushed ourselves off the dirt and sprinted forward another thirty yards before dropping again to the prone.

"Rounds," he said flatly.

I pulled another belt of rounds out of my kit and snapped the final black link onto the belt already dangling from the gun.

We did this again and again and again. For an hour we did this. Until my hands couldn't snap the links anymore. Until both of us were smoked.

I slept heavy but not well.

The next morning, we got word that First Platoon was back in the FOB. After responding as a quick reaction force to our position on the evening of April 22, they had stayed in the field, scouring the hillsides of the canyon, trying to obtain any intelligence concerning those that had planned and executed the ambush.

Other maggots were gathered in a First Platoon tent. One of their team leaders was seated on his cot, filthy and taking off his body armor, having just arrived a few minutes before.

"That's what we found up there," he said, pointing to two bolt-action rifles and one sorry-looking Kalashnikov lying on the plywood floor. The rifles were a hundred years old if they were a day. "There was a couple of blood trails. No bodies. Nothin' else but that. They mighta hauled out any dead or wounded. Don't know. That's what we found. I guess they got a bead on some guy in the nearby village that might know something. Might have connections around here closer to Salerno. Don't know. Sorry we couldn't get 'em."

The ambush became the impetus for more operations. Now that we'd finally gotten someone to shoot at us, the focus was to kill or capture anyone associated with or responsible for the events of April 22. It was comforting to place the blame on a faceless, nameless "enemy," someone other than ourselves who could be held responsible.

By May 1, we were back in the saddle, going on a series of nighttime raids into the surrounding villages and countryside. We reverse-cycled, sleeping during the day and waking at about three o'clock in the afternoon to eat and work out before assembling for our operations order. Then, once night had fallen, we would mount our vehicles in the dark to get some bad guys. This routine was repeated almost daily. The events of April 22 were behind us, except that they weren't.

On May 9, I was called back into the same tent where I had been interviewed by Captain Scott not long before. Another investigation had been ordered by Seventy-Fifth Ranger Regiment Commander Colonel James Nixon. He had appointed his second in command, Lieutenant Colonel Ralph Kauzlarich, to conduct another 15-6 investigation. It struck me as slightly odd and certainly irritating to have to recount the events of April 22 to yet another stranger. But I didn't think much of it. I had seen the army do dumber things.

"Have a seat," Kauzlarich said, he himself already seated. He was six feet and lanky with balding brown hair. He looked bored to tears. "You're Elliott, right?"

"Roger, sir."

"Okay, tell me what happened on 22 April," he said, taking no notes, consulting no map, and without any tape recorder that I can recall. He just sat there while I talked, politely waiting for my lips to stop moving.

I told him what I had told Captain Scott, my memory of April 22 having faded but my memory of what I said to Captain Scott fresher. It became a copy of a copy. I finished in less than ten minutes.

"Great," Kauzlarich said. "Thank you. You're free to go. Send in the next guy in your squad who hasn't been in here yet."

"Roger, sir. Rangers lead the way, sir," I said saluting.

"All the way," he said, standing and returning the salute, the unit motto awakening some measure of attentiveness.

That must be it. Probably just tying up a few loose ends or something, I told myself as I walked away.

That evening there was no mission, so I went to the "church" service being held for special ops guys and conducted by Captain Struecker. Maybe twenty guys were there. A few popular Christian songs were sung and a devotional was offered by Struecker.

"Blessed be the name of the Lord," one of the songs went. "You give and take away. You give and take away. My heart will choose to say, 'Lord, blessed be your name.'"

Why? Why should my heart say that? I thought. *What gives him the right to take?*

I never had the chance to go to FOB church again. But I wouldn't have wanted to.

The raids were running together in my mind. Each day almost exactly like the last. Each night viewed through the same one-eyed, green haze of night vision.

★

Word came that we'd be rotating back home soon, but before we left the FOB, there was at least one more raid for the Black Sheep to conduct. The intelligence was promising: a High Value Target (HVT) with possible ties to April 22.

With darkness upon us, we climbed aboard our Humvees for the hour drive that would take us to the objective. The roads were good by Afghan standards. No wadis to negotiate. We moved briskly through the night. Our vehicle's occupants were the same as they had been on April 22.

We rolled in hot, expecting a fight given the importance of the HVT. Our vehicle was positioned about forty yards away from the front door of the house complex we'd be assaulting. Ashpole and I stayed on the vehicle as part of a blocking position, Ashpole on the .50 cal and me on the 240. Our job was to ensure that nothing got into or out of the objective while the line dogs conducted their assault.

I glanced over my shoulder and could see Sergeant Weeks and the rest of his squad stacked in a line outside the main door. It was strange how I came to recognize the shape and movement of people without seeing their faces.

The feeble door was easily breeched and the "controlled hurry" that was a room-clearing operation ensued. They quickly shuffled inside and we awaited the sound of gunfire, but none came, which was a relief.

After about fifteen minutes, Weeks, the interpreter, and the rest of the assault squad emerged with the man who appeared to be the owner of the home.

I saw Weeks reach for the radio mic on his kit and lean his head to the left, and then I heard his voice over the vehicle's radio: "This ain't it. We got the wrong objective. HVT is not here. Please advise. Over."

Great.

"Squirter, six o'clock!" yelled one of the Black Sheep.

I swung my weapon around only to hear a shot and see an Afghan man fall to the ground.

"Sniper brought him down," Ashpole said. "Looks like he got him in the a—. Great shot."

With no HVT and a new casualty on the objective, our mission shifted. We now provided security for the medevac chopper that soon came and retrieved this anonymous "squirter," someone who made the unfortunate choice to run from the objective. The man would live.

We left FOB Salerno the next day, the same way we had come, via a Chinook that took us to Bagram. After three days there, we climbed aboard a C-17 and left Afghanistan where we'd found it.

★

After turning in my M4 and M9 to the arms room, I headed back up to the Second Platoon AO and the barracks room I shared with McCoy. He was there.

"Steve! Dude, it is so good to see you! How are you, man? Dude, it's crazy what happened," he said, himself pained by the casualties we'd sustained.

"I should've been there, man. I should've been there," he said.

"It's all right, man, you're doing what you're supposed to be doing.

Going to Ranger School. How's that goin'? You're not done already, are you?"

"No, man. I got some leave and wanted to see you guys. I head back to Benning next week. I got these, though. I got copies for everyone," he said, pointing to a stack of *Sports Illustrated* magazines. On the cover was Pat, hair waving as he ran across the gridiron.

I cringed at seeing a dead man as he once was, full of life. I picked up a copy so as not to insult McCoy. His intentions were good; he wanted to help us memorialize a fallen comrade.

"Thanks, Chris. That's really great," I said, setting my copy down as quickly as I could. It would be ten years before I'd bring myself to read the article that had been written. I knew the story and wanted to forget it.

This was a big deal. The media had been busy in our absence. *What are they saying about Pat? What are they saying about us?*

I turned the key in my black Subaru Rally Sport, and thankfully it hummed to life. Josey Boatright, James Roberts, and Evan were in the car with me. It was Saturday, May 22. Five days prior, we'd been at the FOB. After landing at McChord a few hours prior, turning in weapons and grabbing a shower, we had a new objective: finding the best food that money could buy.

I stepped on the gas and pulled onto I-5 on my way to Tacoma.

"Yeah!" Evan yelled as we all laughed with relief. We were off the clock, finally. No sergeants, no regiment, no war. We debriefed the deployment, all of us having gone for the first time with few if any opportunities to talk frankly about our experiences until now. Every topic was fair game—except for April 22. Evan was the only guy with us that night who wasn't part of the platoon, and he knew better than to bring it up. Roberts, Boatright, and I were completely fine with that.

We walked down the streets of downtown Tacoma and entered the steakhouse El Gaucho. The restaurant reeked of class as tuxedo-clad waitstaff ushered us down the grand staircase to our candlelit table. A pianist was deftly playing jazz standards. One could not help but relax.

We gorged ourselves on steak, lobster, and halibut, none of it freeze-dried. The ice in our glasses reminded us of simple luxuries we had forgone the past six weeks. Boatright and Roberts drank but not heavily. Evan and I abstained. We just didn't have a taste for alcohol. War stories were told, all except one.

As our food settled, the joy of simply being alive pervaded us, and we were just getting started for the night.

We were still on Afghan time, so we figured we'd stay up all night and all the next day to get ourselves reset. We purchased cigars at El Gaucho and retreated to an all-night coffee shop in Tacoma to smoke and talk. With each drag and puff, Afghanistan felt farther and farther away.

Sleep was coming for us, though. Jet lag was kicking in. As Saturday night became Sunday morning, we decided to catch a movie to get us through. *Troy* was the unanimous selection. The film is loosely based on the Trojan War of Greek mythology. In a sparsely filled theater, we grabbed the best seats in the middle. I sank into the plush upholstery and marveled at the grandeur of a simple, American movie theater.

The previews began as I fought back yawn after yawn.

Suddenly, Evan was shaking me. I found myself lying down on the seat next to mine, immediately sitting up as I watched the film's final credits. I had missed the war of Troy. I had missed the tragedy of Hector and Achilles.

That story was over as another was just beginning.

7

TRUTH AND
CONSEQUENCES

The first casualty when war comes is truth.
HIRAM JOHNSON

"Beep, beep, beep . . ." I groaned as I turned off the alarm on my wrist-watch. The face of the timepiece glowed and told me it was 5:30 a.m. It was Monday, May 24, and work call was at six.

I reluctantly gave up the warmth and comfort of my poncho liner, a thin, camouflage blanket reverently known as a "woobie," and put on my PT uniform—black T-shirt with the Second Batt scroll on the left breast with black running shorts to match. After I laced my running shoes, I walked across the hall to the latrine. I pushed open the door and froze.

The latrine was empty save for one other Ranger, wearing his black PTs as well. He was walking toward me. It was Kevin. The last time I saw him was on April 22.

Unbeknownst to me, Kevin had driven to Fort Lewis on Saturday to greet the first wave of Alpha Company as they returned from Afghanistan. When he saw guys from the platoon joking and laughing, obviously thrilled to be home, he was understandably upset. How could they be happy when Pat was dead? I was part of the second wave, and he was gone before I arrived.

My first instinct was to bolt, but I couldn't. Walking toward me was the living resemblance of the life that had been lost, a reminder of the cost of war etched into the face of a brother.

At that point, I was certain Kevin knew Pat's death was fratricide and that I was among the Rangers who had fired in his direction. It had been over a month—how could he not know? With hardly any access to media, no Internet in the barracks, and only a flip phone, I had no idea that a nationally televised memorial service for Pat had been broadcast on May 3. I had no idea what anyone had been told. I assumed everyone knew the same obvious truth the rest of the platoon knew. The same truth I had told when questioned.

As we walked toward each other, he on his way out of the room and I on my way in, I could see the pain in his eyes. He likewise seemed to detect the uncertainty, even fear, in mine. With a half smile, he graciously extended his hand. I did likewise and we shook hands briefly, Kevin seeming to comfort me more than I him.

A few minutes later, Alpha Company was assembled in front of the barracks. The maggots, Kevin now among us, stood in our line at the back of Second Platoon and waited for Owens.

"Back to garrison," Bailey said.

"Yeah, Owens'll be back to his old self," Suhl agreed.

"You missed us, didn't you?" Bailey said as he nudged Kevin, trying to lighten the mood. "I know you missed Sergeant Owens. We had him all to ourselves."

Kevin finally cracked a smile.

"Parade rest, maggots!" was the familiar command from the familiar voice that seemed to come out of nowhere.

"Company, attention!" First Sergeant Fuller commanded, and the formation responded. "Platoon sergeants, fall out and conduct PT!"

"Roger, First Sergeant!" was the unanimous reply from Godec and his three colleagues.

"Squad leaders fall out and conduct PT!" was the command, continuing to roll downhill.

"Roger, Sarn't!" came the reply from Owens and the other squad leaders.

"Ready to run, maggots?"

"Roger, Sarn't!" was our obligatory response.

Owens went relatively easy on us. After the squad run, he had admin duties to attend to and placed the gunners—Suhl, Ashpole, and Kevin—in charge.

"Let's grab a lift, Elliott. That run wasn't enough," Ashpole said.

"Roger, Specialist."

"Hey, anyone want to come with us? Elliott and I are gonna go lift."

"Sure, I'll come along with you guys," Kevin said.

The two-minute walk from the A Co. barracks to the battalion weight room was silent. All of us were happy for some measure of physical distraction. Some semblance of normalcy. We attempted to trade a brutal past for a present in which nothing had changed, where life carried on as it had before.

How is Kevin doing? I thought. *What is he feeling?* I was amazed that he seemed to be functioning as well as he was. I wanted simultaneously to know and to forget. To go deeper and to stay shallow. The inertia of the immediate was inescapable. The path of least resistance was to simply not talk about it, so that is what we did.

We entered the busy weight room, music blaring and plates clanging. I was grateful it was too loud to talk. We bench-pressed and spotted each other, keeping the weight from crushing each other as we each reached the point of exhaustion. We continued to lift.

The walk back to the company was even more quiet. Things would never be the same, but perhaps they could be better than they felt today. Maybe we could work with each other again. Maybe there would be better days ahead.

The next afternoon, Denton and I were sitting in the squad room with Suhl and Ashpole. The smell of gun oil filled the air. Weapons maintenance was the order of the day. Ashpole and Suhl tore apart the 240s while Denton and I stripped down our M4s and M9s. A *Family Guy* DVD played in the background. Behind us were our bunks and wall lockers set against the white cinder-block wall that separated us from the other room in which Ping and Kevin were working.

"I love Stewie," Denton said, referring to the baby in *Family Guy*. "He's hilarious."

"Is Quahog an actual place?" I asked Denton. "It's supposed to be in Rhode Island, I think."

"Not exactly, but there's a town sort of like it right near where I grew up."

"Question: If you're from Rhode Island, isn't *everything* in Rhode Island right near where you grew up?" I joked.

"That's hilarious. You callin' my state small? At least we're not outnumbered by cows," Denton said with eager curiosity to see how I'd respond.

"Ooh. Whatcha say to that, Elliott?" Ashpole said, trying to egg us on.

"Fight, fight, fight!" Suhl and Ashpole chanted in jest.

The zinger I had ready dissolved in the sound of a scream and glass shattering against the wall next door.

We froze. Silent. Straining to hear.

We glanced at each other, each searching the face of the others to try to understand what had just happened.

Kevin, I thought.

Owens entered a minute later.

"Hey," he said in a voice not much above a whisper. "There's a mess next door. Would you guys mind cleaning it up? I'm sorry to ask you to do this."

"Roger, Sarn't," Denton and I immediately replied.

We stepped through the hallway and into the squad room next door. Chewing tobacco and saliva were spread in a circular pattern around an impact point on the otherwise white wall. The still-dripping spit guided our eyes to the remnants of a smashed beer bottle scattered across the blue tile. Without a word, we quickly and robotically eradicated the mess, eager to see it gone and to cleanse the memory with Lysol.

We returned to clean our weapons in silence.

Later that afternoon, Sergeant Owens stepped into the squad room, oddly wearing his civilian clothes though the duty day had not yet ended.

"What's going on, Sarn't?" I asked. The rest of the maggots came out of nowhere except for Kevin.

"Kevin's not doing well. I took him out to coffee to talk about it and let him go home. He just found out that Pat's death was friendly fire. He's having a really hard time with that. Especially with the rest of us laughing and acting like everything is okay."

Wait. What? He didn't know?

Everyone in the platoon knows. We knew almost immediately. It has been nearly five weeks. They had a memorial service. How could Kevin not know? What has he been told? What is going on?

What I didn't know in that moment was that the army had disseminated a story about Pat's death that led Kevin, the Tillman family, and the nation to believe that he died gloriously in a hail of enemy fire.

On April 25, Kevin had repeatedly called FOB Salerno from Bagram, asking to speak to O'Neal about what happened. Lieutenant Colonel Jeff Bailey, the battalion commander, finally gave O'Neal permission to speak with Kevin but not before ordering him to say nothing about friendly fire. Before the flight back to the States with Kevin and Pat's remains, Russell Baer was also ordered to say nothing about fratricide.

Bailey reportedly directed Major Hodne to recommend Pat for a posthumous Silver Star, one of the highest decorations that the military offers in recognition of valor in combat. A draft of the recommendation sent April 27 was supported by two witness statements, one from O'Neal and one from Sergeant Mel Ward, also a member of Serial One. Yet neither man signed his statement. O'Neal apparently refused after observing that his original statement had been embellished. Sergeant Ward reportedly didn't even remember making a statement. Nothing in the final citation stated how Pat died. After the May 3 memorial service, Pat's father asked Baer to describe the firefight. Baer told what he could while following orders and leaving out details of friendly fire. Everything that had been done and said—and left unsaid—by our chain of command and by the Department of Defense led to the very clear impression that Pat was killed by the Taliban.

But I didn't know any of this then. The implications of what Sergeant Owens had just said were beyond my grasp.

What is going on?

The next morning, I descended the stairs on my way to the arms room to start retrieving the big guns, the .50 cal and Mk 19, for maintenance. That task always fell to the maggots. The company was quiet as I walked past the first sergeant's office. He wasn't there, but somebody's kit was. The vest we all wore that held our front and back ceramic plates also included pouches where gear was placed. Attached to the front left portion of the vest is a radio handset. Holes in this kit's vest pockets indicated where bullets had left their mark, tearing through the densely woven green nylon.

I didn't stop to stare for long, a few seconds at most—no one wants to get caught hanging around the first sergeant's office. I instantly understood that this was the kit belonging to Jade Lane, the platoon radio operator who was hit along with the PL on April 22. During the ambush, Lieutenant Uthlaut and Lane took positions next to the outside wall of a two-story mud home in the tiny village that was below and west of Pat's position on the hillside. Both fired their M4s at enemy positions on the opposite side of the canyon as our Humvee rolled through the wadi below them. The PL was struck in the face with shrapnel, likely from an exploding grenade fired by Johnson's M203 grenade launcher. Lane was hit twice by bullets, once in the knee and once in the chest, the latter ricocheting off his body armor and searing his right shoulder.

I saw green splotches on the tears in his kit, the residue of belt-fed American weapons like the 240 that I fired and the SAW that Alders manned.

That meant Lane's wounds were caused by either Alders or me

or both of us. Alders was adamant and specific about where he fired, sure that he never engaged Lane and the PL's position.

That left me.

It didn't make sense. I didn't fire at the village, at those guys . . . did I? I had no memory of shooting at that building, yet the physical evidence was undeniable.

Those green splotches.

It must be true. *I* shot Lane. I nearly killed him.

If that was true, what else did I not remember?

I kept walking.

The next day was Thursday, May 27. I was told that Sergeant Godec, still the acting PL, wanted to see Ashpole, Alders, and me.

We sat there, the three of us in our starched green BDUs and spit-shined black boots, tan berets in hand. We waited in the barracks room next to the platoon sergeant's office.

Godec entered.

"At ease," he called out, and before we could stand, Godec said, "Carry on, carry on."

We sat on a couch as he perched himself on the bureau in front of us.

He took a breath and got right to the point. "Here's the deal. You have a meeting later today with Captain Saunders. All of you, along with Baker and the PL, are getting RFSd. That's what the CO is going to tell you. You'll each receive a company-grade Article 15, which will basically stay in your A Co. file but won't follow you. You'll be reassigned to other infantry units in the big army. Don't know where yet, but I'm told you'll have some preference if you want to stay on Fort Lewis."

Alders was enraged. "RFSd, Sarn't? For what?"

"Failure to follow the ROE and lack of weapons discipline," Godec replied.

"Permission to speak freely, Sarn't?" Alders asked with formality.

"Yeah, of course," Godec replied, trying to cut through the jargon.

"If we're such f— ups, why didn't we get sent home from deployment? Why'd we stay in the platoon and go out on missions?" Alders asked.

"Why's the PL getting fired, Sarn't?" Ashpole asked. "He got wounded."

I didn't say a word. It wouldn't matter.

"All I can tell you is that this is coming from higher. It's coming from the BC," Godec replied, neither betraying the chain of command nor supporting it.

A few hours later we sat crammed in Captain Saunders's office—he, Sergeant Godec, Sergeant Baker, Alders, Ashpole, and I. Saunders was fair-haired. His forty-year-old, fit physique juxtaposed oddly with his face, worn with care and stress and aged beyond his years.

I barely heard what he said as I watched his lips move. He simply repeated what Godec had already told us, adding to it that Baker would be fined—$2,000, I believe.

Huh? So that was a two-thousand-dollar mistake? Assessing a financial penalty for anything that had occurred seemed bizarre at best. Either the mistake was epic and required an epic punishment, or it was understandable given the circumstances and required no punishment beyond the guilt we all carried.

As I tolerated the moments in the CO's office, I discovered I hated him. The man who put us in that position *to get back his Humvee* was the man firing us. This man was firing the PL who had fought against the decision to split the platoon. In that moment I hated him.

Maybe we should be sitting here, I thought. *Maybe we should be fired. Maybe we deserve far worse. But you weren't there. You don't get to be the one to fire us unless you're also firing yourself.*

After his statement to us concluded, we followed Godec's lead as we stood and saluted—the rank, not the man.

Word spread quickly. That night Boatright sauntered into my room. Without a word he plopped on a chair in the corner, beer in hand, pupils dilated. He was drunk, and he had something to say.

I sat on the couch across from him.

"Hey, Josey. How you doin'?"

"It's f—ed, man. All that s—. Pat. And now you guys gettin' fired?"

I had nothing to say.

He continued, "You know, I thought I had found something I was good at. I thought I'd found a place I could do something that matters. But I can't stay here. It's you today, and it could be me tomorrow. Higher doesn't give a f—. Hiding behind all that Ranger Creed bulls—. They don't give a f— about us." He took another swig as he stared off.

Was he right? Were we being wronged? There was no question, I had fired on friendlies. I had to pay something for that, right? Or could I off-load that on those with more rank and experience?

"Thanks, Josey. I'm really sorry for what happened out there. I'm sorry we fired at you."

"Ah, man. I probably would have done the same thing. What were you supposed to do? Who's to judge you for that?"

Me, I thought. *I can judge me for that. The CO, the BC, Kevin, the Tillmans, Jade, the media. God.*

The following day, our platoon was ordered to attend a briefing by Lieutenant Colonel Bailey. Bailey was the battalion commander for just a few more days. He was slated to rotate out, having completed his assignment as Second Batt BC. His departure had nothing to do with the events of April 22. It had already been planned.

The herd of Black Sheep assembled and marched across the quad to the battalion headquarters. We sat in the battalion conference room as the BC began his brief complete with PowerPoint slides.

It was a presentation meant to sew shut the bursting wound once and for all. He was selling us on what happened, how we had screwed up, and why the five of us were being fired. There were differing feelings toward Baker, Alders, Ashpole, and me. Some were like Josey and thought it unfair that we should get fired. Others thought it was too lenient, that we deserved worse. Everyone, though, was united in their support of the PL. The guy who fought against splitting the platoon and got a mouthful of shrapnel for following orders was being fired by the chain of command that set the events of April 22 in motion. The wound that Struecker had attempted to close at the critical incident debrief chafed against Bailey's words. It festered, the stitches slowly tearing.

Later that afternoon, as I sat in the barracks contemplating my future, Struecker walked in. I jumped to attention.

"Sit down, sit down. Relax," he said.

"Roger, sir," I said as I sat on the couch, staring at the cross sewn on his collar.

"You're Elliott?"

"Roger, sir."

"How you doin'?" he asked.

"I'm okay, sir."

"Well, I just wanted to check in and make sure you were all right. You hang in there, okay? Don't let this get you down."

"Roger, sir."

"You need anything from me, you let me know. Okay?" he said, raising his voice half an octave to indicate the conversation was over.

"Roger, sir."

"Okay," he said with a smile striving for reassurance. "You know where I can find Alders?"

Struecker's just making the rounds to make sure the BC's PowerPoint didn't make us suicidal.

"Roger, sir. He should be in their squad room, down at the end of the hall. Take a left at the *T*, and their room is on the left."

"Thank you," he said as he stood and saluted, inviting me to do the same.

"Rangers lead the way, sir."

"All the way."

Get me outta here.

That Saturday, Evan and I took a hike. We drove past Olympia on Highway 101 to the south end of the Olympic National Forest to hike to the peak of Mount Ellinor. The drive took about two hours as we bounced along the final stretch of trail roads in Evan's black Chevy S10 pickup. Conversation meandered. Evan would be going to Ranger School soon, which was great news. He didn't know I was getting RFSd.

As we placed the truck in park at the upper trailhead, I knew I had to tell him.

I hesitated. "Hey, there's something I have to tell you."

Evan instantly engaged, his eyes narrowing as he focused on what I was about to say.

"Well, what is it? What's going on?"

"I'm getting RFSd. Not just me but Baker, Alders, Ashpole. Even the PL. The five of us are getting fired."

"For what? I don't understand. I thought Ashpole hit him. Baker was in charge, right? How can they fire you? I mean, what happened, exactly?"

We'd never talked about it. Evan, my best friend, fellow Ranger, and part of the quick reaction force that relieved us on the night of April 22, probably knew less about what happened that day than half of America that read the news.

I felt wronged. I felt petty for feeling wronged. I felt like I deserved none of the concern or outrage people like Josey or Evan were feeling for me.

We hiked, climbing the steep, still-snowy peak. We came down trying to make sense of it all.

I found myself in administrative purgatory. I was still assigned to Second Ranger Battalion but was in the process of being RFSd. Suddenly, I was Schrader—there but not there. A walking cancer for other newbies to avoid. I just wanted to leave.

But before my new assignment could be secured, there was Ranger Ball on June 10. Ranger Ball was a party at the American Lake Conference Center, the Fort Lewis officers' club. The battalion got decked out in class A uniforms and jump boots, and after enduring some chicken breast, rice pilaf, and a couple of speeches, most guys got trashed.

I was relieved to think I wouldn't have to go until Sergeant Owens informed me otherwise. "Elliott, you will attend Ranger Ball, is that clear? It's not optional. You're a part of this platoon, and you will be in attendance."

"Roger, Sarn't."

It felt nice to be included, but it was a forced inclusion. Was this Owens's way of protesting our departure? I didn't know, but I had to be at the ball—that much was clear. All of us did, Ashpole, Alders, and Baker.

As I knotted my black tie and buttoned my class A jacket, I was struck by the plain blue ribbon above my right breast pocket. It was a Presidential Unit Citation, awarded to Second Ranger Battalion for actions taken on D-day. Above that ribbon was my name tag, "Elliott." I was authorized, *required*, to wear that ribbon as part of my uniform as long as I was assigned to Second Batt. It was a mark of shame, an indicator of what I was not.

Evan and I made our way to the American Lake club, and we mostly just hung out with other friends, Dustin Broek, Josey Boatright, and Marc Denton. Lots of guys made it a point to tell me how glad they were I was there. Others ignored me altogether.

We sat at long banquet tables as the program started. Surrounding us were a bunch of new guys that had arrived during our deployment. They looked so young. *Did I look that young?* They were wide-eyed, taking it all in.

One of them snapped to parade rest as I walked to my seat.

"What are you doing?" I asked him. "Relax."

"Roger, Specialist."

"Stop it. I'm Elliott. I'm nobody, okay?"

"You're part of Second Platoon, right? Pat Tillman's platoon? You were over there with him, weren't you?"

What does he think? What has he been told?

"Yeah, I'm part of Second Platoon, but not for long. Just relax, okay? I'm not gonna smoke you for anything. You're makin' me nervous."

He smiled and relaxed a bit.

Lieutenant Colonel Bailey made the opening remarks and dedicated the evening to Pat, the second member of Second Battalion to be killed in action in Iraq or Afghanistan. The lights were dimmed and a slide show accompanied by music began. Still shots of battalion operations appeared and dissolved. The final image was of Pat, sitting in front of the American flag, his tan beret cocked boldly above his brow.

The lights came back up. The screen darkened. The new guys just stared at me—perhaps in awe of my tie to the famous, perhaps out of pity for my infamy. I couldn't tell and would never know. They just stared, speechless.

8

BROOK

Whatever our souls are made of,
his and mine are the same.
EMILY BRONTË

Alders stumbled out of the car, a half-empty fifth of whiskey in his hand. His wife helped him into the restaurant as he joined the rest of us.

The Black Sheep assembled one final time in the tiny town of Steilacoom, situated right outside Fort Lewis and overlooking Puget Sound. Nearby on I-5 to the north were Tacoma and Seattle; to the south, the state capital, Olympia. It was a beautiful evening as summer finally arrived. The days were lengthening, and the ever-present winter rain gave way to blue skies.

Second Platoon would be deploying back to Afghanistan soon, and they were giving Baker, Alders, Ashpole, and me one final send-off.

We still didn't know where we were going. Baker was likely getting out of the army. Alders was in the process of dropping his SF packet to go to Special Forces selection. Ashpole and I were simply hoping to be reassigned to one of the Stryker brigades on Fort Lewis. Neither of us had any desire to leave the Pacific Northwest. No door outside of the Ranger regiment was closed for any of us, but our respective careers with the regiment were over for good.

I was one of the first to arrive at the restaurant, working off the theory that the sooner I showed up, the sooner I could leave. Ashpole was next, then a drunken Alders and his wife.

Then Lane arrived. He was twenty-two but looked even younger.

He limped in using a cane.

He joined in conversation with a few other guys. I talked mostly with Denton and Boatright. Lane eyed me as I did him. I didn't know what to say, so I said nothing.

As the crowd grew, we moved from the dark confines of the pub to the covered patio as beer was drunk and cigarettes lit. I didn't have either.

I sat on one of the white plastic chairs as Sergeant Weeks came up and joined me. "Hey, Elliott."

"Hey, Sarn't."

"Listen, I'm gonna be leaving Fort Lewis soon. I'm heading to Ranger Training Brigade to be a Ranger instructor. I want you to have my number."

I hesitated.

"Well, get your phone out so I can give it to you," he instructed.

I retrieved my Motorola Razr and took down his digits as he recited them. Satisfied that I had his number, he continued, "You call me anytime, you understand? If you need anything, you call me. Do not hesitate."

"Roger, Sarn't. Thank you."

"Listen up, Sheep!" Sergeant Godec announced. "This is the last time we'll all be together. We're here to say good-bye to a few folks."

He continued and then handed out our plaques. Each of us received a framed memento of our time with Second Platoon that included our name, dates of service, and the platoon coin.

Do I deserve this?

I offered my thanks to Sergeant Godec and to all the squad leaders and left as quickly as possible.

I continued to attend church, the same church I had gone to prior to deployment and where I had met Brook. Beyond the social aspect, I wasn't sure why I was there. The sound of the music, the words of the pastor, the whole construct of the place just felt hollow. It didn't make sense. It was what I knew to do so I continued to do it, but I couldn't really tell you why beyond that. I didn't know what it meant anymore.

If nothing else, it was an escape from battalion, a place where my failures didn't seem as real and didn't follow me through the door. I was already running from the past, and I didn't even know it.

On July 1, I walked out of the dimly lit amphitheater after the Thursday evening service was over and made my way down the long corridor toward the exit. On my way out, I noticed a cute redhead standing behind a registration table for an upcoming youth conference. Her straight hair fell to the middle of her back. Soft, poignant blue eyes noticed me as I noticed her. Though we had met and even talked, it was as if I were seeing her for the first time. I felt drawn to the table, or more precisely, to the girl standing behind it.

"Hey, Brook, how's it goin'?" I asked.

"Good," she said. After an awkward pause, she added, "How are you?"

"I'm good. Yeah, I'm good. What's all this for?"

"Oh, it's just registration stuff for a high school conference coming up." A pause.

"Cool. Yeah, that's great. Well, I should probably get back to post. Have a good night."

"You too."

After church the following Sunday, I was invited to hang out with a bunch of folks at a nearby park. Being in no hurry to return to the barracks, I gladly tagged along. Brook was also among the dozen or so who showed up on a bright and beautiful afternoon. For an hour or so we laughed, joked, and threw a Frisbee around.

I tossed the Frisbee to her somewhat gently, assuming her slender build was fragile. Upon catching it with ease, she slung it back to me with accurate force. I smiled and did likewise.

As the afternoon shadows began to lengthen, we gathered our things and made our way to the parking lot. For some reason we were talking about food.

"That's one of the things I love about being up here, all the fresh seafood," I said. "We don't have much of that in Kansas."

"Hey," she said, "my stepdad just got back from Alaska with a bunch of fresh salmon and halibut. We're fixing some tonight. Do you want to have dinner with us?"

I laughed to myself. Brook had just managed to invite me over to dinner with her parents. Her invitation was innocent and endearing, but that was a little too fast for me.

"I'd love to, but I can't tonight. I have to get back for work. But why don't you give me your number and we can hang out another time?"

She silently wrote down her number on a small piece of paper from her purse.

"Thanks," I said. "I'll give you a call."

"Okay. Good night," she said as we parted.

The following afternoon I pulled out the piece of paper and dialed the number.

"Hello," was the greeting on the other end.

"Hey, is this Brook?"

"Yes."

"Oh, this is Steven. Is this a bad time?"

"No, it's good, actually. Gracie is taking a nap, and I was just reading a book."

Gracie was Brook's two-and-a-half-year-old little girl. Her dad, Christian, lived in Seattle. Brook and Christian had never married but were engaged for a time. Gracie was a doll with curly blonde hair and brown eyes. I had seen her occasionally with Brook at church.

"Cool. You like to read much?"

"When I can. It's tough sometimes with Gracie and keeping up with school."

"You're going to Pierce College, right? Seems like I heard someone say that."

"Yes. I'm working on my associate's, taking a full-time load."

"Wow. I'm sure you've got your hands full. Would you want to hang out sometime?"

"Yeah, that'd be great," she said.

"Well, I saw a big discount bookstore in South Hill. You want to go check that out and maybe get a bite to eat?"

"Yeah, that sounds fun."

"Great. How about this Friday night? I can pick you up at your house."

"That sounds fine," she said.

That Friday I arrived at Brook's parents' home to pick her up. I climbed the steps somewhat nervously and rang the doorbell. The sound of two yipping dogs filled the air and then quickly subsided as they were let out back. The heavy oaken door opened, and there she stood. Her red hair draped over a cream-colored sleeveless blouse. Her eyes seemed bluer than before.

"Hi," she said, seeming to know something I didn't. As we entered the house, I was smitten with her subtle yet palpable elegance, an effortless grace that betrayed a strength and beauty I had never seen. I would have followed her anywhere in that moment.

I met her folks, shook hands briefly, and exchanged pleasantries. Gracie was playing in the kitchen, and I made sure to say hello. After a few minutes we were in the car and on our way.

The conversation was awkward yet polite as we drove to the bookstore, punctuated by moments of silence that should have also been awkward but weren't. It felt easy to be quiet with Brook.

"What kind of music do you like?" I asked.

"Oh, whatever," she said.

I turned the dial to the alternative rock station. Johnny Cash was covering U2's "One."

"I have this on CD," she said. "I really like Johnny Cash."

"Yeah, me too," I replied.

The conversational silence returned. The two of us just listened to "One."

We meandered through the bookstore with no particular objective. I spotted Leif Enger's *Peace Like a River,* a book I had read in college, and recommended it. Brook found *Memoirs of a Geisha*, and it was like she had met an old friend.

After we had wandered through the bookstore awhile, we left in search of food. We found ourselves at the Steilacoom Pub & Grill. We ordered our food, Brook kindly insisting that she pay for herself. We ate and walked down the hill toward the Sound. The day was long and warm. It seemed unlikely that the sun would set. We sat on the swings at a park and talked, watching a ferry ripple its way across the water.

We simply wanted to be together but needed something to "do" in order to justify giving space and light for a newfound intimacy to grow. We opted for coffee and drove to a Starbucks on 72nd Street in Tacoma. Having secured our drinks, we sat on the patio.

"What's that?" she asked as she ran her finger over the engraving of a bracelet I was wearing.

"It's a KIA bracelet," I said. I turned my wrist so she could see the name "John Mark Price" engraved on the silver band.

"John Mark was a Black Sheep maggot—he was part of my platoon and my squad. He died in December of 1989 when the battalion jumped into Panama. He was killed on the jump. We're expected to learn the story of a fallen Ranger and wear a bracelet in their honor. We never forget the fallen."

Her attentiveness invited me to continue.

"Have you ever heard of a guy named Pat Tillman?" I ventured. "He played in the NFL and then joined the army." Despite this being our first date, it felt natural to broach the topic with her. To not speak of it felt somehow like a lie of omission, as though I were walking around with the title of "Ranger" without mentioning that the word "former" would soon be attached.

"No, I don't follow sports. Who was he?"

Who was he? A comrade? A hero? A victim?

Having begun, I now had to continue. I summarized the events of April 22 and my current status as a soon-to-be former Ranger. I didn't know what any of it meant; I just knew I had to tell her.

She took it all in, becoming a sadder kind of beautiful.

"I'm really sorry about all of that," she said sincerely.

"Me too."

The summer light was finally fading. It was nearly ten o'clock, and we'd been together for over four hours. It wasn't nearly long enough.

As I drove back to the barracks, reflecting on our time together, part of me cringed at the thought of all I had shared with Brook, and yet how could I not? The attraction to Brook was real and beyond the physical. Likewise, the stakes were higher since Gracie was involved. I didn't feel like wasting time, hers or mine, so if we were going to go down a road together, she had to know the truth.

I called her again the next day. The so-called rules of how often and when you're supposed to call a girl seemed stupid. I wanted to be with her. We were soon spending four or five nights a week together, hanging out at her folks' place, walking and talking at all kinds of different parks. One night, we drove to what was a dark spot on the map for both of us, Olympia. We walked around the state capitol, admiring the architecture, stopping to observe and reflect on the various memorials to war that had been built. Carefully manicured rose and dahlia gardens provided an almost storybook background. If only time would stop. If only summer would never give way to the seasons that follow. But time was unstoppable in its perpetual march, and I would be marching on as well.

I was asked by the battalion S1 (the army's version of human resources) if I had a preference for where I went after leaving battalion. I told him I had no desire to leave Fort Lewis. I loved the Pacific Northwest, and at the time I had every desire to continue my relationship with Brook. There were a number of other infantry units on post, so I didn't think it would be much of an issue.

"Needs of the army" governed all, however, and I was no exception to that principle. Those needs dictated a transfer. In the middle of August, I received orders to report to the First Infantry Division (First ID) at Fort Riley, Kansas, on September 16. Ashpole had been assigned to one of the Stryker brigades there at Lewis. Alders was going to SF selection. Baker was getting out.

Why did they even bother to ask me? I thought.

The First Infantry Division, known as the "Big Red One," was next in line to deploy to Iraq, which explains why I was assigned there. The army was bringing the division to full strength before heading overseas. The Big Red One is regular army, a far cry from the intensity and expectations of the Ranger regiment. Now that I was no longer part of the regiment, I just wanted to leave, but I didn't want to go there. I was still undecided as to my career path. I could go to SF selection like Alders and seek to become a Green Beret. I could drop my packet to go to Officer Candidate School (OCS). Neither of those options were on the table if I was going straight to Baghdad. Needs of the army superseded my career ambitions.

The following night, Brook and I went to the Thursday night worship service at church. I was there because she was there. Afterward a bunch of folks went to a nearby Applebee's, and Brook and I tagged along only to split off on our own once we arrived at the restaurant. After settling in to a table and giving our drink order, I started in: "I got my orders yesterday. I'm being assigned to Fort Riley in Kansas. I have to report there no later than September 16."

I saw her eyes fill with tears, and her emotion triggered a similar response in me. She said nothing, inviting me to continue speaking.

"I'm leaving, but I don't want this to change anything between us. I want to be with you no matter where I am. I understand if you don't, but that's how I feel."

She quickly reached out and grabbed my hand.

There was hope. I still had options within the army beyond going to Fort Riley, and even if I decided to get out, I just had to make it through the rest of my enlistment, which would be over in May of 2007, less than three years away.

I knew we could figure it out. She felt the same. All we had to do was ride out the storm.

9

THE STORM

The sky grew darker, painted blue on blue,
one stroke at a time,
into deeper and deeper shades of night.
HARUKI MURAKAMI

I stomped on the gas, driving nearly seventy miles per hour on the gravel road made of crushed white limestone. A plume of white dust followed close behind. I was off the highway, driving the five and a half miles into the heart of Round Mound Township, heading back to the home place. The wheat had been harvested and the fall crops were ripening.

Having left Fort Lewis a couple of days before, I made a beeline for home and was looking forward to spending the next ten days far away from the army until my report date at nearby Fort Riley. My mom was living with my grandparents at the home place, so I'd have plenty of time to spend with her as well.

I let off the accelerator, found the brake, and slowly turned down the driveway under the white "Luhman" arch. The summer flowers were fading, but the mums were beginning to bud with flashes of orange, yellow, and red. The garden had been tilled save for the tomatoes, whose vines were still laden with fruit. Firewood had been piled on the front porch in anticipation of the winter to come. Everything was as I had left it, though now the glory of the summer was beginning to fade.

I had been in the car for most of the last twelve hours, having come through Wyoming, Colorado, and Nebraska. As I stretched and crawled out of the car, Mom, Grandma, and Grandpa appeared on the patio.

"Well, there he is!" Grandpa called out.

I was embraced, first by Mom and then by Grandma. Grandpa's calloused hand shook mine with a new intensity.

"Have you eaten anything today?" Grandma asked doubtfully. "We'll have dinner in just a bit, but you'll have to help yourself to what-ever you want," she said, concerned as usual for my nourishment.

"It's so good to see you," Mom said as she hugged me.

"It's good to be seen," I said, trying to lighten the moment and assure her that I was fine. That all was well.

What do they know? I wondered. *What do they think? Am I different to them?*

Dinner was amazing. We prayed and ate as we always had. The con-versation focused mostly on logistics. The route I took from Fort Lewis was of particular interest to Grandpa, who himself had driven all over the US with the family over the years. And of course, what lay before me, reporting to Riley on the sixteenth of the month. The mood shifted from the joy of the journey that had brought me here to the prospect of the war toward which I was heading. As if on cue, Mom and Grandma got up, cleared the table, and did the dishes in the kitchen. Grandpa and I remained at the table, both of us eating a bowl of homegrown canned apricots for dessert. The polite and nervous clanking of dishes and cutlery was all that could be heard. Finally Grandpa spoke.

"You know, Steven," he said, "it's just not right." An anger and a hurt bubbled to the surface feeding a pained expression I had never seen. I was startled, waiting for what he'd say next.

"I mean you havin' to leave the Rangers and all. That's just 'cause he was a football player, isn't it?"

"Well, I mean, I don't know really. We were—it was confusing. It was getting dark, and we didn't know where Pat and the other guys were. But we fired at them, you know. We didn't know they were friendlies." It was surreal to speak of it, yet I felt safe talking to him about it.

"That's what I mean," he said, his frustration increasing with his tone as he continued: "You know, we fired an awful lot of shells over there. We's there for a year and a half until the armistice. And—" he unconsciously gazed slightly to the side looking far away, peering into a distant past that seemed all too present in that moment. As he looked away, I looked inside, seeing a part of him I had never seen before. A part of him that I realized was now a part of me.

"You know we didn't always have all the guys we needed on the howitzer. Guys got hurt, some got killed. Sometimes I ran the gun by myself. Loading it, taking in the firing coordinates, and firing it. There was times we found out that we got the wrong coordinates. We found out our shells landed on our guys, you know? Shells that we'd fired."

The only thing worse than the death that war brings is when that death is at the hands of friends. Those with whom you train and fight. Those with whom you are joined in a common cause dying unwittingly, pointlessly, accidentally at the hands of their comrades. There is a hollowness to that, the echo of which rings long and hard with sounds of anger. Sounds of guilt. Sounds of shame.

I thought Grandpa and I would be connected by the experience of serving a cause greater than ourselves. Now, that bond was extended, and our connection was grounded in the tragedy of friendly fire. He was comforting me. He was trusting me. He was coloring in details of his service, dark shades I'd left out in forming a vision of what the war was like for him.

Where he had described a strafing here and there, as though it were a thunderstorm, I imagined the terror he felt as he sought cover, seeing his friends cut down by German aircraft.

Where he had described the German carts they would find to

move supplies, I now saw the bloated horseflesh, riddled with shrapnel and rotting.

Where I had seen a confident young man, steel helmet cocked on his head, a Lucky Strike dangling from his lip, ready to meet the Axis powers head-on, I now saw a farm boy, someone who had lived his life helping things grow and went to Europe as an agent of death. I saw grief—a grief that was his and a grief that I knew was now mine.

"It's not your fault, you know? You's just followin' orders." He said it just as much to convince himself as he did me.

"Yeah, I know, Grandpa. I know," I lied.

That night my mom and I finally talked. She looked tired. My service had taken a toll.

"I just don't understand how it's your fault," she said. "I mean, it sounds like it was kind of *his* fault. Why didn't he take cover?"

I cringed. Her motherly instincts never let up for a moment. I could do little to no wrong.

"It's not that simple, Mom. We shouldn't have been firing there, and he thought we saw him and would stop. He was trying to protect the guys he was with. We were trying to defend ourselves. Whose fault is that? I don't think it's his."

"But then the family keeps asking questions. That won't bring him back, will it?"

"They were lied to," I said. "They just want to know what happened. You'd want to know the same thing. You'd want to know that anyone responsible for what happened was held accountable."

"I guess that's true," she conceded. She just wanted someone to blame who wasn't me.

"What exactly has been in the news?" I asked reluctantly. I had no Internet access in the barracks, on the road, or here at the home place. I didn't watch TV and wasn't trying to follow the story in the press, but I knew they had, whatever it was that was being reported.

"At first, they said he was killed by, you know, the enemy, and there was this big memorial service on TV. Then they said it was friendly fire. Some people were even saying the army had him killed," she said with confused exasperation.

"That's crazy, Mom. Everyone in the platoon loved him. Everyone was crushed by it. It was an accident, and the army was wrong for not telling the truth. We all knew it, and that's what we told the investigators. I'm just glad I'm not there anymore."

But where am I?

"Will you have to go over there again?" she asked.

"Oh, I don't know. Maybe. I think the unit I'm going to is slated to go to Iraq, but I'll just be sitting around the FOB most of the time. It won't be like being at regiment." I was lying some more.

"I'm just glad you're home and that you're okay," she said as she gave me a hug and we said good night.

Am I home? Am I okay?

A couple of days later I made the eleven-mile drive south on country roads to my other grandparents, my dad's folks, Keith and Ida Elliott. The Elliotts were a more stoic clan than the Luhmans but no less kind. Granddad Elliott was also a farmer, raising wheat and cattle just like Grandpa Luhman. Grandma Elliott was just as gifted in the kitchen as Grandma Luhman.

That evening, precisely at 6 p.m., the table prayer was prayed and we ate homemade beef and noodles ladled onto mashed potatoes, garden-fresh peas, and chocolate cake along with iced tea. I could eat that meal seven days a week. Granddad and I retired to the living room to chat. A college football game was playing on TV. Once the dishes were done, Grandma joined us. No mention of the war was made.

As I got up to leave and said my good-byes, Granddad insisted on walking me outside to the car. He'd never done that before. Granddad was reserved, usually keeping people at bay with his intellect and sarcasm, making it far more difficult to know or understand his heart.

As we walked outside and approached the car, he stopped. "You know this isn't your fault, don't you?" he said, staring intently through his silver-rimmed glasses, a toothpick neatly perched in the side of his mouth.

We're talking about this again.

"Yeah, Granddad, I know."

"It's just these gol'darned politics," he said angrily. "We've got the media tearing into everything, just making it all worse."

What does he know? What does he think? I didn't want to ask.

Granddad continued. "It's war. Fratricide has always been a part of war, and it's awful. You were doing the best you could, and we're proud of you."

It must be really bad if Granddad feels the need to tell me that. He had never been remotely as emotive or vulnerable as he was with me in that moment. He wasn't a veteran—he was too young for both World War II and Korea—but he had lived. He knew more than I did. He knew more about how life's pains could affect a man. The sense that this was all behind me was beginning to fade. I left still trying to pretend it was over.

While visiting with Grandma and Granddad Elliott, I learned that my dad, Mark Elliott, was in town. This was a rare occurrence as he had lived abroad since I was ten years old. He was a teacher and coach and worked at various private schools around the world. At the time, he was living in Bucharest, Romania, and was back in Kansas visiting friends and family. At Grandma's suggestion, I gave him a call, and we set a date for lunch in nearby Hays.

My dad had been largely absent from my life, but it became easier to converse and connect the older I became. He and I looked a lot alike, so seeing him was a bit like seeing a glimpse of my future. We sounded a lot alike, and we seemed to think a lot alike. We saw each other infrequently, but it was always strange how similar I was to him having never grown up with him.

As we sat in Quiznos on the brick-lined streets of downtown Hays, we got caught up. My dad was well read, and our conversation meandered easily from sports to politics to history. Soon the conversation took a familiar and, in this case, more fatherly turn. "You know, I read the news. Even though I live half a world away, I know what's going on."

Great.

"It's a part of war. An awful part of war, and it wasn't your fault."

"I know, Dad. I appreciate you saying that."

"You're serving your country, which is honorable, and I'm proud of you. I was never a father to you, and your mother did an amazing job. You're a good man, and this doesn't have to define you."

He saw a wound I didn't know was there. He saw a wound I didn't want to see. All of them did. Grandpa Luhman, my mom, Granddad Elliott, and now my dad. They all saw the implications of my experience far more clearly than I did. Their responses were both comforting and troubling. Their own pained expressions and sincere, hushed tones served as a reflection of the hurt they each observed. A hurt I had yet to fully realize.

★

I reported to Fort Riley on September 16. I expected my time here to be brief as the division was expected to head to Baghdad within a month. I slept in the comfort of Fort Riley's Reception Battalion, and after 6 a.m. breakfast chow the morning of the seventeenth, I was preparing to tackle the in-processing checklist. I stood in formation after eating with the rest of new arrivals. I no longer wore the tan beret of the regiment and instead wore the black beret of the regular army. On my right shoulder, the Second Battalion scroll was sewn, indicating I'd been to war with the unit. Combat scrolls were very uncommon in the big army and attracted immediate attention. The guy standing next to me was annoyingly impressed.

"Wow, you're a Ranger?" he asked.

"No, I was. I'm not anymore. I'll be with the Big Red One."

"Why aren't you wearing your tan beret? I mean, you're technically still with the unit until you're assigned to the First ID, so why don't you wear it?"

"Because I'm not there anymore. I'm not one of them anymore."

"Man, I'd wear it if I could."

I bet you would.

We were soon released to complete our various in-processing tasks. Before I could work on my checklist, however, I was told to report to a particular office at the Reception Battalion. I did so, standing at parade rest while a sergeant first class asked me a bizarre question: "Specialist Elliott, how would you like to go to South Carolina and be a driver for a general?" By the glint of excitement in her eyes, you'd think I had just won the showcase on *The Price Is Right*. It wasn't clear if I should be thrilled by the offer or if she was selling me something.

I briefly considered my options. I had joined to go to war, but part of me was missing. The heart and the taste for that was gone. "Yeah," I said, "I think I'd like to do that, Sarn't."

"Well, all right then. We'll get you new orders cut, and you'll be on your way."

Later that morning I climbed back in my car, new orders in hand, and drove from Kansas to Fort Jackson, South Carolina. I was now a member of the Twenty-Fourth Infantry Division Forward at Fort Jackson. The unit's mission was to oversee training and mobilization for national guard and reserve units being sent overseas. My boss, the assistant division commander, was Brigadier General Richard McPhee. General McPhee was from upstate New York, a West Point graduate who had recently returned from commanding an artillery brigade in Iraq.

Apparently, General McPhee had put in a request for a driver who wasn't a driver. He wanted someone who had combat experience and preferably some education. His boss, a two-star, Major General Hardee, was at Fort Riley, which is how the invitation had come to me.

I nervously entered the Twenty-Fourth ID FWD headquarters building situated at the heart of Fort Jackson, across the street from the main parade ground. The building itself was a World War II–era structure, single story and painted white. I was greeted by Captain Kevin Newell, an infantry officer who was serving as General McPhee's aide-de-camp. He and I would spend a lot of time together.

"Great to meet you, Specialist Elliott. Wow, didn't know you were a Ranger," he said, eyeing my combat scroll. "Let's go in and meet the Boss."

I'd never met a general before. I'd hardly talked to a captain before. I was now the most junior enlisted person in an office filled mostly with captains and above. It was strange, to say the least.

I entered General McPhee's office guided by Captain Newell and saluted while standing in front of his desk as he rose to do likewise, a huge grin spreading from ear to ear. McPhee was bald and stocky and looked like he was captain of the wrestling team, which, it turns out, he was in his days at West Point.

"Specialist Elliott! Welcome! So good to have you here!" he said, pumping my hand. He eyed my combat scroll and combat infantryman's badge. "Kevin, we got us a Ranger!"

I wondered what file, if any, had preceded my arrival. What did he know about me? What did he know about why I was here? Did he recognize my name? Apparently not. Apparently the past was the past and I could start fresh.

Later that afternoon, as I prepared to go to my barracks room on post, a sergeant I had not yet met approached me at my desk. I immediately jumped to parade rest and was told to relax. An eager grin spread across his face, reminding me of a tobacco-stained Cheshire cat. He asked, "So, you were part of the whole Tillman thing?"

S—.

"Yeah. Yeah, I was, Sarn't."

His grin widened as he slowly shook his head in amazement. "Well . . . now you're part of history."

I didn't know whether to be angry with him or to pity him. He had simply mistaken infamy for fame.

My infamy and place in history apparently secured, I left and tried to forget what he said.

General McPhee worked long hours, which meant that Captain Newell and I worked long hours as well. When we weren't traveling, I usually had weekends off. On one of my first Sundays in South Carolina, I ventured off base to go to church. The muscle memory was still there. I chose a large church just outside the gates of Fort Jackson called Shandon Baptist. A large church was appealing as it meant I was less likely to have to meaningfully interact with other people. It would be easier to be a stranger.

The service was fine. It had a more Southern flare than I was used to.

Why am I here? Why am I doing this? Where is God in all this? The same questions resounded in my heart with growing intensity.

When the service concluded, I found myself overcome with a terror that only well-meaning Christians can produce when eagerly engaging a stranger who is just realizing he doesn't want to be engaged. My appearance—fit, young, close-cropped hair, obviously alone—and the proximity to post marked me as a member of the military. The well-meaning congregants descended upon me like vultures on a rotting carcass. They did exactly what you would hope any group of churchgoers would do to welcome a stranger. To me, it was terrifying.

I stood up and attempted to leave when a middle-aged Baptist approached and shook my hand. He then introduced himself and his wife. "Are you new here?" he asked.

"Yeah, I just got assigned to Fort Jackson."

"So you're in the army then?"

"Yes, I've been in for a little over a year."

"Have you been to combat?" he asked, his curiosity and concern increased.

"Yeah, I was in Afghanistan this past spring."

"Wow. Well, thank you for your service."

Other people were listening to our conversation and moving closer. My blood pressure rose. I was surrounded. The questions kept coming, now from other people in the crowd:

"What do you do at Fort Jackson?"

"Where are you from?"

"Can we take you to lunch?"

I tried my hardest to be polite and to stifle the growing sense of panic. I needed to escape. I briefly visualized myself low crawling under a pew, ducking their questions as one would try to avoid enemy fire. Instead, I resorted to the only weapon I could think of: lying.

"I really appreciate your hospitality," I said with a smile, "but I have to go. I've got another commitment for lunch. I'll take a rain check though." I broke free to daylight and walked quickly out of the sanctuary, suppressing the urge to sprint to my car.

Those people were nice—Southern nice, which was a whole new level of nice that I wasn't prepared for. My choices were clear: I could either engage with people and answer their questions honestly and with respect, or I could lie to them and keep them at a distance. I chose a third option, to disengage entirely and avoid telling the truth or having to maintain a facade. Sunday-morning church was no longer an option, not as long as there were other people there.

I sat in my car in the parking lot of Shandon Baptist. I breathed deeply, in and out, trying to calm myself. The crowd was stifling. My adrenaline was pumping. Something inside hurt.

Outside work, the only person I talked to was Brook. We both hated talking on the phone, but it was all we had. We would talk for hours sometimes, thankful to be connected but feeling so unsatisfied to be apart. We reminded ourselves that I could be in Iraq for a year. To talk with each other and to have me stateside was a luxury that many in the military couldn't enjoy.

There was a brief time of relief from being out of regiment. I had an office job now and didn't have to worry about getting yelled at or hazed. At the same time, I had an office job—a job I had chosen while others went to war. I worked fairly long hours but had no life. No family. No friends. The freedom of being out of regiment was wearing off. I was here, and I was alone.

My new home at Fort Jackson was a private barracks room in a newly constructed complex. The room itself was ten feet by fifteen feet and contained a bed, a desk, and a TV. There was a kitchenette complete with a fridge and microwave adjacent to the bathroom. It soon began to feel like a cell. I was increasingly alone with my thoughts and feelings, two things I had tried to avoid since deployment, and before there had always been people and events to keep me occupied. Now there was nothing. Just me in this room. Here because of what I'd done. Here because I had chosen this. I hated it.

Anger, guilt, and shame mixed with boredom. I had never drunk alcohol before besides half a glass of sparkling wine at Christmas. I had never had a taste for it. I had never wanted it. But for some reason, drinking just began to make sense. An escape seemed appealing.

Sleep was also becoming harder and harder to come by. It was so hard to wind down. Even if I had worked out hard or gone on a long run, those things just seemed to make the anxiety worse. They made the vigilance more intense. I just wanted to rest, but I couldn't.

On a Friday night, after picking up some Chinese takeout off post, I stopped by a convenience store on Fort Jackson and perused the alcohol section, which easily took up half the store. *Where do I start?* I had no idea what would pair well with cheap Chinese food, so I just grabbed a bottle of red wine, a Chianti that had a medieval knight on the label.

Once I got back to my room, I popped in a movie that had just arrived in the mail from Netflix. I sat in my black office chair, eating sweet and sour chicken and sipping the wine. It tasted awful and I felt better. Distracted. Different. Numb. The room didn't seem as terrible.

I should be happy to have this room, I thought. *Some people are at war. Some people are dead.*

I woke up, my head pounding. *Where am I? What time is it?* I thought. My wristwatch told me it was a little after three in the morning. I was asleep on my bed with my clothes on. I had no recollection of anything past finishing my meal. I swore I'd never drink again. Who would? I felt awful. Yet as bad as I felt that first night, a pattern was set.

I got better at drinking and better at hydrating to minimize the effects the day after. As I drank, my emotional defenses lowered. Guilt and shame metastasized into anger. Anger at myself. Anger at the regiment. Anger at the army. Anger at God.

The storm was gaining strength.

★

I was standing there manning the 240 on the Humvee. Ashpole was on the .50 cal in the turret. We were in the canyon in Khost, hemmed in by sheer rock walls that rose up into the darkness, inching our way around the curves. I knew we shouldn't be there. We were trapped.

Just like before, the enemy opened fire. I heard explosions and the echoing sound of gunfire, theirs and ours. Muzzle flashes sparkled on the hillside, only now the cliffs all around us were glowing red and yellow, dripping with lava. There was nowhere to run. My feet were stuck in place. Rangers ahead of me were on fire. I strained but couldn't see their faces as they writhed and screamed.

Suddenly, I was lying in the dirt, still gripping my weapon, the buttstock pressed painfully into my shoulder. Rocks jabbed into my legs and elbows as I shifted around, trying to find comfort. The smell of gunpowder was thick.

Terrified and angry, I took aim with the 240. I needed to stop these men. I needed to kill them. I locked onto an enemy position at the top of the cliff and fired. Somehow my sight followed the trajectory of my rounds. As the 7.62mm bullet closed in, I saw one of the enemy clearly. He looked Middle Eastern—dark complexion, dark eyes, a beard. He held an AK-47. Even though he wore the tiger-striped uniform of an AMF soldier, I knew he was the enemy. I observed from just a few inches away as the rounds from my weapon shredded his uniform in a neat line across his chest, blood exploding from his torso. It was startling how quiet the damage was upon impact. My view shifted to another bullet and another enemy fighter who suffered the same fate, then another, and then another. In one case, a round ripped through a man's head, exploding out the back. The bodies fell neatly onto the rocks at the top of the cliff. Pools of blood quietly grew around the corpses.

I was sickened by the sight. The look of terror was frozen in each face as lifeless eyes stared back.

An incessant beeping overpowered the sound of screams and gunfire. I blinked. It was an alarm clock. I was in a dark room, lying in bed. This wasn't Afghanistan. I was in the barracks at Fort Jackson. The clock read 7:00 a.m.

It was a dream—a nightmare. Nightmares were becoming more and more frequent; the alcohol didn't seem to keep them from me. Almost every night, in some form or fashion, I had them.

I breathed deeply, trying to lower my heart rate. I had just slept but I was exhausted. I was here but I was just there and I felt the same as I did the day after the ambush. Worn out, tired, and old.

I rubbed my face and eyes, trying to erase the memory.

The wind was driving a heavy rain. The waters were rising. The storm had landed.

10

BROKEN

I loathe my very life;
therefore I will give free rein to my complaint
and speak out in the bitterness of my soul.
JOB 10:1

Before long, General McPhee and the rest of the Twenty-Fourth ID
FWD were on to the next mission, overseeing the training for the
Forty-Eighth Brigade, which was part of Georgia's National Guard.
The brigade was going to Iraq, and their mobilization would take
place over a four-month period at Fort Stewart, Georgia. During that
time, we lived off post in nearby Savannah.

I began to focus on getting reassigned to Fort Lewis. I was even
happy to deploy as an infantryman with a big army unit at Lewis.
I just wanted to be close to Brook. It seemed like it should be simple.
I worked directly for a one-star who was eager to help me in my
career. I was an infantryman, and we were at war. I thought my
time working for General McPhee would be a brief interlude before

heading back to the Pacific Northwest, but the infantry branch was consistently uncooperative, and assignments that seemed an obvious fit for me and for the army were filled by others.

Brook and I were serious about each other. She had visited my family and me at the home place over Christmas, and we counted the days until she and I would see each other again in Savannah.

Finally, she arrived at the Savannah airport on St. Patrick's Day to spend the four-day weekend with me. She was gorgeous. Seeing her was a ray of light. It was soothing to touch her, to kiss her. We played the part of tourists, visiting Charleston and Fort Pulaski National Monument just south of Savannah and taking in a blues concert by Buddy Guy.

My frustration with the army was obvious, but beyond this, Brook had no idea I had been drinking like I was. She had no idea I was sleeping poorly, if at all. She didn't know about the nightmares.

I was living in a town house in Savannah with a guy in my unit, Corey. On the last night of the visit, Brook and I were downstairs on the couch, watching a movie. We tried watching *The Notebook*, but I just couldn't take the melodrama, so we started watching something else. I don't remember what.

As we watched, without warning, emotion welled up in me, and I found myself crying. My stomach tightened as I fought back sobs that wouldn't be stopped. I quickly retreated to the nearest bathroom to try to regain my composure. After a few minutes, I returned to the couch where Brook was still sitting. The movie was still playing. I didn't say a word, staring straight ahead at the screen.

She hesitated and then asked, "Are you okay?"

"What do you mean? Oh, yeah, I'm fine," I said. "What'd I miss?"

She didn't press the point. Before long, she went to bed upstairs, and I settled into the couch trying to forget the weakness I'd exhibited, unclear as to what it meant and embarrassed that someone else had seen it. *What is wrong with me?* I thought. *What do I have to cry about?*

I tried to put it out of my mind based on the premise that if I could ignore the symptom, then the problem didn't exist.

I took Brook to the airport the following morning to catch her flight back to Seattle. Grateful for the time together and heavyhearted at having to part, we said our good-byes. She returned to her world and I to mine.

★

"E, you got the coordinates for the training site?" General McPhee asked.

"Roger, sir. They start the exercise at 1000 hours, and it's about a forty-five-minute drive, so we should be there in plenty of time."

"Good, good. Let's get outta here."

I put the rumbling Humvee in gear and began to pull out of the command group parking lot toward the wide-open vistas of the Mojave Desert. I had two passengers, General McPhee seated to my right and Captain Newell directly behind me. As we drove through Fort Irwin, soldiers who noticed the red plate with a single white star on the front of the vehicle would stop and salute. The Boss saluted back, his eyes fixed straight ahead.

We had been sent to the National Training Center (NTC), the closest approximation to a Middle Eastern landscape you could hope to find in North America. The desert itself is nearly fifty thousand square miles of the driest land on the continent. The isolated location, which is a mix of mountains, high mesas, and lots of sand, makes for ideal training conditions.

Fort Irwin's original purpose was to train conventional ground forces for the possibility of a massive clash with the Soviets in Europe. Armor officers in the command group told stories of their younger days playing war at the NTC in their tanks, practicing for a Cold War Armageddon.

There were, however, no tank battles raging on the plains of Fort Irwin as we drove to the training site. Instead, the post was used as a finishing school, a final box to check, for any reserve or national guard unit that was deploying to Iraq or Afghanistan. It was General McPhee's job to ensure they were ready for deployment, and we found ourselves at the NTC observing Georgia's Forty-Eighth

Infantry Brigade as they completed their final training before heading to Iraq for a year.

The main post of Fort Irwin was relatively small and extremely isolated. We lived in the motel on post and worked twelve- to fifteen-hour days virtually seven days a week. If the Boss was working, so was I because I was his transportation. Most days Captain Newell and I would get General McPhee at 5:30 a.m. for a workout, grab breakfast, visit the office briefly, and then spend a day in the field observing the training while the Boss coached the Forty-Eighth Brigade staff. The day almost always ended with a call from General McPhee to his boss, Major General Hardee back in Fort Riley, apprising him of the day's events and offering his assessments. I heard many conversations well beyond my pay grade and took cues from Captain Newell in the art of listening while pretending not to hear.

Work was a grind, each day exactly like the last, and while I would have loved some time off, there was nothing to do there. We might as well have been working. We were in the United States, but all of us were away from friends and family. As General McPhee put it, "What are you gonna do? Go back to the room and watch the idiot box? Might as well be workin'."

Yes, sir.

The closest town to Fort Irwin was Barstow, California. It was thirty-seven miles away on a two-lane desert highway that was one of the most dangerous roads you could find. Soldiers were all too likely to have a few too many and attempt the drive back to Fort Irwin only to never make it. You could hardly go a mile on that road without seeing a wreath or a cross marking someone's loss. Because of that, we were under a strict no-alcohol policy.

Nightmares continued with varying levels of severity. But I was always there, in Afghanistan. Always at war.

I had decided to focus my energies as best I could on the next goal. The door to regiment was closed, and I accepted that. I didn't know what I wanted to do long-term. The option to stay in the army was still on the table. The question I was asking was, How can I still make something of my service beyond driving General McPhee around?

The immediate answer to that question was Ranger School. Although I had completed Ranger selection and served in the regiment, I was not "Ranger qualified," and that represented unfinished business for me. I continued to carry around the black-and-gold Ranger tab in my wallet as a reminder of what I still needed to do. Getting my tab would be my way of redeeming what was lost, of proving to the army and to the world that I wasn't a failure.

I couldn't change the past, but I could control my future. With enough effort, I could control what would happen to me. I didn't need anyone else.

We arrived back at the office at Fort Irwin at about three o'clock in the afternoon after a day of driving around the "sandbox," as it was called.

Stuck to my otherwise empty desk was a Post-it note instructing me to call a JAG (Judge Advocate General) officer at Fort Bragg, North Carolina. JAG officers are essentially military lawyers. It wasn't clear to me why a JAG officer at Fort Bragg would want to talk to me. I thought nothing of it. It was late on the east coast by that time, but I picked up the phone and dialed, expecting to leave a message. He picked up.

"Specialist Steven Elliott?" the voice asked with polite professionalism.

"Yes, sir. This is Specialist Elliott."

"Specialist, I've been asked to inform you that Brigadier General Gary Jones has been charged with conducting an investigation into the death of Corporal Patrick Tillman. General Jones will need a statement from you regarding the events of 22 April 2004."

I immediately detached. A sort of shock set in. My heart was on pause while my mind simply processed the information needed to complete the conversation.

"Yes, sir. When do you need the statement? I'm at Fort Irwin right now."

"As soon as we can arrange it. I understand you'll need to speak to your chain of command. Please contact me as soon as you've done so."

"Yes, sir."

Speak to my chain of command?

This won't end.

I sat at my desk, my strength slowly leaving me as I considered the implications. I'd have to tell General McPhee. What would he think of me? Would he fire me too? I'd likely have to tell him some version of what had happened. They wanted a statement—but why? I'd already given two. What else did they need to know? Attorneys were involved—why?

The Boss was in his office, door closed and on the phone. I couldn't believe I'd have to bother him with my past, my failure. I started with Captain Newell. Kevin Newell was a tall, dark-haired Pennsylvanian. He had commanded an infantry platoon in the early days of the Iraq invasion and had received a silver star on that deployment but never talked about it. I never asked. He was quiet and approachable, but my legs felt heavy as I walked into his cubicle.

"Sir, I need to talk to you about something."

"Sure, take a seat."

Where could I start? Where could I start to tell someone what happened? How I served with Pat and may have killed him?

"Sir, I just got off the phone with a JAG officer at Bragg."

"Okay." He was listening more closely.

"I don't really know how to say this, sir, but the reason I left the regiment is because I'm one of the Tillman shooters. I mean, I don't know for sure if I hit him, but I was one of the guys that fired on Pat's position not knowing they were friendlies. That's why I'm here."

I felt as though there were blood on the floor. As if I were taking the dressing off a wound that had been tightly compressed and could no longer be contained. At least, I lacked the power to contain it.

"Okay. We've got to talk to the Boss. You just hang tight, and we'll figure this out, okay? It's gonna be all right."

Captain Newell immediately went and stood outside General McPhee's office, checking impatiently through the window to see when he was off the phone. As soon as the Boss hung up the receiver, Kevin entered and closed the door. I sat outside and waited.

What is he telling him? What will they think of me?

After about twenty minutes Captain Newell came back. "Boss wants to talk to you. Come on," he beckoned kindly.

General McPhee was seated at his desk with a look of stern focus as if he were staring down an archenemy. Standing beside him was his chief of staff, Lieutenant Colonel Lewis "Buck" Buchanan. Buck had flown Cobra attack helicopters in Vietnam. He was half Korean, half Cherokee, a larger-than-life military hero, and his expression mirrored that of McPhee. I sat down, Captain Newell behind me leaning against the closed door. There was no escape.

"E," McPhee started, "you tell me what happened."

"Sir," I began, "our platoon was split, and it was getting dark. We were supposed to get a broken Humvee back to Hardball Road. When we drove through a canyon, we started taking fire. We didn't know where the other serial was. Some of them were firing over our heads as we left the canyon, and we fired back. We all knew within a day of the ambush that it was friendly fire, and that's what we told the investigators."

"I understand it was friendly fire, E. I get that. But what happened when you got back? What did the regiment do?"

"Well, nothing for a while, sir. There was an investigation, two of them actually at the FOB. I think they were called 15-6s? We told them what happened, and then we went on some more missions, and then we went home. It wasn't until we got back that things started hitting the fan."

"So then how did you end up here?" he asked.

"Sir, we—the shooters and the PL—were given company-grade article 15s and RFSd. They said we failed to follow the ROE."

His face reddened and a vein above his left eye began to bulge as his right hand formed a fist. He glanced up at Buck, their eyes locked in agreement.

"It's not right, E," he finally said. "It's just not right. Everything. How they handled it. All of it. We are going to help you, do you understand? We're gonna get you an attorney. We'll take care of it. It's just not right."

"Yes, sir."

I became the Boss's number one priority. The following day was spent not in the field but in the office as General McPhee worked the phones and made arrangements. He relieved me of my duties at Fort Irwin and instructed me to go back to Fort Jackson immediately. He contacted the JAG office at Fort Jackson and arranged for me to meet with legal counsel before I made any statement. He worked with General Jones's people to set up an interview via video teleconference so I wouldn't have to go to Fort Bragg but could instead be interviewed by General Jones while I was at Fort Jackson.

I sat with the Boss as he and Buck recounted all that had been set in motion, ordering me to focus on this and not worry about anything else, reiterating that I wasn't letting anyone down. Finally, he told me he had made one other phone call. "I have a friend at the chaplain school there at Fort Jackson. His name is Chaplain Jones. He's a former SF guy. I think you'll like him. Here's his number. You can call him anytime you need to, and he's happy to meet with you if you want. We just don't want you doing anything stupid."

Anything stupid. He meant suicide. I guess now I was Landry except I had a one-star sitting in the chair making sure I didn't end it all.

"Thank you, sir."

My flight from Las Vegas back to South Carolina was set for two days out. I still worked in the interim, which was a welcome distraction.

My last morning at Fort Irwin, a little after five o'clock in the morning, I awoke in the darkness of my motel room. Predawn light sliced through the gap in the curtains that never seemed to fully close. I sat on the edge of my bed and attempted to go through the motions of another day, but I couldn't. My chest was heavy. My gut was in knots. It felt as though a weight were trying to crush me into the carpet fibers.

I reached for my flip phone and found the number for Chaplain Jones. I pressed the button to dial, not knowing what I'd say, not quite knowing why I was calling him or how I expected him to help me. The anxiety I was already feeling was amplified by the anxiety of calling a stranger at a time of need. That feeling grew.

"This is Chaplain Jones," said the warm voice that greeted me.

"Hi, this is Specialist Elliott. General McPhee gave me your number and told me I could call you."

"Yes, Specialist. I'm so glad you did. What can I do for you?"

With that question the bubble of anxiety popped.

I wept.

After a few moments I realized I had been crying while still hold-ing the phone to my ear, which was weird. It felt strangely rude and stupid.

"I'm sorry, sir. I'm really sorry" were the first words I was able to speak.

He had stayed on the phone listening quietly.

"No need to apologize. Take your time. It's okay. I'm very glad you called. Would you like to get together when you get to Jackson?"

"Yes, sir. That'd be great," I said as I wiped my eyes with the palm of my hand. "That'd be great."

We set an appointment for later that week, and I hung up the phone.

I exhaled and got out of bed.

★

I arrived at Fort Jackson and immediately met with the JAG officer the Boss had been in touch with. We sat in her office as we discussed the legalities of my situation.

"Specialist Elliott, this is a very unusual matter. General Jones is conducting yet another 15-6 investigation, which is not a crimi-nal investigation. It's simply a fact-finding endeavor, an attempt to discover what happened. You've already been punished with the company-grade article 15, so it would seem difficult to charge you again for the same crime."

Crime, I thought.

"I don't mean it that way," she corrected herself. "What is pos-sible, however, is that the findings of this or any of the other 15-6 investigations could be used to bring charges of criminal negligence. But for now, it looks like they're just asking the same questions they have been up to this point, to try and understand what happened."

"So what you're telling me, ma'am, is that this is just the third round of the same thing I've already gone through and that this inves-tigation has no threat of a criminal prosecution. Is that right?"

"Yes."

"But you're also saying that the army or even the Tillmans could use this information to go after me in some sort of criminal charge?"

"Yes, or even a civil charge, I suppose. Sorry, I don't mean to scare you. I just want you to understand that this matter is—well, it's unique. There's a lot of attention being paid and a lot of attention in the media. I can't really advise you all that well on what could happen because I just don't know. I know that you have to testify to General Jones. There's no legal reason for you not to, and you'd be providing the same information you've already given anyway, right?"

"Yes, ma'am. There's nothing new."

"Okay. Well, then I think you just make your statement as accurately as you can and see what happens."

See what happens.

I thanked her and left.

The video teleconference was scheduled for the following week. I had nothing to do at Fort Jackson but work out, drink, and try to distract myself. In the spirit of distraction, I decided to start taking classes toward my MBA, utilizing the distance-learning program through Oklahoma State University. It felt good to work toward something, and I completed the paperwork to begin my studies there at Fort Jackson. I read books from the post library during the day in my room, worked out for an hour or so in the late afternoon, and then ate dinner and drank until I fell asleep.

I talked to Brook every day, sometimes more than once. We wrote to each other at least every week. Getting my mail and seeing an envelope with her handwriting on it was the best part of the day. Her schooling was going well, and she was a straight-A student. Gracie would be entering preschool. It was a relief to hear her talk about her life. It hurt to be away from her. I loved her.

I told her about the investigation. She was the only one I talked to about it. I felt bad sometimes for doing so, but she wanted to know and I needed to talk to somebody. Her confidence was greater than mine that everything would work out okay. I needed to hear that but found it hard to believe. The incident and all its ramifications kept coming back, worse every time.

My sleep continued to deteriorate as did my diet. I drank coffee all day and then switched to alcohol for the evening—wine and beer mostly. I'd lost about twenty pounds since I'd left battalion. I ate little and had to force myself to eat when I did.

I reported to Fort Jackson's video teleconference center as ordered. The technician escorted me into the room. It was cavernous, decorated in bureaucratic shades of brown for both the walls and carpet. To my left was a large seating area bordered by a half wall that reminded me of a jury box. In front of me was a massive flat screen. I sat alone at the center of a ten-foot conference table.

The voice of the technician came through the speakers. "You ready, Specialist Elliott?"

"Roger, Sarn't," I replied.

"Okay, here we go."

The image of Brigadier General Jones sitting at a desk flickered to life on the screen. He was a large man, bald, with Special Forces patches clearly visible on his uniform. He was polite and direct. For the next half hour, I answered what felt like the same battery of questions I had answered twice before. Reliving the details, straining to remember something I may have missed. Ultimately, offering a statement that was more a memory of the previous statements than it was of the ambush itself.

I left and went back to my room.

The next day I drove over to the chaplain's school at Jackson. Chaplain Jones was an instructor there, and he and I sat down in a conference room for a chat. I still wasn't sure why I had come or what it would accomplish. After a little small talk, Chaplain Jones got to the point.

"Sounds like you're going through a lot right now, Steve," he began. "What would you like to talk about?"

I hesitated and finally said, "I don't know, sir. I just—I just want it to stop, but it won't stop. I just want this to be in the past. The family won't let it go. The media won't let it go. I just want it to be over."

"I can understand that. You went to Oral Roberts, is that correct?"

"Yes, sir. I graduated from ORU."

"Okay. Can I assume that you come from a place of faith?" he asked.

"Yes, sir. I grew up in the church."

"Okay. Can I ask, where do you feel God fits in all of this?"

I exhaled sharply. "That's a great question, sir. To be honest, I don't have a clue. I mean, well-meaning people have told me things like 'God works all things together for good.' Or 'everything happens for a reason.' And I think, really? So, Pat had to die and people had to get hurt for me to learn some lesson or for God to have some raw material to make something with? Everything happens for a reason? No s—. It's called cause and effect, and it's how the whole universe works. Pat's f—ing head was caved in because people shot him. Cause, effect." I paused. He was unfazed and maintained eye contact.

"I'm sorry, sir. I didn't mean to let loose like that. I don't know. If God's there, why is he letting this happen?" I didn't expect an answer.

He pondered for a while before responding.

"I don't know, Steve. I don't know. I know it's all a tragedy, and I know that the decisions of people caused it. Does it help you to talk about it?"

"I guess. I don't know. I don't think I feel worse. It doesn't fix anything, though."

"Well, you're welcome to talk to me any time of the day or night. Everything is confidential. There's no right or wrong thing to say. I'm here if you need me."

"Thank you, sir. I appreciate that, and I'm sorry."

"You don't have to apologize, Steve. I'm glad you're here."

Chaplain Jones gave me a referral to the mental health clinic at Fort Jackson. I didn't have to go—he reiterated that multiple times—but I had little else to do and figured, why not? A couple of days later I found myself sitting with a shrink for the first time in my life. That in and of itself felt like failure.

She sat, notepad in hand, as we began.

"What brings you here today, Steven?"

"I'm not sleeping much. When I do sleep, I have nightmares quite a bit. I work out, but I guess I'm not feeling all that well."

"You were deployed to Afghanistan last year, is that correct?"

"Yes, ma'am."

"Is there anything about that deployment you'd like to talk about?"

"Well, ma'am, I was part of a friendly fire incident. I was a Ranger, and our platoon was ambushed. It ended up being kind of a high-profile incident because it involved Pat Tillman. I was one of the shooters, and I was released from the Rangers because of it."

Does she need to know that? I thought. *Does she know who that is? Is that even relevant? Does it matter that it was Pat and not somebody else? Would I feel the same?*

"Hmm," she said as she scribbled. "Okay. Well, here's a prescription for Zoloft." She handed me a piece of paper.

"Zoloft, ma'am?"

"It's an antidepressant that should help you sleep. It will take a little time for you to get used to it, so I'm starting you on a half dose. You can't drink any alcohol while you're on this, so just know that."

No alcohol? That was hilarious.

"Thank you, ma'am," I said as I left. I threw the prescription in the trash on the way out of the building.

I would meet with her a half dozen more times during my brief stay at Fort Jackson, which remained my permanent duty station, though I would be on temporary duty extensively at other posts. My file read "chronic posttraumatic stress disorder." I had no idea what that meant.

What I did know was that I wanted to be with Brook. I wanted to marry her. I was increasingly tired of being at the whim of the army and sought to control whatever I could. I refused to let the army keep us from moving forward with our lives. The challenge was logistics. We had looked at rings in Savannah, so I had an idea of what she liked, but it was hard to be spontaneous with a proposal when I lived on the other side of the country and had to arrange leave to visit her.

As the topic was broached more openly, we found ourselves accidentally planning a wedding.

"I think I can get some extended leave at the end of August," I told her. "Why don't we plan a wedding for then?"

"Well, you have to propose first, you know," she informed me.

"Of course. I don't want to be presumptuous. You need to at least have the chance to shoot me down."

"Well, how are you going to do that?" she asked. "I thought you were working all the time."

"I am, but I'll just fly back for a weekend. I'll fly from Charlotte on Friday night and fly back from Seattle on Sunday night."

"Really? Are you sure?"

"Positive." I already had the ring, and it was burning a hole in my pocket.

"You said you have a choir concert coming up in a couple weeks, right? I'll come back for that."

"You'll fly all the way across the country for a choir concert?" she asked, amused.

"Of course! You don't think I value the arts? It'll be worth the flight."

The concert was at Pacific Lutheran University in Tacoma. After a cross-country flight, I found myself sitting with Brook's parents and Gracie as Brook and the other members of the Pierce College choir performed.

The concert ended and her folks took Gracie for the evening while Brook and I left the performance hall alone. We walked along brick-paved paths lined with grass and gently covered with trees, soaking in the aging spring that would soon give way to summer.

We came upon a secluded bench whose only companion was a Japanese maple. Evening was turning into night. I didn't care to waste any more time.

"Can we sit down for a minute?" I asked, my heart racing as I gripped the ring between my thumb and index finger as it lay hidden in my pocket.

"Sure."

We sat side by side facing each other.

"I love you," I said. "I want to be with you. I want us to be married."

I couldn't read her expression, but I at least appeared to have her attention. I drew the ring from my pocket. The small diamonds surrounding the princess-cut pink sapphire still managed to sparkle in the fading light.

"Will you marry me?"

A smile formed across her lips as she nodded and said yes.

We kissed and, hand in hand, made for El Gaucho in downtown Tacoma to celebrate.

I flew back to Charlotte the next day, and Brook started planning an August wedding.

I was immediately back in the grind at Fort Stewart but elated to be engaged and excited to ponder my future with Brook.

Then the Boss got a call. It was GOMO, the General Officer Management Office. This was the office in DC that essentially managed the general officers of the army. A member of the recently deployed Forty-Eighth Brigade had already been killed. His remains were set to arrive at Dover in a day or so, and his funeral was set for the following week. It was the duty of every general officer to be available to serve as the senior officer for the funeral of any service member. The call came to General McPhee, indicating the need for a general to serve that function for this young man. He agreed to do so, telling me, "It's not something you want to do, E, but it's something you got to do. When that call comes, you just do it."

The following week General McPhee, Captain Newell, and I found ourselves in a small chapel in rural Georgia. We waited in our class A uniforms at the back of the room for the service to start. Sunlight flooded through the side windows, lighting the podium as well as the shiny black box situated in the front. The casket was open. All I could see from where I stood was the chin of the corpse, a nineteen-year-old private killed by an IED.

I'd been to lots of funerals for old people but only one funeral for someone who seemed too young to die—a friend I worked with at Wendy's in high school, Dan. He hadn't been wearing a seat belt and was thrown from his truck in a rollover. He didn't need to die. It seemed to me that this kid didn't either.

Slowly, the dozen or so people that made up the family entered the chapel. I assumed the young woman leading the procession was the widow, but she looked like a kid. As she caught the first full glimpse of her dead husband, she broke away from the family and threw herself on the casket. Her wails and sobs echoed off the otherwise silent walls.

I looked down and tried not to think about it. *How many times has this scene played out? How many times will it play out?*

The chapel service ended quickly. I don't remember what was said or who said it. Six pallbearers in their class As carried the closed casket down the center aisle and out of the chapel, passing directly in front of us. This was their job. They did this all the time. They looked fatigued as they carried the dead and placed his remains in a hearse parked outside.

We got back into our Suburban without speaking and followed the procession to the grave site nearby. Captain Newell and I stood back from the funeral party. General McPhee stood next to the chaplain as he spoke. The chaplain's remarks concluded, a bugler played taps, and General McPhee gave the pallbearers the command to ceremoniously fold the American flag that had been draped upon the casket. Silently, the flag was transformed into a blue triangle with white stars and placed in the Boss's hands. He turned to the seated widow and presented her with a flag on behalf of a grateful nation.

I never wanted to see that again.

Within the week, all of us had returned to Fort Jackson. The Forty-Eighth Brigade was now fully deployed to Iraq, as evidenced by the casualties they were sending home. Our job was done until the next unit got the call for mobilization.

To celebrate our return to Fort Jackson and the completion of the Forty-Eighth Brigade mobilization, General McPhee hosted a staff lunch at an Olive Garden in Columbia, just a few miles from Fort Jackson. We waited for our soup and salad while munching on the breadsticks. I was sitting next to one of the staff officers, Captain Joe Ritchie. He was a former company commander with the 101st Airborne. I always enjoyed talking with him, and we shared a somewhat common cultural connection having both spent time in the airborne infantry world. Captain Ritchie had his Ranger tab, a common achievement for any officer wishing to advance. General McPhee made some remarks, and we began to eat when our food arrived.

"So, Specialist Elliott, what are your plans?" Captain Ritchie asked.

"Well, sir, I have almost exactly two years left on my enlistment. I'm not sure if I'm staying in or not. If I do, I'd likely try and go SF or drop my OCS packet. But I know for sure I want to finish Ranger School."

"Really?" He chuckled. "You want to go to Ranger School? You know I went there because I had to, right?"

"Roger, sir, I know."

"I'm not trying to talk you out of it. That's great, and your motivation is admirable, but if you don't mind me asking, why do you want to get your Ranger tab? Why not just wait until you need to get it, if you need to?"

"Well, sir, I've already completed my Ranger School physical and just completed another PT test for school. I think I'm ready now."

"Yeah, but why? For what? You might get out in two years. You really want to spend a couple months plus sucking at Benning? Again, go for it. That's great. But why?"

"I guess it's just a goal I had, sir. Part of what I set out to do when I joined."

"That's awesome, Specialist. You should do it."

Why? It wouldn't change the past. It wouldn't change what I'd done or who I was. Why?

That night, I decided to go to a Wednesday night service at Shandon Baptist. Wednesday seemed a lot safer than Sunday, but still I was sure to arrive fifteen minutes late and sit quietly in the very back pew.

The senior pastor was teaching a series on the Psalms, going through them one by one. I didn't hear much of what he said. I was distracted by how foreign the once-familiar setting of church was beginning to feel. I stared at the backs of strangers' heads and wondered what had brought them to church. I wondered why I was there and failed to come up with an answer. The pastor read from the text of Psalm 13: "Look on me and answer, LORD my God. Give light to my eyes, or I will sleep in death, and my enemy will say, 'I have overcome him,' and my foes will rejoice when I fall. But I trust in your unfailing love; my heart rejoices in your salvation. I will sing the LORD's praise, for he has been good to me."

He has been good to me.

I got up and left.

That Saturday I ran and spent a good part of the day off post at a Starbucks to study for my GMAT, the test I had to pass to complete my application for the OSU MBA program. I got back to my room later in the afternoon and started drinking immediately, beer mostly. As the evening wore on, I sipped whiskey and listened to music. Metallica was blaring as I stared at the trifold wallet on my desk. The open side of the wallet was facing me, so I could see the yellow edge of the Ranger tab tucked inside and peeking out. I pulled it out and massaged it in my fingers.

Hope turned to despair and despair to frustration. Frustration finally became rage. I wanted to destroy it and everything it represented. I wanted to crush the fabric in my hands. I wanted to feel the release and satisfaction of its destruction.

I threw the wallet at the wall and was pleased to hear the leather smack the concrete. I grabbed a lighter I used when I smoked an occasional cigar and drunkenly made my way into the kitchen. I leaned on the counter, lighter in one hand, Ranger tab in the other. With intense concentration I managed to hold the flame beneath the corner of the tab. At first, only a wisp of smoke was visible, and then the word *RANGER* melted in the fire.

That was the last thing I remembered.

I woke up in bed, still dressed. My right hand was throbbing. I flexed it painfully and saw that three of my knuckles were scraped and bloody. The joints were badly swollen.

Images of the previous night flashed in my mind. I lay there, wondering if it had been a dream.

I slowly sat up and saw streaks of dried blood on the white cinder block wall. I got out of bed and walked into the kitchen. A small pile of ashes sat on top of the burned linoleum countertop.

It wasn't a dream. It was real.

11

FREEFALL

"You aren't one of his disciples too, are you?"
[Peter] denied it, saying, "I am not."
JOHN 18:25

I sat, wearing my army PT uniform, waiting in the early-morning heat to get this over with. It was July, and for the next thirty days I would be at the Fort Stewart Noncommissioned Officer Academy to complete the Primary Leadership Development Course (PLDC). The course was an army requirement for anyone about to be promoted to sergeant or who had just recently been promoted to sergeant. The course included classroom instruction, physical fitness assessments, and field exercises. For me, it was a box to check to wear the rank that General McPhee had pinned on my collar a few months prior.

On May 1, I had stood in the command group conference room as the Boss conducted the promotion ceremony: "We are here today to promote Specialist Elliott to sergeant. He is a warrior, he has served our country, and he has served honorably." General McPhee delivered these words with focused intent and particularly emphasized the word *honorably*.

He pinned on my sergeant's chevrons and saluted me as "Sergeant Elliott." With a shake of the hand and a slap on the back it was official. It was a good step forward. I'd make a little more money and get a slightly larger NCO apartment at Fort Jackson. Every little bit counted, particularly given that Brook and I were engaged and had set a date for the wedding, August 27. Being stuck in an army schoolhouse for thirty days with scant access to pay phones or e-mail was not ideal when our wedding was five weeks away. I'd graduate and then be on a plane for Seattle almost immediately for our wedding and honeymoon. Between now and then, however, was thirty days at Fort Stewart's sweltering version of PLDC.

The class was composed of soldiers from all sorts of units. That was one of the values of a course such as this: it allowed people from different parts of the army to learn and train together before going back to their respective units. The uniform of the day was PTs, so it was impossible to tell names, units, or ranks as people filed in. My objective here was the same as it had been in previous courses: keep my head down, do what I was told, and stay out of the limelight.

The crowd of quiet, PT-wearing students had grown to about forty. As we waited for the cadre to begin our in-processing, a new herd of soldiers barged in. There were about twenty of them—all men, all with the same haircut, all physically fit, and all cracking jokes and making fun of each other in their "big army" PT uniforms. It was as though the cool jocks had just entered the gym for a school assembly.

Where are these guys from? I wondered. Then it struck me. *They're First Batt Rangers.*

First Ranger Battalion was right down the road at Hunter Army Airfield, practically in downtown Savannah. Fort Stewart was the only post around and would be the obvious destination for any First Batt Ranger that was about to be or had already been promoted to sergeant. It was a peculiarity that even though the regiment was its own highly insular community, Rangers still had to go to big army schools and hang out with big army people as they climbed the ranks.

Nothing against PLDC, but this would be a joke to them. They had all gone through Ranger selection, as I had, they had all earned their Ranger tabs, and they had all undoubtedly been to combat. Now they were going to be forced to spend a month locked up here to check their own boxes for promotion.

It wouldn't be long before they figured out who I was. They'd see the combat scroll on my right shoulder when I wore my BDUs. They'd see I wasn't in the regiment anymore. They'd see I hadn't earned my Ranger tab. They'd know I was RFSd almost immediately. They'd know I was a screwup. Some might even put the pieces together and figure out why. In regiment, getting RFSd is its own proof of guilt. The regiment wouldn't kick someone out who didn't fully deserve it. I would be Schrader, a cancer to be avoided. A pariah.

We were assigned to our barracks, and I was surrounded by all the guys from First Batt. My bunkmate, Grimes, was a second-generation First Batt Ranger. His dad had jumped into Panama in 1989. Turns out they had all come here practically straight from deployment. This was the only block in their stateside schedule that would allow for PLDC, so instead of spending time with wives, friends, and girlfriends who were just a few miles away, they were stuck here for the next month. Grimes and I chatted a bit. I was careful to provide only the information he asked for and managed to avoid sharing the fact that I, too, had been in regiment.

We took an army standard physical fitness test that next morning. I maxed my score, which seemed to impress some of the First Batt guys. They didn't know who I was, my military occupational specialty, or my unit, but I was fit. After that, we were changing into our BDUs for a day of classroom work and orientation. As I slid my right arm through my BDU top, I saw Grimes's eyes fix on the Second Battalion scroll on my right shoulder.

"Wait a second, you were at Second Batt?"

"Yeah, I was there for a little while. I was assigned out here to work for a general officer. They wanted someone with combat experience and some education, which I had."

"Huh. But you didn't go to Ranger School?" He wasn't buying it.

"No, I got reassigned before I could go," I said, continuing to offer half-truths.

"Oh. Okay. When did you deploy?" he asked.

"Last spring, in 2004, to Afghanistan."

"Yeah, it's a lot of fun over there." He smiled as he laid off the gas. He clearly sensed something was off, but my performance on the PT test that morning didn't fit the profile of a guy kicked out of regiment for a DUI or for not meeting some physical standard. An uneasy calm settled in. Offer nothing, explain as little as possible, and maybe I could navigate the month without the truth coming out. The truth of who I was and what I had done.

The day passed uneventfully enough. I came back to the barracks to put away my notebook before dinner chow and found Grimes talking closely and quietly with another Ranger, Brown. Both of them were in my squad. The look they both gave me as I came closer made it clear that they had been talking about me.

"What's up, guys?"

Brown's expression was unreadable. I couldn't tell if he was angry, sad, or confused. Brown spoke with awkward plainness. "Look, Elliott, you see Thompson over there?" He nodded to another Ranger across the aisle about thirty feet away who was himself engaged in conversation but clearly observing ours.

"Yeah, what about him?"

Brown took a breath. "He went to Ranger School with Pat and Kevin."

The whole group is three steps ahead of me.

"Well, Thompson's a f—in' idiot, okay? You understand? But he wants to kick your a—. Me and Grimes talked him down. He knows you were one of the guys RFSd for what happened."

I didn't respond. Brown continued, trying to somehow take the edge off all he had just shared. "He ain't gonna come after you, understand? Thompson says he was close to Pat in Ranger School, which is probably just bulls— anyway. Sergeant Major'd destroy him if he tried something like that. He's all talk."

"Yeah," I said.

"But, look. I'm sorry. We just gotta ask. What happened out there?"

I'd been given the benefit of the doubt because my accuser was a jerk. Now I would be judged by my response. I desperately wanted to defend myself and offer a full justification for my actions that day. I also felt unworthy of any defense. Maybe Thompson was right. Maybe I deserved to have my a— kicked.

"It was just all f—ed up. Our platoon was split, and we were supposed to get a broken Humvee to Hardball Road. We didn't move out until dusk. We had no comms with the other serial. When the ambush started, we were stuck in a canyon. When we finally got moving, we saw more muzzle flashes as we exited the kill zone, and our squad leader fired there. I was on the 240, and I fired there too. I had no idea. No idea there were friendlies anywhere."

Grimes and Brown hung on every word. A two-man jury in deliberation.

"So then why were you RFSd? You fired where a team leader fired." Grimes's accusation, though veiled, was evident. The regiment doesn't make mistakes.

"BC said it was lack of weapons discipline and failure to follow the ROE."

"That all sounds f—ed up, man," Brown responded, committing neither to judgment nor acquittal, stopping short of a full pardon. "Just don't worry about Thompson. I hope he does try something so I can kick his a—."

Grimes said nothing. His bunkmate had been kicked out of the unit he and his father served in for playing a part in arguably the most embarrassing incident to occur in modern Ranger history. Guilty or not, I represented bad luck at best and a miserable failure at worst.

They all knew. They were all talking about it. Offering their own opinions. Coming to their own conclusions. Examining me, trying to tell if I deserved worse or was wrongly accused. You could see the wheels turning as guys in the barracks tried not to stare. I couldn't tell if I was pitied or hated.

After PT the next morning, I walked into the chow hall for breakfast. I picked up a tray full of food and turned to search for a seat. Rangers were seated throughout the chow hall, some together and some with other students. Guys like Brown and Grimes ignored me. Others shot me a glance making it clear they weren't interested in my company. I sat by myself and would get used to eating alone over the next few weeks. It was just easier to be alone.

Before class started that morning, one of the cadre called me into his office and informed me that I would be one of the two platoon sergeants for our class. This meant that for half the class, which was called Second Platoon, I'd be the liaison between the cadre and the students. I'd be their peer leader, responsible for communicating schedules, time hacks, and packing lists for training events. I'd be the one who would stand in front of the formation, and with the cadre's direction, call them to attention and march them to and from the day's events. I would get to be singled out, to stare at all of them and give them orders as they stared back at me. He said it was because I had a bachelor's degree.

"Sergeant Elliott, here's the schedule for today. I expect you to form up your platoon and march them to their classrooms no later than 0900 hours. The uniform of the day is BDUs and patrol caps. Make sure everyone has notebooks and writing utensils. If they're late or out of uniform, it's on you. Any questions?"

"Negative, Sarn't."

I walked back to the barracks and found Grimes on his bunk. The rest of Second Platoon was just hanging around, waiting for instructions. Waiting for me.

"All right, listen up!" I yelled, standing in the center aisle of the two rows of bunks.

Slowly conversations stopped and guys emerged to hear what I had to say.

"I've just been named platoon sergeant for Second Platoon. You can listen to me or not. You guys know how this works. I don't have any actual power. I'm just here to tell you what the cadre tell me and get us from one point to the next. That's it. If we work together, this can all be a little bit easier. If not, then someone else can have this job. We'll form up outside in five minutes and march over to the classrooms. Class starts sharp at 0900. BDUs and patrol caps is the uniform, and be sure to bring your notebooks and something to write with. That's it."

I walked outside to wait for the platoon to form up, half wondering if anyone would show, half hoping they wouldn't so the cadre would have an excuse to name someone else as platoon sergeant.

One by one and two by two they all emerged and dutifully stood in formation, special operations combat veterans taking drill and ceremony commands from a guy who'd been fired from their unit.

"Platoon, attention! Right face! Forward march!" And we were off. Not a dissenter in the bunch.

The month passed without incident. Every day I hoped to get fired from being a platoon sergeant, and every day I still had the job. My solace and hope in all this was Brook. Most nights I could manage ten minutes or so on the pay phone and greedily listened as she filled me in on the wedding she was planning. *Our* wedding. It was an escape to another world, a world I would soon join her in.

As PLDC came to an end and all the points were tallied from assignments and field exercises, I found myself with the second highest score in the class. The only student who scored higher than me was a First Batt Ranger. This made him the distinguished honor graduate and me the honor graduate. This further compounded the other Rangers' confusion as they tried to reconcile my place in the world as one who was RFSd from regiment but performed better than all but one of them at this school.

The First Ranger Battalion sergeant major was the speaker for our graduation. As the ceremony concluded, the distinguished honor graduate and I were recognized, and the sergeant major came forward to shake our hands and present us with the First Ranger Battalion coin as a commemoration of this moment and of a job well done.

If he only knew, I thought.

"Sergeant Elliott, congratulations. Great work," he said as he shook my hand, placing the coin squarely in my palm.

"Thank you, Sergeant Major."

He noticed the Second Battalion scroll on my right shoulder and looked at me, puzzled, as he asked, "What brought you out here, Sarn't?"

"Unfortunate circumstances, Sergeant Major."

His confused expression deepened, beckoning me to offer more detail.

I complied. "Pat Tillman, Sergeant Major."

He let go of my hand and walked away.

★

Two days later I was on a plane for Seattle. Brook had done an amazing job coordinating all the details for a wedding on a budget. I couldn't wait to see her. We hadn't been together for nearly two months, and that was the quick weekend when we got engaged. The pressure to make the most of every day, every moment we were together was growing. The days leading up to the wedding were hard. Expectations were high, and it turns out that getting married is stressful.

August 27 arrived as a perfect Northwest summer day. The ceremony was at a friend's property in Eatonville. Mount Rainier glistened in the background. Evan was my best man, and Dustin Broek was there too. Both had just earned their Ranger tabs. Boatright was still at Ranger School and would successfully complete the course but couldn't come to the wedding. Family from Kansas and California had come too. We had far too little time to spend with some of the most important people in our lives.

I stood on the lawn in front of an iron arbor that served as an altar. Evan was next to me, both of us in uniform, mine somewhat ill-fitting as I had lost nearly thirty pounds since being in regiment. I learned that the best man has a very practical function beyond serving as a legal witness. He's there to make sure the groom can physically complete the ceremony. Getting married was amazing and horrifying. It made sense and was nonsensical. The gravity of the commitment being made cannot possibly be understood by those making it. Broken people, unable to fully tend to their own needs, pledge to care for the needs of another. For life.

"You doin' all right?" Evan asked.

"Uh, yeah," I said, mildly dazed as I waited to bind my life to another.

He laughed. "No you're not."

I felt better. Knowing he knew I wasn't quite myself was a comfort.

Brook emerged from the house. Her red hair, veiled with white lace, fell on her shoulders. She was stunning. Her dad, Denny, walked her down the aisle, hugged her, shook my hand, and gave her to me.

I remember the pastor saying something. I remember us saying something. I remember Gracie, three and a half years old, walking down the aisle with our rings with the help of Brook's brother, Brandon. I remember a kiss, applause, and pictures. I remember cutting cheesecake and hearing voices offering toasts.

Suddenly, we had changed our clothes, said our good-byes, and climbed into our new car, an unexpected wedding gift from Brook's dad. We began to drive away, en route to the San Juan Islands for our honeymoon. We were finally together. We were finally married.

Brook started bawling. That was not the response I was hoping for.

Tears were scary to me. I fought the urge to throw myself from the moving vehicle as she sobbed and finally, as the emotion ebbed, managed to ask her, "Are you okay?"

"Uh-huh," she finally managed, mascara staining her cheeks.

"What's wrong?"

"I love those people, and we hardly got to see them or talk to them, and they came so far and did so much," she said as she continued to cry.

Her heart for others broke through something in me. I found my lip quivering and tears welling up.

"I know," I said. "We're really lucky, and it's not fair to not have more time."

The next hour-and-a-half drive was a collective sigh, a release of tension and expectations.

We arrived at the ferry terminal at Steilacoom as the sun was beginning to set. We would spend our first night together at a bed and breakfast on Anderson Island before making the drive the following day up north to the ferry at Anacortes, Washington, that would take us to the San Juans.

We drove onto the boat and parked. We got out to go up to the observation deck to enjoy the evening light. As we walked toward the stairs, Brook grabbed my hand and we walked together, in that moment complete. In that moment, one flesh as we began our journey together. It was the greatest moment of my life.

★

I stood there in the dark. A ridgeline in the distance. The darkness flashed into strobes of light as I was drawn closer to the cliffs. The ridgeline was empty and quiet save for one person. Bryan O'Neal. He smiled at me strangely.

Bryan was in uniform, but two items were missing. The cloth camouflage cover that fit tightly over the Kevlar helmet was gone. The dark green helmet stood out sharply against the brown rocks. He wore no BDU top, only a brown T-shirt with his BDU pants and boots.

The strobes continued as my vision of Bryan zoomed in and out like a telescopic lens gone haywire. One moment I was overwhelmed with intimate detail—the dirt on his face, the sweat stains on his T-shirt—and the next I was straining to discern the nature of his silhouette on the distant horizon.

My eyes blinked open and quickly focused on the textured wall next to my bed as the nightmare bled into the waking world. I ran my fingers across the wall as I studied the minute shapes and ridges of the vertical surface, seeking to ground myself in reality and leave the images of my sleep behind. I zoomed out, got up, and took a shower.

The morning after the ambush as we were cleaning up our vehicle, I remember seeing Bryan, standing there on the ridgeline with no BDU top or helmet cover. It was an odd but otherwise benign image at the time. I eventually figured out why his helmet cover and BDU top were missing. They were biohazards, covered in Pat's blood and brain matter. Sometimes the horror lies in what is missing, not in what is there.

I was back at Fort Jackson. After the wedding and honeymoon, Brook and I were again apart. The pain of that separation deepened as we grew closer. My disdain for the army grew, as it was the most obvious force that kept us apart.

We were in a logistical quandary. She was enrolled full time in school, and Gracie's dad, Christian, had regular visitation with Gracie every other week. I was assigned to Fort Jackson but was often gone due to the Boss's travel schedule. In short, it made little sense for them to uproot themselves from the West Coast and follow me to the East Coast when I would be gone most of the time anyway. On top of that, by the fall of 2005, I had decided I wouldn't be staying in. Brook and I would mark time as best we could until my enlistment ended in May 2007. We were counting the days.

General McPhee had just moved on to another assignment, and I was working for a new boss, Colonel Weeks. Our unit was in limbo as the army implemented the Base Realignment and Closure process, which meant that some units were being moved around, some installations closed, others beefed up. The word was that our division would be moving to Fort Meade, Maryland, just north of Washington, DC, and would continue its mission overseeing all national guard and reserve mobilizations for units east of the Mississippi. Colonel Weeks was there to oversee that process along with his trusty chief of staff, Lieutenant Colonel Buck Buchanan (known simply as "Colonel Buck"), and to hand off control to a new, yet-to-be-named two-star general. I didn't yet know what role, if any, I would play in that new division. In the interim, I continued to work on my MBA.

With no smartphone or Internet at the barracks, I went to the learning center at Fort Jackson to use their computers, do research, and occasionally check the news. A new Internet company had just emerged called Google. Apparently, they had the best search engine. Having completed my work for the evening, I couldn't help myself.

What does the Internet know about me? I wondered. *How much control do I still have to keep myself and my association with Pat's death in the dark?* My name, at least, was innocuous. There were a million Steven Elliotts. Still, what was out there? What could people find out? What could follow me?

I started searching. "Steven Elliott" turned up nothing of interest. I then reverted to searching for me through another name. I typed "Pat Tillman." I wished I hadn't.

Article after article, page after page. News articles were everywhere. I would read them in reverse, scanning desperately for any mention of my name first and then reading the article for its content. Not always, but often enough, my name was there, usually alongside Baker's, Alders's, and Ashpole's. Usually missing one of the *t*'s in Elliott, a common misspelling.

Maybe that will be enough, I thought. Maybe the missing *t* would provide the anonymity I desperately wanted.

It was there in black and white over and over again. It became more real, and it was far from over. The family kept asking questions, and the army kept coming up short in its responses. Conspiracy theories filled the void left by an unknown truth. I was horrified.

As I clicked and read, I stumbled across a *Washington Post* story written at the end of 2004 that detailed the Tillman family's search for answers and their attempts to make sense of inconsistencies. Until that moment, I knew less about the broader events surrounding Pat's death than your average news junkie. I was so close to it, so painfully close in such an awful way, I didn't want to know. I already knew too much.

Another article stated that "the medical examiner's report said Tillman was killed by three bullets closely spaced in his forehead." My mind raced. I visualized what Pat must have looked like. This was the first I had read of any medical examination.

I had been working under the vague and unverified assumption that rounds from the .50 cal had killed him. I was no ballistics expert, but this article, stating the medical examiner's findings, made that impossible. A .50-cal round would cut a person in two. There would have been no head to examine. He must have been killed by a smaller-caliber weapon. Three rounds closely spaced seemed to leave me or

Alders. Alders swore he never fired on that position, and firing a SAW from your shoulder while on a moving vehicle would not provide a high level of accuracy. That seemed to leave me.

I was firing short, three-to-five-round bursts from a mounted weapon, a much more stable firing position than what Alders had. *Could my shot group have been that tight? Especially as we were moving? How would the rounds disperse? How would they hit? Who else could have done it if not me?* I was falling down the rabbit hole of speculation, a new layer of guilt descending. A new layer of shame emerging.

Was it me? Am I responsible?

I called Brook that night and for the first time since our first date talked with guilty necessity about the ambush. Necessity because I felt like I would burst if I didn't talk to someone about all that I had read. Guilty because she was the last person I wanted to dump this on.

"I read a bunch of articles about the ambush," I said. I was on my second beer, which provided some level of calm and made frank conversation a bit easier.

"Oh. Is that a good idea?"

"I don't know. But it's all out there. There's a medical examiner that says Pat was killed by three rounds to the forehead." The horror of the imagined image weighed heavily on me.

"Okay. So what does that mean?" she asked.

"It feels like it means it was maybe me. All this time I thought it was Ashpole. I didn't want to know, I guess. It just seems like, unless there were some other shooters we don't know about, which I can't even fathom, it was Alders or me."

She fought to comfort me. "Well, how much does that matter? I mean, I know it does—I'm not saying it doesn't—but you all were in a horrible situation that wasn't your fault. It seems like your commander is more responsible than any one of you."

"Yeah, but he didn't fire the rounds. I did. *We* did. We were manning those weapons systems. They were our responsibility, and we messed up. I don't know."

"Well, try not to let it get to you, okay? Are you praying about it?"

My anger spiked briefly. "Yeah, I am."

"It's in the past, and it's not fair, but you can't change it. You were doing your best."

My best, I thought. Splattered brain matter and a caved-in skull. My best.

"I know," I said. "I shouldn't even be talking about it. What's the point, right?"

"It's late out there. You should get some sleep," she said.

"Yeah, I should. All right. I love you. I miss you, and I'm sorry."

"I love you too. It's okay. Good night."

I slept a dreamless sleep and awoke to a Sunday morning. I took a run in a neighborhood off post, showered, and drove to a coffee shop to study. It was a fight to focus. The polite relevance of supply and demand curves and marginal utility calculations diminished in the light of "three rounds to the forehead."

I sat there in the corner of the coffee shop, surrounded by strangers and feeling exposed as never before. Logic fought against the irrational fear that everyone knew. As if my crime was tattooed on my forehead. I felt naked.

And then I felt dumb. *You're not important enough to be that guilty,* I told myself. *You're a nobody, a Steven Elliott hiding in a sea of Steven Elliotts, some with one* t *and some with two. It'll be forgotten. Nobody cares that much. You were just a no-name trigger puller.*

But I had pulled the trigger.

Back at my room, the lonely solitude was oppressive. I pounded a beer first thing and turned on music to feel less alone. I continued to drink. I hadn't prayed. I couldn't remember when I had stopped praying. I was afraid of what I'd say. I was afraid of hearing nothing.

As I became more drunk, my emotions became more malleable, moving with the music. A ballad played. "Just to be with you, I'd do anything . . ." was the chorus. *God's love was supposed to be like that,* I thought. *Jesus came to save us, didn't he? "For God so loved the world . . ." I was "saved" wasn't I? Is this what his love feels like?*

The void was closing in. As drunken tears began to fall, I sat on the floor, my back to the wall, sobbing.

"Why don't you love me?" I cried, pounding the floor with my fist. "Why don't you love me?"

I was startled by my own voice but not surprised that I heard nothing in response.

★

Things were on the move. Though I was still technically stationed at Fort Jackson, I was spending more and more time at Fort Meade during the fall and winter of 2005. I worked mostly with Colonel Buck, working through logistics for what would be a new division, First Army Division East. General Hardee, General McPhee's former boss, was spending more time at Fort Meade as well, helping with the transition and preparing for the new division commander who had yet to be named.

Fort Meade was synonymous with its largest and most notorious tenant organization, the National Security Agency (NSA). Apart from the NSA, it was a very quiet little post. First Army Division East would be occupying one of the largest buildings on the installation and would bring a whole new division command along with the personnel required to support it. Some turf wars ensued as long-term tenant units at Fort Meade chafed at the idea of having to give up real estate to a new unit. The political aspect of the new division was what brought General Hardee to Fort Meade as he worked to smooth over rough places and prepare the way for what was coming to the post, like it or not.

His schedule was packed, and I was increasingly functioning more as an aide-de-camp—setting up meetings and planning itineraries— than just a driver. As busy as he was, he insisted that we visit Walter Reed Medical Center a few miles to the southwest. He wanted to visit wounded soldiers that had served in units that he and his staff had helped train.

General Hardee exuded an understated, all-American sort of confidence. It was obvious why he had risen through the ranks. He happily sat in the front seat next to me in our government sedan as we drove to Walter Reed. He had no desire for pretense and preferred simplicity. We talked about our families. He asked me about my plans, encouraging OCS but not pushing it. People like General Hardee made me think twice about leaving the army.

We arrived at Walter Reed, parked in a space reserved for general officers, and linked up with the liaison officer who would be taking us to the half dozen or so soldiers we'd be visiting.

I hadn't visited hospitals often, but when I had, it was usually to visit old people. Walter Reed was full of young people. Young people whose youth had clashed with violence on behalf of their country.

As we made our way to the first soldier, we passed a young man wearing a gray Marine Corps T-shirt who was being pushed in a wheelchair by a beautiful brunette. They were my age. It wasn't what was there but what was missing. His right arm was gone. His left arm also. Both absent past the shoulder.

What have I lost? I thought. *What right do I have to feel sorry for myself?* My whiny prayers and sense of injustice felt so pathetic. I felt as though I didn't have the right to hurt, not in the face of such suffering and sacrifice, particularly since the pain I experienced had, in some degree, been caused by me and particularly since others had paid a far higher price. Pat. Jade. What right did I have?

We made it to the first room. General Hardee began to go in and noticed I was staying behind in the hall.

"Come on in, Sergeant Elliott. They'll want to meet you. That'll mean something to them to meet a Ranger."

Two kids sat on the floor on the far end of the room, staring up at the TV and watching the movie *Chicken Run*. A woman sat in the chair to the left. In the bed was her husband. He was wearing standard army PTs, and the black shorts exposed his left leg into which were stuck multiple steel pins all held in place by a brace.

As we entered, he quickly struggled to sit up.

"Sir!" he said offering a salute.

"At ease, at ease," General Hardee said smiling, returning the gesture and immediately shaking the man's hand and kneeling next to him, his posture one of humility in the presence of the wounded.

"You should be more careful," General Hardee joked, pointing at the man's leg. They both laughed.

"Yes, sir," he chuckled.

"Where were you deployed?" General Hardee asked, intent on hearing his story.

"Well, sir, I'm a combat engineer, and we was in Baghdad. IED hit us, and my leg got crushed. They thought I'd bled out, but I made it. I made it." He repeated the phrase as if to convince himself that there was some providence in his survival and therefore hope for the future.

"How are they treatin' you here? You gettin' enough to eat?" General Hardee continued.

"Oh, yes, sir, they're real good to us. Nurses are great. Docs are good."

"Good, good," Hardee replied. "Oh, I want you to meet Sergeant Elliott," he said motioning me to the bed as he stood up.

"Hey, man, good to meet you," I said, shaking his hand. He noticed my combat scroll on my right sleeve.

"You're a Ranger?" he said with excitement.

"Yeah, I was in the regiment for a while."

"Can't believe it. We got a general and a Ranger visiting us. You guys are somethin' else."

"Yeah, I guess so," I said with a plastic smile, playing the part he needed me to play.

"Sergeant Elliott, give me one of those coins, would you?" General Hardee asked.

I dug in my pocket and retrieved one of the several Twenty-Fourth Infantry Division coins. It was the size of a silver dollar but gold in color with the green taro leaf of the Twenty-Fourth ID engraved on one side and the two stars of a major general on the other. The coin would become a reminder of this moment. A token of affection and admiration for this wounded man.

General Hardee took it, placed it in his right hand, and again shook the hand of the wounded soldier. "We thank you for your service and your sacrifice for this nation," he said. The man's Adam's apple bobbed as he fought for his composure. They continued to chat, and I turned to his wife, who was wiping her eyes.

"How are you?" I asked.

"Oh, we're just thankful he's okay, but this is getting old. He's on his fifth surgery and has at least two more. We're practically living here. It's just really hard, but we're grateful."

"I can only imagine," I said. "I hope the surgeries go well. Best of luck to you guys."

We left, the morale of the room noticeably lifted, and repeated this ritual another five times. Five more young men broken from war. Five more families trying to make it work. Five more coins offered in respect and gratitude. Each of them figured I was something special, plucked from the ranks of an elite unit to work directly for a general. I wanted to believe that was true.

General Hardee left the next day and so did I, returning to Fort Jackson for a couple of weeks. There was little to do at the office but wait to see what my next assignment would be. I reported every day and mostly did homework for school but quickly reverted to whatever task I was given by Colonel Buck. Another week passed, and another long, lonely weekend presented itself. One that I would largely drink my way through.

I sat yet again in my room listening to Nirvana. Drinking. Thinking. Considering the notion of God, who he is. *If* he is. Alcohol continued to lower my inhibitions. I reasoned that if God was all-powerful, then he's mean, lazy, or both, because he doesn't seem to do anything about the pain and suffering in the world. But if he's all-loving, then he lacks the power to make that love felt and the Bible offers some moral ideals for us to aspire to—which is fine—but doesn't solve the problem of pain. All-powerful *or* all-loving. Not both.

My money was on the first scenario. I decided that God just doesn't give a s—. And if that's true, why should I give a s— about a being that has the power to take away pain but refuses to do so?

I gave you the reins to my life. I followed you, and you screwed it up. I can do that. I can be a f— up. I don't need you for that.

The evidence was damning. People I had considered my friends were wounded, physically and emotionally. Pat was *dead*. Just the fact that war and all its horrors existed was confirmation that God had little regard for his creation.

"God," I said aloud, "can you explain yourself?"

Kurt Cobain's lyrics built to a crescendo along with my anger. All my life, God had been my "insurance policy"—I had paid the premiums of Bible reading, church attendance, and "moral" behavior, but when I needed the benefits, they weren't paying out.

I sat back in my chair, rocking as I gulped my beer with shallow satisfaction. With the same sense of authority and justification I might have derived from firing a lackluster employee or canceling expensive cable service, I ended it. No words were spoken. No analysis beyond my experiences was conducted. I was simply done.

What if he's not even there? I pondered that for a moment. I took another drink and laughed quietly to myself. *I bet he's not.* With that thought, I, the created, shut the door on the Creator. I savored the relief it brought. I was free of attempting to reconcile the idea of a loving God with a hateful world. With loss. With guilt. With shame.

The relief was short-lived. I was suddenly untethered. As I slowly rocked in my chair, I felt as though I were falling.

I took another drink.

12

LOCK ME UP

My guiding principle is this:
Guilt is never to be doubted.
FRANZ KAFKA

"Sir, some of these documents are kind of fragile. You sure you're okay with me handling them?" I asked as I sorted through stacks of papers, many yellowed with age and dating back to the early 1970s.

"You callin' me old, Sergeant?"

"Oh, no, sir, I didn't mean that. It's just that, well—"

"Maybe we can get someone from the National Archives who knows how to handle historic documents to help you make copies of my medical records?" Buck said with a smile, happy to needle me a bit.

"I'm just kiddin', Sergeant Elliott. I know I'm old as sin. Just do the best you can and let me know when you've got 'em copied."

Buck was getting out. After nearly forty years of service in the army, he was retiring and would be looking for a job as a government contractor. I was giving him a hand, getting documents in order for his exit term of service while we waited for things to firm up with the new division. We were still at Fort Jackson, but all of us would soon be going our separate ways. It was still unclear what my next assignment would be.

By this point I had given up on getting back to Fort Lewis. I had less than a year left, and the odds of the army permanently reassigning me to a new unit with so little time on my contract was slim. Brook and I just had to wait it out. I was halfway through my MBA and focusing on securing a job for when I got out in May of 2007. My problem was singular: the army. It stood in the way of Brook and me being together and moving on. As soon as I was out of uniform, everything would be different. Everything.

Before that day would come, there was still work to do. Buck called me into his office, which was unusual.

"Have a seat, Ranger," he said as he sipped from a black mug upon which was emblazoned the symbol for Delta Force. Buck was one of the original members of that unit. It seemed as though he'd seen everything.

"What's up, sir?"

"I got work for you, Sergeant. It was just confirmed that Major General Jay Hood will be the commander for First Army Division East at Fort Meade. He and his wife, Lynne, will be arriving at Meade within the next two weeks."

"Okay, sir. What does that mean for me?"

"Well, Sergeant, it's going to be a number of months before General Hood's staff is assembled. He'll get a driver, a civilian secretary, and an aide but not for a while. I need someone to basically be all three. Someone to make sure he and his wife are taken care of. He's an old airborne guy. Spent years in the Eighty-Second as head of the division artillery and even the chief of staff for the division. I think you two will get along. And you're too d—ed smart, Sergeant. So I'm gonna work you like a major for as long as I have you."

"Yes, sir. Whatever you need. Where are General and Mrs. Hood coming from?"

"Gitmo. He's been the commander of Joint Task Force Guantánamo in Cuba."

"Yes, sir."

"Pack your bags and head on up to Fort Meade. You'll be responsible for making sure the Hoods get properly in-processed to the post and helping to square away their housing and household goods. If he likes you, I'm sure he'll keep you busy."

"Thank you, sir. I'll head up there day after tomorrow."

After a long drive on the I-95 corridor, I arrived at Fort Meade and helped pave the way for General Hood's arrival. I visited every office and bureaucrat necessary to ensure housing was secured, the Boss's goods would be received, and any other logistical items were addressed in their transition. A week later the Hoods arrived.

My flip phone sprang to life, and I could see the name "MG Hood" on the caller ID.

"Sergeant Elliott speaking."

"Sergeant, how are ya? This is Jay Hood. Colonel Buck tells me you're available to help us out. Is that so?"

"Yes, sir, whatever you need."

"Why don't you meet me at the office, and we can start taking care of some business."

I waited in front of the Division East headquarters as instructed, the steel-gray government-issued Dodge Stratus idling. Before long, a lean figure was striding to the car. His reddish-brown hair was cropped close at the temples. The blue jeans and polo shirt he wore could not hide the air of authority with which he walked. He sort of sneaked up on me even though I was looking for him. Before I could get out of the car and salute, he was in the passenger seat.

"You're Sergeant Elliott, I assume," he said as he buckled himself in.

"Yes, sir."

"Well, what do you got for me, Sergeant?"

"Sir, we'll need to head over to the Reception Company and get you registered here on post. From there I can help with your housing and household goods. Unfortunately, your billet isn't ready for you yet, but your temporary housing is." The last part didn't go over well, and his expression became more annoyed.

He paused, saying nothing, narrowing his gaze slightly as he sized me up.

"Well, I guess we'll just see how smart you are," he said with an unsettling lack of confidence.

"Yes, sir."

The logistics went off without a hitch, and I quickly became General Hood's right-hand man. A few days later, I picked him up at his house for a series of official meetings that day. Both of us were in uniform for the first time around each other, having only worn civilian clothes up to that point. He opened the door of the dark blue Chevy Tahoe and sprang lightly into the seat. He immediately stared at my right shoulder, at my Second Battalion combat scroll, and froze.

He immediately asked, "Sergeant, why are you here?"

I attempted my normal course of evasion. "It was just unfortunate circumstances, sir."

He leaned in closer, speaking more slowly as he emphasized each word, "Sergeant, why are you here?"

I found myself trapped in a four-wheel-drive confessional with the "priest" asking the questions and demanding a reply. I was cornered and about to be exposed for who I was. For what I had done.

He continued before I could reply. "You're under my command now. You're mine. I need to know why you're here so that I can help you if needed. I have to know."

I took my hands off the wheel and exhaled with a mixture of relief and trepidation. I had no choice. The two silver stars on General Hood's black beret made that clear. I couldn't hide the truth from a major general, and I couldn't escape the confines of the vehicle. "I'm one of the Tillman shooters, sir," I said.

General Hood gritted his teeth, his jaw muscles flexing as he stared out the passenger window.

After a few painfully long seconds, he broke the silence and turned to me. "I am sorry," he said. "The army failed you."

"Yes, sir."

"How did you get here?" He was exasperated. I told him the whole story—the Cliff Notes version, anyway. From that point forward, I was his. I was welcomed into his home and broke bread with him and his wife. I even walked their dog on occasion, a feisty beagle named Belle. I felt like an orphan coming in from the cold. Their kindness was life.

Two weeks later, General and Mrs. Hood and I were heading down the Baltimore–Washington Parkway to DC. The French embassy was hosting an event in the Boss's honor for his service to NATO in Kosovo. I was invited and continued to serve in my aide/secretary/driver role. The night was a joy. The Hoods reminisced on their younger days while stationed in Europe, and we mingled effortlessly with French officers and other dignitaries. I got to pretend that night that I was something special, part of some inner circle, having arrived there on the basis of my merit.

Within a few months, the army saw fit to assign the Boss his secretary, Sally. We got along great, and she offered welcome relief as the Boss's calendar and professional life became more complex. General Hood had not been assigned an aide, normally a captain or a major, so I continued in that capacity.

"Hey, Sergeant," Sally said as I walked into the office.

"What's up?"

"I got a voice mail for you. You'll probably want to give them a call today," she said as she handed me a Post-it note with a phone number and three letters—"CID."

"Okay. Thanks."

I didn't know what CID meant. I got all sorts of calls from all sorts of places, usually in relation to travel and logistics for the Boss, so I thought little of it as I listened to the dial tone.

"Special Agent Smith" was the greeting.

"Hi, this is Sergeant Steven Elliott, and I was given a message to call you."

"Hello, Sergeant. Thank you. Yes, we're conducting a criminal investigation into the events of 22 April 2004 that resulted in the death of Corporal Patrick Tillman. Our job is to determine if there was any criminal intent or negligence. We need to set up a time to take your statement."

I went numb as I heard the word *criminal*. Then I felt a mixture of fear and irritation. I don't remember how the call ended, but I remember hanging up the phone. I stared at the Boss's open door, knowing I'd have to tell him. I wondered what Sally thought. CID is the army's Criminal Investigation Division. She would have known what that meant even if I didn't. *I might as well get it over with*, I thought as I knocked on the door of General Hood's expansive office.

He looked up, peering over his dark-framed reading glasses, which he quickly took off. He hated anything that made him look old, especially reading glasses. "Come on in, Steve."

I sat and told him. He pondered. This was clearly new territory for him as well, which was less than comforting.

"I know Stan McChrystal," he said in tired frustration. McChrystal had been in charge of Joint Special Operations Command when we were deployed. He was implicated in the criminal probe with particular interest as to what he knew and when and if he was part of any cover-up of the truth of Pat's death.

"We served together at the Eighty-Second. I just can't believe all this," Hood finally said. "Steve, it's gonna be okay. You go there and you tell 'em the truth as best you remember it. I know this is hard, but please just trust the system."

Trust the system.

"Yes, sir."

I didn't need more reasons to drink because I was doing just fine on that front, but this certainly provided a new, more tangible focus for my anger and anxiety.

Criminal, I thought. The fact that there was such an investigation, the fourth investigation, was its own strange evidence of guilt. You don't get to this place without placing blame. Someone was guilty. Someone would pay a price.

Soon afterward Brook visited for a long weekend. She had never been in or around DC. We visited Annapolis and Baltimore and walked from the US Capitol to the Lincoln Memorial. I would often walk the

Mall by myself on the weekend, stopping in the National Art Museum to find a quiet space to sit. Being in the museum, surrounded by priceless works of art, was soothing. Just to see something beautiful brought a sense of calm. The museum was far more wonderful and far more beautiful with her.

She, of course, dismissed the investigation as only a loyal wife could. It was obvious to her that I was innocent, that it was an accident, and it would of course be just as obvious to anyone else. That's the kind of support you expect to receive, the kind of support you need, and also the kind of support that leaves more than its share of doubt.

Her visit brought both joy and heartache as it was a welcome relief and also far too short. The distraction brought by her presence was soon gone and my reality was unchanged.

Criminal.

In September I made the hour drive from Fort Meade around the beltway to the army installation at Fort Belvoir, Virginia. I was early, so I had time to drive around post, which didn't take long. I soon approached my destination. It was a concrete bunker surrounded by barbed wire. Gates and doors were opened, and I found myself in a windowless, soulless office, not sure if I would be leaving as easily as I had entered.

I was escorted to a small room that contained a desk with a laptop and two chairs. The agent I spoke to on the phone walked in. He was not much older than I was and was dressed in khakis, a button-down shirt, and a tie. As I'd heard three times before, the agent would be asking some questions about the events of April 22. After offering the standard preamble, he leaned back in his chair.

"Before we begin," he said, "I want you to know that I'm former infantry. I just want to tell you that I'm really sorry for what you're having to go through."

Is this all just a formality? Are they just going through the motions investigating me, or is he offering sympathy for what's yet to come? I wanted to accept what seemed to be kindness, but it was hard for a guilty heart to receive it as such.

"Thank you," I said, somewhat confused.

The questions were nearly identical to those asked in the previous investigations. So were my answers. When the interview concluded, the agent shared that he and his CID team had traveled to the site of the ambush in Khost, examined the terrain, and attempted to re-create the lighting conditions from April 22. I couldn't believe it. I couldn't believe that others had to go back to that place to try and figure out what had happened.

I started meeting with an Air Force shrink at Fort Meade. I just needed someone to talk to about it, and I didn't want to burden Brook with everything rattling around in my brain. He was exactly what you'd think a military shrink should be—quiet, professional, and understated. I shook his hand and fought the urge to apologize to him. That's how I felt every time I talked to a chaplain or a psychiatrist. I just felt bad. I wanted to tell them, "I am so sorry that you have to sit here and listen to my problems. But thank you just the same." I knew it was silly. It felt like I had a burden that was mine and that I was failing if I couldn't carry it by myself.

"How are you?"

"Not great," I said.

"How's your sleep?"

"Bad. I drink myself to sleep most nights. When I don't, I tend to have more nightmares."

"Are you eating?" he asked.

"If doughnuts and Cup O' Noodles are considered 'eating,' then yes. I generally don't have much of an appetite."

"Are you taking any drugs or medications?"

"Just caffeine and alcohol."

I described the ambush to him, half making a case for my innocence in highlighting all the mitigating circumstances and half inviting his condemnation.

"How does all this make you feel?"

"Confused. I don't know, sir. I mean, I know logically that I didn't cause all of that to happen. I know that. I don't need one more person to explain that to me. To tell me it wasn't my fault. And yet, I pulled the trigger. I have to own that, don't I? There's a price to pay for that, isn't there?"

"Do you feel a lack of control over your life?"

"Yes. I joined. I volunteered, right? I was in a war zone because I chose to be there. I get that. I took steps to put myself in what I understood to be a dangerous situation. But what are the odds, you know? What are the odds that I'm sitting in that seat, on that weapon, on that vehicle, on that day? What are the odds that I even have a chance to misidentify the target and shoot at Pat or Jade or anyone else? And of all the people, you know? It just feels like I won some horrible lottery and I'm waiting for the next shoe to drop. I feel like I'm waiting for the next awful thing to happen."

"What do you want to believe about the situation?"

"I want to believe that it wasn't my fault, but it's hard to buy into that. Pat's dead, you know? Jade walks with a limp. That happened. If I'm guilty, I just want to know it and they can lock me up so I can pay whatever price there is to pay. I just want to know one way or the other, I suppose. I just want to believe that this can be over."

The waiting continued as CID completed their investigation, and I kept myself busy between work, school, and drinking.

An old friend had arrived at Fort Meade. Buck, newly retired, would be the assistant G3 for the division. He would be at the heart of overseeing the unit's operations and mission to train national guard and reserve units. He was also a confirmed bachelor who knew how to cook, and before long he invited me over for a meal at his new home off post.

"Come on in, Steve!" was the reply when I rang the doorbell. "I'm burnin' some meat for us out on the grill. You want a glass of wine?"

"You bet," I said.

We sipped our wine on the deck as Buck grilled filet mignon, shrimp, and vegetable kebabs. We sat and ate, working our way through a bottle of wine. I ate until I could eat no more. It was the best meal I'd had in a very long time.

"Did you get enough to eat?" he asked. "We need to fatten you up."

"Yes, sir, it was amazing. Thank you."

"Stop with the 'sir.' I'm just Buck now."

"Okay, Buck." It felt strange to say it.

"Hey, I wanna show off my new surround sound and TV," he said as we moved from the dining room to the living room. On the far wall was a massive flat screen, and the room was wired for sound.

"You like the Eagles?" he asked.

"Sure."

"Well, here's a concert of theirs," he said, queuing up a previously recorded live concert of the Eagles, which to him was the perfect vehicle to show off his audiovisual setup.

"You want a scotch?" he asked. "I've got a Glenlivet I've been waiting to open."

"Sure."

I sat on his couch, full from dinner and feeling the warmth of the alcohol. It was nice. I felt relaxed. We watched and drank for a while, and then Buck spoke in between sips of scotch.

"You know I flew helicopters in Vietnam, right?"

"Yeah, I knew that. Cobras, right?"

"Yeah, that's right," he said as he took a longer sip. He continued. "I'll never forget a day that I couldn't miss with a rocket. I mean, I was hot." He slowly lost eye contact with me and stared off at the floor as he spoke. "I came in and hit the objective that we'd been assigned, came back around . . . and all I could see were the charred butts of these dead kids." The words cut through the sea of music and alcohol.

He looked straight at me, his black eyes penetrating. "It's awful," he said. "It's war. There isn't a day that goes by that I don't think about that, that I don't regret that, but you've got to let yourself off the hook a little bit. You've got to find a way to forgive yourself."

"Tequila Sunrise" played in the background.

★

By the time December came around, General Hood had an aide, a helicopter pilot named Jeremy Bell. Captain Bell wasn't much older than I was and had done his time in Afghanistan flying Chinooks. We got along great, and he was more than happy to have my help.

We sat in the office talking when he pulled a small stuffed bear out of his pack.

"I can't believe I have to do this," he said.

"What do you mean, sir?"

"This bear is my daughter's class mascot. She's in kindergarten. Each kid gets to take it with them for a week, and you're supposed to take pictures with it. You know, like it's having its own adventures," he said trying not to roll his eyes.

"Okay, sir," I chuckled.

"My wife insisted that I bring it here so the bear can 'meet' General Hood and we can take his picture. I've been trying to find a good time to ask him, and I have to do it soon. Otherwise I'll be in trouble."

"Sir, just promise me that I'm around to watch." I didn't have to wait long. General Hood came out of his office and was passing our desks on his way to the coffeepot.

"Sir," Captain Bell started and then explained to him what he had just explained to me. To our surprise, General Hood was happily compliant. We watched and laughed as he picked up the bear and grinned, ready for the photo. His expression changed once Captain Bell retrieved his camera.

"What is that?" General Hood asked sternly.

"It's the camera, sir," Captain Bell replied.

"You want to take my picture with that camera?" he asked, his eyebrows rising as he pointed.

"Yes, sir," Bell replied, somewhat confused.

"Not a f—in' chance," Hood said and proceeded to elaborate while holding the bear. "This is a digital camera. Any picture you take can last forever. Anything in a digital medium in the Internet age can multiply and go anywhere. No way."

He put the bear down and smiled. "Nice try, though."

The Boss left, and I died laughing. I hadn't laughed that hard in a while.

"You feel better?" Captain Bell asked as his ego recovered from the incident.

"Much better, sir. At least you can tell your wife you gave it a shot."

Once the laughter wore off, I couldn't stop thinking about what the Boss had said. *Anything in a digital medium can last forever.* The thought was chilling. *What will people know about me? What can the Internet tell them? I'm being investigated for a crime. Will potential employers know that?*

I was able to return to Washington State for Christmas. Brook had bought us a home in Puyallup, practically across the street from her folks, and I was visiting for the first time. It was, as all our visits were, wonderful and difficult. It always took a few days to get used to being around each other again, and then, just when we were settling in, it would be time for one of us to leave. The challenges of those visits were easy to rationalize. It was easy to blame the army and our unnatural circumstances. Once I was out, everything would be fine.

This time, I was back in part for job interviews. I had decided to pursue a career in financial services and was interviewing with all manner of insurance companies and brokerage firms. My best prospect was with Smith Barney, one of the largest wealth management firms at the time. There was a job opening in the Olympia branch, and having already interviewed with the branch manager, I reported to the Columbia Tower in Seattle on a typically wet December morning for my final interview with the regional director.

I sat nervously in the mahogany-enameled waiting room as my tie gripped my throat with discomfort. I looked the part but didn't feel the part. *What do they know about me? What will a background search turn up? Will my past follow me?*

I was soon invited into the regional manager's office, which overlooked the Seattle skyline on two sides. I braced for questions regarding my past even though logically I knew that was unlikely. Still, the voices of accusation continued. I struggled to remain calm as the interview commenced. I struggled to remember the advice I'd been given: "If you want the job, make sure you ask for it. Make sure you close him. Don't wait for him to just give it to you."

We chatted, his questions seeming to assume a formal relationship we had yet to establish. Finally, I asked him, "I don't mean to be overly forward, but I want to work here. I want the job, and I'd like to know if you'll give me that opportunity or not."

"Steve, I think you can excel in our industry, and we'd love to hire you. I'm so glad you asked."

"Thank you. Thank you so much."

They apparently hadn't done a Google search.

There was no news from CID when 2007 began. Only silence and no clear indication as to when that silence would be broken. On an overcast day in late January, General Hood, Captain Bell, and I were on the road to Fort Dix, New Jersey. The Boss had been asked to speak at a memorial service there, and he was scribbling thoughts on a few note cards as we drove, trying to capture the words he would offer to those who had lost their loved ones.

"Steve," he said, "what do I say to these people? What do they need to hear from me?"

I thought for a moment. "Sir, I think they need to know that their loss isn't a waste. They need to feel somehow that it matters."

He considered this and continued writing.

The speech he gave was beautiful—not necessarily because of his eloquence but because of his heart. His voice cracked as he spoke of the fallen. His tough and driven exterior gave way to something inside. His compassion was the essence of his strength.

I hope he's right, I thought. *I hope this matters.*

On March 26, 2007, I sat with Major Dave Stacey, the secretary to the general's staff. His office was across the hall from mine, and he along with Buck had been there for me since my first days at Fort Jackson. Major Stacey was an infantryman as well and a constant source of support. He was a friend.

We sat, just he and I, staring at the TV, which was tuned to C-SPAN. Army officials were finally ready to publicize the result of the CID investigation.

I realized that this was it. CID was where the buck stopped as it related to criminal proceedings. If they exonerated me, it was over. I'd be out of the army in two months, and Brook and I could finally begin our life together. If they didn't, I'd have to face whatever consequences that entailed.

The acting inspector general of the Department of Defense came to the podium and offered some initial remarks. Brigadier General Rodney Johnson of CID then took over. He walked the audience through the investigations, the ambush, and the shooting. At one point, Johnson reported that "head wounds to Corporal Tillman are consistent with either 7.62- or 5.56-millimeter munitions"—which would mean my 240 in the former case or someone else's rounds in the latter. The evidence was still inconclusive beyond that.

Johnson added, "During the course of our investigation, we examined the rules of engagement, or ROE, governing operations in Afghanistan and found no violations of the ROE. We also looked at applicable training manuals and standard operating procedures, or SOPs, and again found no violations."

Then Johnson showed a slide with CID's executive summary, which stated, "Investigation determined that members of Serial 2 did not commit the offenses of Negligent Homicide or Aggravated Assault. It was determined that although CPL Tillman and AMF Soldier Thani were killed during the incident, members of Serial 2 believed they were under enemy fire and were returning fire at enemy combatants. Under extreme circumstances and in a very compressed time frame, the members of Serial 2 had a reasonable belief that death or harm was about to be inflicted on them and believed it was necessary to defend themselves."

The acting inspector general then returned to the podium. Among other things, he said the chain of command had made "critical errors in the reporting and assigning investigative jurisdiction in the days following his death." The report recommended "appropriate corrective action" regarding the unnamed officers responsible.

"That's great, Sergeant Elliott!" Major Stacey said as he clasped my shoulder.

"Thank you, sir," I said, trying to find the same joy and relief that he seemed to be feeling.

I walked back across the hall and peeked into General Hood's office. He stood behind his desk examining a stack of documents and looked up at me, smiling.

"CID just made their announcement, sir," I said.

"I know, Steve. I told you it'd be okay."

"Yes, sir. Thank you. Thank you for everything."

I went online and found the CID report that had just been issued. I wanted to print a copy for myself, my own proof in black and white of the words that had just been spoken. That night, I drank and I read, poring over the document, writing in names that were otherwise redacted. Most of the report, all but two paragraphs, dealt with the chain of command and their failures leading up to the ambush and, in particular, their failures in the aftermath. I read the paragraphs pertaining to us, the shooters, over and over again, hoping that the pronouncement of innocence would sink in. It didn't.

I pulled out other documents. Letters that had been written on my behalf by Lieutenant Uthlaut and Sergeant Owens. They gave me letters of recommendation on regimental letterhead attesting to my professionalism and capability. Lieutenant Uthlaut, whose lip was still in stitches from friendly shrapnel at the time he wrote it, said he'd "take me back to combat in a heartbeat." *Surely these mean I'm innocent?* They didn't.

I looked at my award from PLDC, the one naming me the honor graduate. *Surely this proves I'm not a failure?* It didn't.

I examined the draft of my final Noncommissioned Officer Evaluation Report that Major Stacey had just given me. This would be the final word from the army as to how I performed during my last year on active duty. General Hood was my senior rater, and I would be rated as an aide-de-camp, an honor in and of itself as that position was generally reserved for captains or majors. Each box was marked "excellent," and the final bullet read, "No duty in the US Army is beyond this sergeant's ability." No duty, that is, except for not firing on friendlies.

The paper trail was clear. I was capable. I wasn't a failure. It was an accident. I wasn't a criminal.

Yet the physical evidence was damning. "Three bullets to the head . . ." and a young man who now walked with a cane.

13

HELLO, GOOD-BYE

---

*We walked to meet each other up to the time of our love,
and then we have been irresistibly drifting in different directions.
And there's no altering that.*
LEO TOLSTOY, ANNA KARENINA

This was it. All I needed was a copy of my DD-214 and I was done with the military. The DD-214 is a single piece of paper. It is the army's report card for those who have served, the document employers and lenders would ask for as proof of my military service. Once this document was printed, it was finished. It was over. I was out.

The civilian who was completing my out-processing clicked *print* as I waited anxiously. That paper was all that was between me and freedom. My car was packed, fueled up, and ready to go.

"Huh, printer error," she mumbled to herself as I nearly lost it. Watching her move, ever so slowly, to troubleshoot the printer gave the feeling of time moving in reverse.

After what felt like hours, she shuffled back. "Let's try this again."

My blood pressure rose as she clicked the left button of her mouse. She had all the power. Without that form, I was still in the army. Maybe I'd be stuck here. Maybe I'd never leave. Trapped in the military by a printer error.

"There we go," she said as the machine whirred to life and spat out my one-page declaration of military independence.

I fought the urge to rip it from her hands as she gave it to me.

"Please double-check to make sure everything is accurate," she said.

I scanned the document quickly and noted that the nature of my service had indeed been marked as "honorable."

"Looks great," I said. "Thank you, ma'am." I carefully and quickly placed the paper in my binder. I briskly walked out of the office, hopped in my car, and drove to the post gym to take off my uniform and put on civilian clothes. I moved with the speed of a man pursued yet trying to avoid suspicion. I knew it was dumb, but I half expected military police to track me down because some box wasn't checked or some signature was missing that was needed to make my exit from the military official.

I was in my Rally Sport in a flash and felt anxiety recede as I passed through the post gate. I entered the freeway and stepped on the gas. The speed slowly calmed me. No one was on my tail.

I'm actually out. It's over.

It took time to believe that and, just to be safe, I didn't stop until I needed to refuel, somewhere in Tennessee.

I drove straight through Tennessee, Kentucky, and Missouri and then found myself on Interstate 70 West on the way to the home place. On May 21, four years to the day from the beginning of my enlistment, I pulled under the "Luhman" arch for my first real pit stop on the way to Washington State.

"Well, there he is!" Grandpa said as he approached the vehicle, rake in hand, having come from working in the garden. "You're not a *soldat* anymore." Grandpa spoke German in the home before English and rarely missed a chance to use a German word or two. *Soldat* is German for "soldier."

"Nope. I'm all done with that," I said smiling.

He and I continued into the house and found Mom and Grandma inside. Dinner was ready and waiting. The mood was one of celebration.

"Hey, it's the veteran!" my mom said as we hugged.

Grandma was right behind her. We embraced and I was quickly ushered to the dinner table. We ate and laughed as we had before. Plates were cleared, leaving Grandpa and me seated across from one another.

"I'm awful glad that's all behind you now," he said. "I can't believe all the investigations and all that stuff. I'm real glad that's behind you."

"Me too," I said.

"How long you plan on stayin'?"

"Not as long as I'd like," I replied. "My new job with Smith Barney starts on the eleventh of June, so I need to get home to our new house in Olympia and get settled in."

"Now, you'll be a financial adviser, is that right?" he asked, intent on understanding my new career.

"Yeah. I'll be managing money for folks and doing financial planning, but first I have to get my securities licenses. The big one is the Series 7. The first couple of months on the job is just studying for that. It's kind of a big deal because if I don't pass the first time, then I'm out of a job. After that, I'll be expected to build my own practice within the firm."

"That's somethin'," he said. "And you got yourself a house?"

"Yeah, Brook bought us a house there in Olympia, which I haven't seen yet except the pictures. It looks great, though."

"And now what grade will Gracie be in?"

"She'll start kindergarten next year. I think she'll go to a Waldorf school there in Olympia, but we're still figuring that out."

"Well, you's always awful bright, so I'm sure you'll manage it all okay. It's all beyond me. I guess you'll be goin' west. 'Go West, young man.' That's the saying, isn't it?"

I stayed for two days and couldn't wait to get back on the road. The home place would always be home in a way, but it wasn't my home now. My home was with Brook, and I was tired of marking time, waiting for our life together to start. Tired of talking on the phone. Tired of writing letters. I just wanted to be with her and Gracie.

I drove straight through, stopping only for a half night's rest at a campground in Idaho. I was approaching Washington from the south through Oregon along the Columbia River. Each vista that opened before me was a gift. I greedily drank in the landscape and the freedom it embodied. My freedom.

On May 26 I crossed the mighty Columbia River passing from Oregon to Washington, with only a hundred miles to go to Olympia. The sky was clear and the sun was bright as I continued north along Interstate 5.

What will it be like? I wondered. *How will it feel to finally be together?* My apprehensions were drowned out by my excitement and relief.

I followed printed directions to the house, hoping I wouldn't get lost. I finally turned down a dead-end street and noticed our car in the driveway of a newly built rambler.

Home.

I pulled into the driveway and listened to the quiet for a moment after killing the engine. I knocked on the door and waited to see who would answer.

The door opened, and there was Brook.

"Hi," she said.

"Hi," I replied as I stepped across the threshold and kissed her.

The warmth of the afternoon sun had followed us inside as we basked in the simple joy of being together. The joy of having a home.

I spied two eyes peering around a corner.

"Who's that?" I asked.

The eyes disappeared while a five-year-old giggle was heard.

Brook escorted me through the entryway and into Gracie's room.

"Wow," I said. "This is awesome."

Gracie laughed again and gave me the tour, both of her room and the rest of the home that was now mine.

★

The newness of it all, of being together after already having been married for almost two years and of starting life together in a new community, quickly wore off as I began to focus on the next challenge. Work.

The threat of the army was gone, and it was quickly replaced by the stress of a new career. I exchanged my BDUs for a suit and tie, and for the next three months I studied for the Series 7, Series 66, and insurance exams, all of which I needed to pass in order to actually keep the job I had landed.

I worked from 7 a.m. to 5 p.m. every day, studying but also seeking to demonstrate my dedication to the other advisers. Everything had worked out so well up to this point, but what if it all fell apart? What if the other shoe was about to drop?

I trusted only in my own abilities. It was up to me to provide for my family. It was up to me to succeed. Old patterns quickly emerged as I drank little more than coffee all day, ate little more than junk food, and switched to alcohol the moment I came home. The joy of being home soon met the work and expectations of being home. Brook made meals that I hardly touched. She planned dinners and events that I couldn't stand. Being around people, being in crowds even in our house, was exhausting. I fell asleep on the couch, drinking and watching TV most nights. The distraction and the alcohol made nightmares less likely or intense but left my side of the marriage bed cold.

It was the stress of work, we rationalized. Once the testing was over, it would all be better.

Down the street from our house was a church, one of the larger nondenominational Christian churches in the area. I was a husband and father now, a leader in the home, and as such, even though I had closed the door on God, I felt an obligation, a faint muscle memory for us to go to church. It was just "good for us." Something we were supposed to do. Something that would maybe make us better people.

We stepped into the large sanctuary as worship songs were sung. *Who are these people?* I thought. *Why are they here? What is this for?* I felt as though I were an outsider observing some strange tribal ritual. I needed someone to explain this to me.

After a couple of Sundays of this, I was done, and Brook was okay to follow my lead based on the expectation that we would eventually find a community of faith to which we could belong. She was somewhat suspicious of Christian culture having not grown up in the church but wanted to grow with God. In truth, I was done with all of it.

We were "good" people, I reasoned. We understood right from wrong. We didn't require the complications of theology to live a good life. We didn't need to go to some designated building at some designated time and give money to some designated ministry to make a difference in the world. If that helped other people, fine. We didn't need it.

It was soon time to take my Series 7 exam. Testing was an all-day affair and covered all aspects of securities laws and regulations. I passed with flying colors. My place at Smith Barney was, for now, secure. However, the relief Brook and I expected from being finished with the test was short lived. I had simply earned the right to more work. The test was over, but I needed to build a business. I needed clients. Once that was done, once I was making enough money, we thought, I'd be fine. It would all be better.

That problem was soon solved with the unexpected departure of two financial advisers. They struck out to form their own company and left hundreds of clients behind. I was new, but I, unlike many others in the branch, had capacity, so I was assigned to keep as many of these folks as I could and in the process was given an incredible foothold in the industry. I had been given a gift—instant clients—and all I had to do was keep them.

Now I would actually be dispensing advice and managing money. Now, having gotten out of the army, having passed the tests, and having secured a clientele, I would be fine.

But I wasn't. My internal angst simply found a new external object to blame. Now it was the clients and the markets. They were the problem. Once I had built relationships with these folks and markets were stable, I'd be fine. I'd relax. I'd stop drinking. I'd sleep. I'd connect with Brook and Gracie.

I rarely journaled, but shortly after the windfall of being assigned those clients, I wrote the following:

So many good things have happened in the last few months;
a few have been nothing short of miraculous. I'm blessed in
so many ways and yet half the time I feel worthless. I haven't
forgiven myself for what happened. I get scared having to
be around people, especially Brook, because feeling nothing
around her ironically hurts and creates a gateway to
depression and further anxiety.

I feel so far from who I was; nights like these, I feel old
in my spirit and wish death would come soon. I mostly feel
melancholy. This is as close to peace as I experience. For me,
melancholy truly is the joy of sorrow.

I refused to talk to Brook about any of this. I told myself I was
protecting her, that she didn't need to be burdened with what was
going on inside me. But to not burden her with the truth was to not
allow her to know me at all. It was to shut her out, to keep her on the
outside as she watched me medicate the disease she could barely
understand.

If I couldn't connect emotionally with my wife, there was no way
I could do so with Gracie. She was beautiful and precious, and I was
a failure. Her childish impulses were simply a source of stress to
my anxiety-riddled brain. I couldn't handle the unpredictability of a
child. I couldn't deal with the normal, less-than-perfect behavior of
a child. I needed control. I needed quiet. I needed to be left alone.

Early in 2008, the initial rumblings of a full-blown financial crisis
began to be heard. Home loans were souring at an alarming rate, but
we were told it could all be contained. At the age of twenty-seven I
was responsible for offering advice and direction to clients represent-
ing tens of millions of dollars in assets. Clients were looking to me for
answers. I looked to other advisers who had been through a crisis or
two and assured my clients we'd be okay.

Work was my escape. I could be someone else, the business version of me. I could be useful and find a measure of identity. Yet I was
nagged by doubts. *What happens if I fail there? Who am I if I'm not
effective and appreciated at the firm?*

On my birthday, March 13, 2008, the unraveling continued as the most vulnerable of investment banks, Bear Stearns, announced they were almost out of money. By the end of the week, the feds had taken over and sold the company, hoping this would be the only casualty.

Clients were increasingly scared. The gilt-edged name above our door and the mahogany that lined our office overlooking the water told people we knew what we were doing, that our knowledge and experience would count in the face of systemic failure. I hoped that was true, but I doubted it. Questions were turning from "What happens if I lose thirty percent?" to "What happens if my bank fails?" I didn't have answers, and those who had gone before me didn't either.

The stress of work was my break. I returned home to the failure of being a husband and a father. I returned home to memories of the past that wouldn't go away.

"Can you at least join us for dinner?" Brook pleaded politely one night.

"Sure," I said as I peeled myself off the couch, tie loosened and beer in hand. I sat at the dining room table and watched her and Gracie eat.

"Aren't you hungry?" she asked.

"I don't know. Not really. I'll have some chips or something."

"That's not good for you, you know. It could be part of why you're not sleeping and feeling so much stress."

"It's fine. It's just work. Once markets settle down, it'll be easier."

"Will it?" she asked with an increasingly common edge to her question.

"Yeah, it will. Do you have any idea all that's going on out there?"

"No, but I know what's going on here. I know you sleep on the couch and drink every night."

"Not every night," I interrupted between sips from my bottle.

"You don't even know. You're not even aware of it anymore."

"Look, I'm sorry. Can you just cut me some slack? I'm doing the best I can."

"Well, maybe you need some help."

"What's that supposed to mean?"

"Well, you've been through a lot and, I don't know, if you don't want to talk to me, then maybe you should talk to someone about it."

"There's nothing to talk about, and even if there was, it doesn't change anything. I can't bring people back from the dead with my words. It's just a waste of time. Sorry. Thank you for suggesting it, but that's not going to help right now. Not unless a counselor can stabilize the debt markets and get rid of billions in bad home loans."

"I don't know what that means, but the way things are can't go on forever. You know that, right? That this isn't okay?"

"Yeah, I know. You're right. I'm sorry."

"Can I go play, Mom?" Gracie asked.

"Sure, baby," she said.

I changed the subject. "So, you still thinking you want some garden boxes and a playhouse out back? I think I can build them."

This lightened the mood as Brook began to describe the garden she wished to plant and the place she wanted for Gracie to play.

I got to work that weekend. Brook wanted a couple of garden boxes. I turned the entire front yard into a fenced garden, digging up the turf by hand with a pick and shovel. I worked from the moment I got home on Friday until late into the evening, drinking as I dug and shoveled and hammered. The work was a meditative if not manic distraction. *Maybe if I work myself long enough, I'll sleep,* I thought. *Maybe I just need to be physically exhausted to find rest.* But the peace, the ease that had previously accompanied hard manual labor, was gone. There was still something there. Something nagging. Something haunting that wouldn't go away.

Gracie wanted a little playhouse, maybe something you tack together on a Saturday using old pallets. I built her a two-story, hundred-square-foot house in the backyard. Lined with cedar siding and shingles, it was gorgeous and unsettling all at once. It was a towering expression of inadequacy. I couldn't sit with her or read to her or play with her, but I could build her an expansive place to sit and read and play. I couldn't be with either of them, but I could make things for them. Gardens, a playhouse, money. I could give them things as long as the thing wasn't me.

We went over to Evan's house for dinner in Puyallup, about forty minutes away. Actually, it was his soon-to-be in-laws' house. We had a blast, drinking a few Jack and Cokes and playing a long, dramatic, and ultimately hilarious game of Monopoly. Evan was out of the army by now and would soon be married, and he and his fiancée, Rachel, were planning on planting their own church.

Evan was the one person who knew me from before the army. Not even Brook knew who I was before becoming a Ranger. As the night wound down, the girls found their accommodations in the guest bedroom, which left Evan and me to camp out in the living room, he on the floor and I on the couch. Evan was inquisitive. Beyond inquisitive. Sometimes his questions could be construed as downright intrusive if they weren't accompanied by a heart of compassion, which they always were.

The conversation died off and the silence that marked the beginning of rest was broken by his question: "Steve, I just have to ask, how are you? I mean, how are you really doing?"

"I'm good, man. I'm doing really good. I mean, we've got a house, I've got a good job, Brook and I are together now. I'm good."

There was a pause and then he laughed and said, "No you're not."

I should have been upset but I wasn't. I felt loved at the frightening prospect of being known.

He continued, "It's going to be okay, man. You're gonna be okay. We're praying for you—you know that, right? You know that we're here for you if you need anything. Anything at all."

"Yeah, oh yeah. Of course. Thanks. I really appreciate it, but I'm good."

A month later, in August, Brook and I went to Port Townsend to celebrate our three-year anniversary. Port Townsend is an idyllic, Victorian-era seaport nestled on the Puget Sound, a couple of hours north of Olympia. It was fun. It was a distraction. We stayed for two nights, and after dinner on Saturday evening, I asked to grab some beer to take up to our room.

"Is that necessary?" she asked. "You had a couple glasses of wine with dinner. Won't that mess with your sleep?"

"No, we're celebrating!" I said. I secured a six-pack of some microbrew, and we headed back to our bed-and-breakfast, itself an old Victorian house.

We did things that couples do on anniversary trips and then proceeded to talk. I was on my third beer, my fifth drink of the evening, when Brook's questions became more pointed.

"Why do you drink so much?" she asked directly.

The alcohol had lowered my defenses. "I'm ashamed," I said honestly. "I'm ashamed of what I did and of what my military service stands for."

There, I said it.

"You mean with Pat?" she asked.

"Yeah, what else? Is there something else I should be ashamed of?"

"No, I just didn't know that was still bothering you."

"Well, I guess maybe it is. You know, people thank me. They f—ing thank me for my service. What do they know? What are they thanking me for? Are they thanking me for shooting at good guys? Are they thanking me for being investigated four times? Are they thanking me for driving around a general or booking plane tickets? I mean, what was all that for?"

There was silence.

"What's the solution?" she asked.

"I have no idea. I know Pat's dead. I can't change that. I know Jade is partially disabled thanks to me. I can't change that. I have no idea."

"Is that the solution?" she asked, nodding to the beer in my hand that I was opening.

"It's better than nothin'," I said, my tone indicating that even in my drunken state, I was done with the conversation.

"I just wish you'd talk to someone," she said.

"Yeah, I should. You're probably right."

Maybe church would help, we thought. Maybe the problem with the last place we had gone was that we had tried a Christian church. Maybe we needed to broaden our horizons. Shortly after our return from Port Townsend, Brook, Gracie, and I went to what could be described as a Universalist, New Age gathering. They met at a school down the street.

The people were super nice, but the whole thing was pretty weird, at least weird to me. There was no structure. There was a "god" if that helped you and if you decided there was. The god could be a deity of your choice or the word *yes* or the idea of love. Ultimately, *we* were gods; the light was within if we could just find it.

I couldn't buy it. It was all too trippy for me. There was nothing to hang my hat on. What was truth? How could we know it? Who was responsible for creating this world we live in? Who was responsible for the pain? I didn't need some idea, some crutch; I needed the truth. This place answered none of those questions, even though the people were really nice.

I continued to worship daily at the temple of finance that was our branch office in Olympia as financial markets unraveled. By September 2008, we were in full-blown crisis mode. The market volatility was nauseating. Lehman was collapsing before our eyes, and we wondered who would be next. Our parent company, Citigroup, had a stock price in the single digits and going dramatically lower by the day. What would happen to us? My already terrible sleep worsened. My already excessive drinking became more excessive. I would come home, change clothes, and go in the office to drink by myself while watching Netflix on the computer and checking after-hours market news, dreading the next day that awaited me.

My life was one of pain and self-medication. I medicated with money, with media, with alcohol, and with pornography. The emotional openness required by the physical intimacy of the marriage bed was often too much. The emotional commitment required to connect with a nameless image was all I could manage, and with that I further detached from Brook and found yet another source of guilt and shame.

In truth, all I wanted was to be left alone. By that time, Brook and Gracie were learning to oblige me.

★

"Jen's coming over for dinner tomorrow," Brook announced as I undid the top button of my shirt and pulled a beer from the fridge.

"Who?" I asked with irritation.

"Jen. She's an old friend of mine I met up in Seattle years ago. She's studying for her PhD at Antioch University in Seattle. I think she's doing work with veterans or something. Anyway, I want you here for it. I know you hate company, but I think you can handle it for one night."

Jen arrived on time with her little dog, Lucy. She had more tattoos than your average Seattleite, and we sized each other up somewhat uneasily. She wasn't quite sure what her old friend Brook was doing with a former military guy from the Midwest, and I wasn't sure what her angle was on the whole veterans thing. I was afraid of being diagnosed by an aspiring head shrink.

The conversation flowed easily enough. We discussed her academic pursuits and her desire to work with vets who had experienced wartime trauma, be it PTSD or some other mental illness. As she talked, I imagined the type of person she would be working with. Homeless, wearing an old surplus jacket, and begging for change on the corner. *Yeah, those guys need help,* I thought. *Good for her.*

"I'm reading an amazing book right now," she said. "You might even like it. It's called *On Killing* by this guy named Dave Grossman. He does a historical deep-dive on the psychological cost of learning to kill."

For some reason that resonated with me. I knew I needed to get ahold of the book.

The evening ended amicably enough, and I bought Grossman's book the next day. I read, "Some psychiatric casualties have always been associated with war, but it was only in the twentieth century that our physical and logistical capability to sustain combat outstripped our psychological capacity to endure it." Grossman also wrote, "It is the existence of the victim's pain and loss, echoing forever in the soul of the killer, that is at the heart of his pain."

The book unfolded as a revelation. Dave Grossman, himself a former army Ranger, was telling me that humans weren't wired to kill other humans. That doing so can cause harm to our hearts and minds. That such wounds have always been a part of war. That I wasn't alone. That maybe I, too, had permission to be broken.

I had heard of posttraumatic stress disorder by virtue of my own medical files. I had the diagnosis for "chronic PTSD," but I had no idea what that meant. I thought it was just a medical acronym used broadly to describe someone having a hard time upon returning from combat. I thought it meant I was just one of the weak ones.

Brook had even suggested back when we were living apart and she was taking her Psychology 101 course in college that maybe I had PTSD. Though she was absolutely right, I had thought little of it—people in Psych 101 classes have a habit of diagnosing everyone around them with something. But now, as I continued to read Grossman's description of the disorder, something clicked. He wrote that PTSD is "'a reaction to a psychologically traumatic event outside the range of normal experience.' Manifestations of PTSD include recurrent and intrusive dreams and recollections of the experience, emotional blunting, social withdrawal, exceptional difficulty or reluctance in initiating or maintaining intimate relationships, and sleep disturbances."

It was as though the words were written to me.

I bit the bullet and called the VA to see what sort of counseling options were available. I soon had an appointment with a guy named Keith whose office was in Olympia. Brook was so relieved.

I sat in his office as I had sat in offices like this before, wondering what sad stories these walls could tell and feeling bad for having my own to offer. Keith was incredibly kind and professional. I described my past and the reality of my present, feeling a bit better to just name it. He offered a Zoloft prescription, which I took for a few weeks and then stopped. I hated it. It just numbed me out. I wasn't interested in trying other treatments.

I reasoned that I would only use drugs or some other treatment if I really needed it, and as long as I wasn't availing myself of treatments beyond alcohol, I wasn't really sick. I saw the treatment as evidence of a disease. No treatment, no disease. In truth, I was deathly afraid. *What if I keep taking your meds or whatever else you offer and they don't work? What happens if I try everything there is to try and I'm still sick? Then what?* I clung to the hope of solutions left unapplied. That was my twisted and fear-ridden thinking.

I went back to Keith a few times, each time with the same problems. Poor sleep, nightmares, depression, anxiety, and each time I heard the same good advice. Take a hot shower, try to moderate the drinking. Take care of myself. He was right, and after a few times I didn't see the need to waste the time, his or mine, hearing advice I wasn't going to take.

Markets were swooning. Oil prices had plummeted, and gas prices had done likewise. Gracie would be with her dad for Thanksgiving, so Brook and I decided to take a road trip down to San Francisco. The drive would be cheap, and it was one of her favorite cities and one that I had yet to visit. My lack of sleep and continued alcohol abuse had made a common cold much worse, but we'd go just the same. This, we thought, would be the adventure Brook and I desperately needed.

But the trip was pure misery, largely due to the fact that I now had pneumonia, a disease I continued to treat faithfully with alcohol. We saw some beautiful sites, but I was sick and simply awful to be around. Brook got a front-row seat to watch my self-loathing play itself out. I was ill and yet I drank.

She was angry—angry that I wouldn't listen to her and angry that I refused to care for myself. I did receive some sympathy for the fact that I had pneumonia, but it was clear upon returning home that we were no longer a married couple. She was done expending emotional energy for someone who wouldn't receive it and wouldn't reciprocate. At that point, we ceased to be married. We were simply housemates.

She started smoking again, a habit she had long since given up. She started partying again, never neglecting Gracie but happy to go dancing and drinking with her friends. Like me, she was in pain and sought a numbing agent. Something, anything that could distract her from reality. By the beginning of 2009, she was done.

With the new year come resolutions. Brook and I resolved to sleep in separate bedrooms on the advice of one of her friends. I took the futon in the office, where I spent most of my evenings anyway, and she kept the master bedroom. Perhaps if we gave each other a little extra space, that would help. It didn't. We simply went further, faster down the separate paths we had been on. Paths that were diverging more by the day.

On February 16, for the first time in a year and a half, I again wrote in my journal:

> I'm not sure I know who I am anymore. I feel so different that sometimes I'm shocked to see a familiar face staring back at me in the mirror. I don't believe in Christ. I believe he lived, taught, died, and had his teachings hijacked. So much of my spiritual understanding came from concrete biblical teachings; now I don't know who I am or how to frame the world. My paradigm is dissolved. I feel empty and old. I love Brook and Gracie but don't show it very well. I've been feeling trapped by the routine. My mind and heart can wander. Some days I have fun and some days I just wish I was dead; it all feels so futile and pointless. The struggle, for what? It feels like pain interrupted with moments of comic relief to break the tension.
>
> Why am I here? Who am I?
> Help me.

By my birthday in March, markets had reached new lows, and we all wondered how much lower they could possibly go. Fortunately, there were no additional bank failures to accompany my birthday. Instead, Brook bought us tickets to see a performing troupe in Seattle called the Circus Contraption. The event was staged in a Theo Chocolate warehouse in the Fremont district. It was set up like a one-ring circus and was a mixture of genres—play, musical, vaudeville, and cabaret—all of it dark and edgy.

Brook and I sat in our bleacher seats as I tolerated what I should have enjoyed and appreciated. I didn't like the crowd or the noise. Brook's gesture fell flat as she persisted with a good attitude in spite of me making fun of the whole thing.

This was the inverse of a first date. This was saying good-bye. As we walked down the damp sidewalk to the car, I felt as though I were walking with a stranger—a kind stranger, but one that I knew less and less. She was living her life, and I was living mine. This was farewell.

A month later, I walked out the sliding glass door in the back of the house to join Brook on the covered patio. She was leaning against a post, smoking a cigarette. I approached and leaned against the nearest post, looking up at the yet unfinished roof of Gracie's playhouse.

"What are we doing?" she asked.

"I don't know."

"We're just housemates, you know," she said as she flicked the ash.

"Yeah, I know."

The next words I spoke were obvious, rational, and painful.

"Maybe I should just move out. I mean, if this is what it is, then this is what it is. There's no use pretending."

"How would that work?"

"You and Gracie can stay here until we figure it out, but it seems like we should just end it. If this is what it is."

"You mean divorce?"

"Yeah, divorce. I mean, do you want to be with me?" I asked.

"No," she said.

The next week I found a room to rent and moved out. Not long after, I went on an overnight trip to Seattle just sixty miles north. I was one of the top advisers in my recruiting class at Smith Barney, and the reward trip to New York had been downsized, thanks to the financial crisis, to a seminar and a night in Seattle.

There's something that can be revealing about hotel rooms. You're out of your element. There are no chores or distractions. You're alone. The order and cleanness of the suite seemed to accentuate the disorder within me.

I sat on the bed, drinking overpriced room service beer and

nibbling at an overpriced room service burger. *Here I am,* I thought. *This is what success feels like.*

I will be a divorcé, I thought. Someone who had been married but now wasn't.

I thought about Brook. The space inside that had been carved out for her was now hollow and somehow weighty in its emptiness. The person I had married was gone, our marriage over in all but the legal sense. I grabbed the hotel stationery and pen and began to write:

Kissing her for the first time on the front porch
Proposing to her
Walking on the ferry as newlyweds
Coming home

Each of these had been moments of joy. Moments of color and life. Moments to remember. Now, as I wrote them down, they turned to ash. The paper I wrote upon was the soil in which they'd be buried. The round-stick BIC pen, the spade that turned the dirt. The words themselves were now gray and lifeless though black on the page.

I remembered. I wrote. I buried.

14

STOP

While he was still a long way off,
his father saw him and was filled with compassion for him;
he ran to his son, threw his arms around him and kissed him.
LUKE 15:20

The intercom buzzed on my office phone and a voice spoke. "Steven, your ten o'clock is here."

"Thanks," I replied as I got up and walked to the front desk of our branch office.

My ten o'clock was seated in the lobby and looked anxious and uncomfortable.

"Hey," I said.

"Hi," Brook replied, trying to maintain a business posture.

"Come on back," I said as we turned and walked back to my office and closed the door.

We proceeded to review an agreement, a document I had drawn up to clearly articulate the financial support I would provide to her and Gracie. I didn't want them to feel insecure, and I likewise didn't want to have an open-ended financial commitment once we were divorced.

Our stuff and our money became symbols of our life together. The joy of building something together was gone. Now was the work of dividing what we had.

We went over everything. Monthly support, house payments, Gracie's school, and costs for Brook to begin working as a nutritional counselor. My goal was to ensure they would be okay. My actions had brought us to this point, so I felt that was the least I could do.

"You're being generous," Brook said as a flicker of compassion flashed and then went dark.

"It seems fair to me. I'm glad you feel okay with it," I replied.

"How does the divorce filing work?" she asked.

"Well, it looks like Lincoln County doesn't require the parties to be physically present to file the paperwork. We can do it through the mail. Once we file, then there's a mandatory ninety-day waiting period and then, assuming we haven't changed our minds, it becomes official and they mail us the divorce decree."

"Okay," she said. "What do I have to do?"

"You just have to sign this stuff," I said as I retrieved more documents from the file. "It's a petition for divorce. I made it so you're the one making the petition. I figured you'd want it that way."

"I don't really care, but that's fine," she said and quickly signed.

We were done. *Do I make small talk? Do I ask her how she's doing?* I walked her to the front door.

"I'll keep you posted if I hear anything on the petition, and just let me know if you need anything, I guess."

"Thanks," she said. "We'll be fine." She walked away, the glass door with brass handles closing quietly behind her.

That evening I went home. To my new home, that is. A newly built rambler on the outskirts of Olympia with two new roommates, Kellen and Joel. Kellen was an up-and-coming home builder who was finishing his business degree while he acquired properties to build on. Joel was going to school and working at the Home Depot.

We quickly became friends and spent many a night drinking and watching movies or playing video games. It was a terrific distraction and relief. We didn't have to talk about our feelings; we just wanted to hang out and do stuff together. That "stuff" mostly included drinking beer and playing video games like Mario Kart and Star Wars Battlefront.

Part of me felt like a kid again, which was amazing. But part of me felt—well, like a kid again, which was awful. I once had a family. I once had a home. Now, save for my adult job and adult paycheck, I was a kid again.

What happened? This was the question that wouldn't stop as I killed more time distracting myself with alcohol and video games.

It was as though I had crawled inside a festering wound. Separating from Brook and initiating divorce proceedings had indeed been a relief. To simply call it what it was and not pretend anymore. To not come home and feel like I had to be available for anyone. To just worry about myself.

But just as it brought relief in some ways, it brought pain in others. A new organism had been given life—the one-flesh union that was once Steven and Brook. That organism, our marriage, was now being destroyed. Years of waiting and expectation for nothing. Years of sacrifice and investment, gone. A person I once loved didn't seem to exist anymore.

I was ripping at a hurt deep inside, and in my attempt to find relief, I found myself inflicting new forms of pain on myself.

Even the distractions, the drinking and playing video games, were becoming work. They gave me no joy. I did these things because I didn't know what else to do. The only thought that brought true comfort was the thought of my mortality, that at least someday I'd be dead. At least someday, this would all end.

What happened?

The question was incessant as I sat on the couch and stared at the wall.

How did I get here?

I didn't mean to come to this place. I didn't start off with this as a destination, yet here I am.

Something had to give. I picked up the phone and called a counselor that Keith had referred me to. This counselor was a specialist in a particular technique for treating trauma called EMDR (Eye Movement Desensitization and Reprocessing). It sounded ridiculous when Keith described it, which was why I hadn't followed up on it. But now I felt more willing to try something else. What did I have to lose?

I had learned, in part through reading Grossman's books and through my meetings with Keith, at least one aspect of what was going on with me. Physically, my brain chemistry was malfunctioning. The portions of the brain where the infamous "fight or flight" mechanism is housed were going haywire, triggering adrenaline and cortisol to be dumped into my bloodstream even if I wasn't in danger. Smells, sights, feelings, subconscious workings—all of these could trigger my mind and body to act as though I were at war when I was really in my living room.

My ability to reason couldn't compete with that response. You cannot reason your way out of a panic attack. You can't simply rationalize the primal reaction to protect yourself. On one level, as it related to PTSD, that's what was wrong with me. My experiences had left a physical and neurological imprint. A switch had been thrown, and I didn't know how to turn it off.

Every night when I lay down, whether on the couch or in a bed, as the waking world began to fade, I could feel the buttstock of my weapon in my shoulder. It literally felt like it was there. It was as though I could take my left hand and touch the 240 or take my right hand and place it on the handle and around the trigger well. Feeling that imprint was bad enough. Feeling crazy for feeling as though I had a gun on my shoulder was worse.

Who could understand this? Who would accept me if they knew this?

I went to the new counselor, Susan, and we discussed the events I had experienced. We identified certain traumatic memories, memories I had to logically deduce were traumatic because the waking recollection of them didn't cause me to hit the deck or openly weep. I just sort of knew they weren't good, so I related those to her.

She explained to me how EMDR worked as she set up and plugged in a two-foot slim black rectangle that had nothing on it but a series of blue LED lights running from one end to the other. When the device was plugged in, the lights traced continuously from left to right.

"How this works," she said, "is that I'll ask you to relax and allow your eyes to follow the lights. As you do this, I'll ask you to recall certain memories and see where that takes you. You might find yourself remembering other things that you'd otherwise forgotten. Just let it happen and relax. There's no right or wrong memory. Just answer with whatever is coming to mind. If nothing is coming to mind, that's okay."

"What is this supposed to do for me?"

"The traumatic memories you have are essentially misfiled in your brain. Your mind has categorized them in such a way so as to still provide a stimulus response when they're recalled. Their recollection can happen consciously or subconsciously, even when you're sleeping. We need to address the memories and get your brain to refile them so that there isn't that surge of adrenaline or spike in anxiety. By allowing your eyes to simply watch the lights, you relax a part of your brain that will enable that refiling to take place."

"Okay, let's give it a whirl," I said with complete resignation. I'd spent ninety-five bucks on dumber things, so why not?

Our first session was exhausting. At Susan's advice, I had scheduled our appointment for a Friday afternoon with nothing afterward, which was fortunate, because I was mentally and emotionally spent. I felt like I'd been doing long division by hand for six hours while crying at the same time.

During the session, other, smaller memories came up that I had forgotten. Pat's memorial service at the FOB was an event I didn't realize I remembered, and when it came up during a session, it hit me hard. I cried. That happened multiple times. Moments that were buried within and adjacent to other moments were unearthed.

After a few weeks of these Friday sessions, I could feel part of the gloom lifting. I physically felt lighter. Mentally, clearer. Emotionally, still distraught over the breakup with Brook, but it felt as though there was some light at the end of the tunnel and perhaps that light wasn't from an oncoming train.

Evan called. I had finally called him and left a voice mail to let him know what was going on with Brook and me.

"Hey, what's up, man?" I answered.

"Dude. I'm so glad I got ahold of you. Sorry I couldn't pick up when you called."

"Oh, that's fine. Don't worry about it."

"Man, I am so sorry to hear what you guys are going through. How can we help? What do you need?"

"I don't know. Thanks for asking, and I wish I knew how to answer that. It's just—there's nothing there, you know? It's just dead."

"What do you mean?" he asked.

"Well, I was so detached for so long, and then she got fed up, which I don't blame her for. We'd been waiting to be together for two years, and then when that finally happened, it turned out to be terrible. Then she started checking out. Partying. Going to clubs. Almost acting like a teenager again. I wanted to change; I just didn't know how. She's not the person I married, and I don't think I am either. It's like we both got duped."

"Wow. How is Gracie doing?"

"I don't know. I haven't seen them in a while. She has her dad and grandparents and Brook, of course. I wasn't really there for her anyway, so I'm not sure she'll really miss me. I think she'll be okay."

"Okay. Well, I just want to tell you two things if I can. First, I want to encourage you in that I think there's always hope and that, man, divorce is death. I can't imagine what you're feeling—and I totally get it—but it will cause other problems you didn't have before."

"Yeah, I don't disagree with you."

"But I also want you to know that, whatever happens to you guys, we love you. We are here for you. All of you. The Lord can heal this regardless of what happens. I know he can. He loves you. He loves your family, and we do too."

"Yeah, I hope you're right."

★

I awoke on Thursday, July 2, to the first day of a four-day holiday weekend. The weather was incredible. Blue skies and seventy degrees. As the day progressed, I thought it actually might be fun to go on a hike. I hadn't been hiking since I had been in the army although I used to love it. I used to love running, playing soccer, going to the gym. All of those things had died. But at that moment, I felt a surge of excitement.

I began consulting the Internet and a few hiking guides we had lying around. I settled on a seventeen-and-a-half-mile loop on Mount Rainier's Carbon River Glacier. The weather would be perfect and, with an early start and not having to pack much gear, I should easily be able to complete the hike in a day.

The hike soon became more than just a form of recreation. It became a challenge. A dare. A battle to be won. As that Thursday wore on, I became fixated on my plan to complete the hike. Proving to myself that I wasn't dead. Proving to myself that I could reclaim some semblance of the life and vigor I once knew.

By 8 a.m. on Friday, I pulled into the parking lot in the northwest corner of Mount Rainier National Park. I threw on my pack and stopped off at the ranger station to get a map of the Carbon River recreation area.

"Where you heading?" was the park ranger's friendly question.

"I think I'll hike the loop up to Mowich Lake and through Spray Park. Looks like a great day for it."

"I don't know about that," he said. "We still have quite a bit of snow on the trails at higher elevations, so that may not be possible."

What does he know?

"Yeah, well, I'll see."

"Just please stay on the trails. It can get dangerous in a hurry, and the weather can shift pretty quickly up there."

"Of course," I said. "Yeah. Well, thank you."

I moved quickly on the trail. The forecast called for clear skies and temperatures in the high seventies, so I wore a T-shirt, shorts, hiking boots, and sunglasses. In my day pack was a fleece jacket, compass, map, knife, first-aid kit, lots of water, and two Clif Bars. Part of the challenge was to do the hike with minimal food. I'd reward myself with a steak dinner at the house later on.

The weather was perfect. The warmth of summer reflected back in the scent of sunbaked pine needles on the forest floor. A cool breeze met the beads of sweat that formed on my forehead. Each step, invigorating. Each breath, proof of life.

After the first few miles or so, I was well ahead of schedule, moving at a healthy four-mile-per-hour clip. This was the infantryman's standard pace, albeit with a much lighter load. I came to a fork in the trail. To the right was the route I had planned that would take me to the top of Ipsut Pass, alongside Mowich Lake, and ultimately up five thousand feet across part of the glacier before descending again to the trailhead.

"Due to snowfall, Ipsut Pass closed" read the sign at the fork in the trail.

I stared at the top of the pass. I could see that the switchbacks leading to the top were covered in snow. The trail was nowhere to be seen. But the pass could be climbed. It was steep but not that steep. I could do it. It would just make for a better story.

Ignoring the sign, I began to walk and climb straight up the six-hundred-foot pass. It was moderately taxing but the slightly melted snow allowed for good footing. I reached the top and looked down feeling both accomplishment and concern.

Climbing up the pass had been difficult. Going back down the pass would be nearly impossible. Climbing down is very different from climbing up, and it was at that moment I knew I was committed to my route. The only way back to my car was to complete the loop I had set out to complete or ask someone for help at Mowich Lake. The second option was no option at all to me. I'd have to finish the loop.

I looked for the trail to Mowich Lake and couldn't find it. Too much snow. *Imagine that.*

I pulled out the map and my compass, and using good old-fashioned dead reckoning, I set myself walking through the snow-laden forest straight to where Mowich Lake should be. The snow was deep but firm. After a while I saw a flat glimmer of ice, and the frozen lake began to emerge from the trees.

There was a ranger cabin on the edge of the lake, and I could see the trail next to it. The cabin, along with the frozen lake and snow-tipped fir trees, was a breathtaking sight. It was as though I had stumbled into a Christmas card.

Emboldened by my progress despite the snow, I stopped for a moment at the ranger cabin, which was locked and empty. I scanned the map, ate half a Clif Bar, and drank some water. Seven and a half miles down and only ten to go, and it wasn't even noon. I was making great time. Few things gave me joy like making great time.

I set out on the trail, but as the elevation climbed, the patches of snow became more frequent, obscuring more and more of the trail until finally it was gone.

The rule when you encounter snow on the trail, snow that completely hides the trail, is to turn around. That's it.

I stopped. I looked at my watch. I looked at the map. I considered having to ask for a ride from Mowich Lake.

I kept walking on the snow, the trail nowhere in sight.

An hour later, after walking through the snow-packed and rising woods, I broke into a subalpine paradise. I was suddenly bathed in the intense warmth of the afternoon sun. Before me stood Mount Rainier, unobscured. Seemingly endless fields of undulating ice and snow filled the horizon. Who cared about the trail? This was amazing!

I consulted my map, having given up on finding anything resembling a trail at these elevations. I pointed myself in what seemed to be the right direction and took off, scampering along in my own personal wilderness.

I moved laterally along the northwest flank of Mount Rainier, up and down a series of snow-covered ridges. As before, the slightly melted snow offered great traction, and I even found myself jogging along portions of the new path I was blazing.

The freedom was intoxicating. Experiencing the raw beauty of nature was beyond my power to describe. Experiencing beauty because you've gone somewhere you shouldn't have is better still. To think, I would have let a little snow and a silly rule get in the way of seeing this landscape!

An hour passed. Then another. Then another. The terrain just kept coming. A twinge of doubt began to grow as I glanced at my watch with increasing frequency.

By 6 p.m., the shadows had noticeably lengthened, and I had yet to begin my descent, though I could see the Carbon River below me in the distance.

This is so big, I thought. *There's so much wilderness. So much untouched.* I suddenly felt small.

The reality that I would likely not get back to the Carbon River Ranger Station and my car before dark began to set in. Moving at night seemed foolish, although I'm not entirely sure why I decided to draw the line between wisdom and folly there. Backtracking to Mowich Lake and asking for help was out of the question. I hated backtracking with the same intensity with which I loved making good time.

I'm alone out here. That fact began to dawn on me. *A wrong step, a sprained ankle, a concussion . . . I'm alone. No one even knows I came here today.* I put the thought out of mind as I continued to walk.

I began to descend, having reached the apex of the various ridges and folds of this part of Mount Rainier. I was working my way down the mountain and into the trees. The terrain was steep and the forest was darkening as day turned to evening.

I'd have to stop. I was tired, I hadn't eaten enough, and the hike was getting more dangerous. I'd have to find a place to spend the night and wait for morning to finish.

I soon found a promising spot. An old-growth fir perched on a rocky outcropping offered a patch of dirt and brush at its base. I cleared away a spot to sit under the massive tree, thankful I wouldn't have to sit in the snow. I put on my fleece and ate the last half of my last Clif Bar. I placed my bare legs inside my pack as my body temperature began to drop.

The sun disappeared, and the air quickly cooled until it was nearly freezing. I shivered as I looked at the cloudless sky, watching a waxing gibbous moon make its faithful arc.

What happens tomorrow? I thought. *How much farther do I even have to go? Five miles? More? What happens if I get hurt? Is this really worth it?*

I fought to drown out those questions by focusing on the objective. "It will be okay," I said aloud. "You can do this. It's fine. You're almost there. You can do this."

This game went on for a while, one part of me offering questions of reasonable concern and the other seeking to crush that voice in favor of finishing the hike. In favor of "winning" and proving whatever it was that it would prove.

I faithfully played the self-talk loop of positive reinforcement as hunger and cold began to bite. I warmed myself with the meager flame of my own strength. My own initiative. My own plans.

My will was set and unwavering. I would finish for no other reason than that I had decided to finish.

The loop continued to play as I rocked and shivered against the towering tree.

What happened next defies my logic and my ability to describe it. Anything I could write or say about it would be wholly inadequate to convey what happened.

A voice spoke, but to say it was a voice like mine or any other human voice would be incomplete. It was more than that.

To say it was a sense or a feeling would be true but also incorrect; it was more than that.

To say it was my thought, derived from my heart or brain, would be wrong. It wasn't. It ran contrary to every intention of my being in that moment. It was not from me.

A voice that was more than a voice spoke. A feeling that wasn't simply emotion overwhelmed me. A cry broke forth and shocked my very being into warmth and silence.

It spoke simply and echoed loudly.

"Stop."

That word resonated through my being—body, mind, and spirit.

I was dumbstruck. I felt simultaneously rebuked and loved like never before. The voice wasn't simply true; it embodied truth. It didn't have authority; it was authority. It was more real than the ground upon which I sat. It simply was.

I stopped.

I wept.

I repented.

I was embraced.

I felt in that moment that the road I had chosen to walk down—a road where I answered to no one but myself and my own, immediate desires—had grown dark and cold, as such roads always do. It was a road leading to death.

I stopped because I could do nothing else when confronted with that force, the force that I knew immediately was the Lord.

I wept because I lamented my waywardness and pride, and because the confrontation was the essence of love with no hint of condemnation.

I repented, which is to say I turned from the path I was on, because I missed him and simply wanted to be embraced.

"Lord, I'm sorry. I'm so sorry. Thank you," I said.

I knew it was him. I can't tell you how I knew; I just did. I was corrected, not condemned. My pride was broken, and I was brought to a place of submission in spite of myself.

The force of his voice unleashed a torrent of rational thought.

"What am I doing here? This is so dumb!" I said, laughing as I wiped away the tears.

I'm here because of me! I walked here! I chose to be in this place. No one kidnapped me and dumped me on the side of a mountain. I walked here, one exhilarating, stupid step at a time. I shook my head in disbelief.

I'm here because I couldn't find the trail. I'm here because I chose to walk along the snow, which means that getting back to the trail near Mowich Lake will be easy. I just have to follow my tracks. I'll find a ranger, throw myself on the mercy of the National Parks system, and get a ride back to my car. What was I thinking?

I slept, comforted by that thought, and was awoken by the dawn. There was no sense waiting for the sun to rise. I was cold and wanted to get moving. I stood and surveyed the way I had come. I could see my footprints in the snow that led to the tree.

I took a step onto the snow, placing my foot directly next to my footprint from the day before, and quickly found myself lying on the ground. The snow that had been baked in the summer sun and had offered such perfect footing the afternoon before was an endless, bluish-white sheet of ice.

The sun wouldn't warm this ice to snow for hours. I could wait for better footing or move the best I could. I chose the latter, and for the next six hours I walked, I stumbled, I fell, I cursed, and I slid, all the while staring at the footprints that marked my journey from the day prior.

The Lord had spoken the night before, simply yet poignantly. His grace and his mercy had caused me to repent. I felt an assurance of his love that was new and that I didn't understand and still can't explain. He should have left me to my own devices, but he didn't. To this day I don't know why.

Love and forgiveness do not, however, suspend consequences. I had chosen to walk there. Every step taken in pride away from the trail was a step that would hurt in trying to find it again. As I traced my steps back to the trail and back to Mowich Lake, each fall and each slip was a reminder, a lesson as to the cost of going it alone, blazing my own trail in hubris and isolation. Grace is by definition free, but each step away from the trail cost me something.

Around noon, the snow finally abated, and my footprints melted back into the familiarity of a dirt path. I walked to the cabin at the lake. It was still locked and empty. I took off my wet boots and socks so they could dry a bit. I sat in the sun, drank water, and stared at the sheet of ice and snow that was the lake.

I awoke with a start, checking my watch to see what time it was. I had fallen asleep for twenty minutes or so. There was no ranger in sight. I had half hoped that someone would just find me there and take me back to my car without me having to ask or explain my predicament. That didn't seem likely. So I put my socks and boots back on and walked down the trail to the Mowich Lake parking lot, hoping to find someone willing to drive me back to the Carbon River Ranger Station.

I passed a few hikers on their way up to the lake on this beautiful Fourth of July Saturday. I couldn't bring myself to impose on any of them to walk back down with me. Finally, I spotted the familiar Smokey the Bear hat atop the head of a park ranger. *He has to help,* I thought. *He gets paid for stuff like that.* I still felt like a fool.

"Hi," I said.

"Hey, how's it goin'? Can I help you out?"

"Yeah, actually you can. So, I, uh, I sort of got stuck in the park last night. I parked down at Carbon River, went up Ipsut Pass even though I wasn't supposed to, and well, I can't get back to my car. I need a lift. Sorry."

I braced myself for a lecture on being a responsible hiker. I waited to be admonished for my stupidity.

"No problem," he said as he turned on a dime, and we headed back down the trail.

"Are you okay? Do you need water? Food?" he asked.

"Oh, I'm fine. I'm a little tired, I suppose, but no, I'm good. I feel good."

"Well, that's good news. We were wondering whose black Subaru that was. That's yours?"

"Yeah, that's mine."

"Good deal. I'm just glad you're okay."

"Me too," I replied.

"You know, you shouldn't be out there when there's snow like that," he said smiling.

"Yeah, I know it was really dumb. I'm sorry."

"Oh, that's okay. I'm just glad you're all right. Believe it or not, I've seen folks do a lot dumber things, so this is pretty mild."

"Oh really? Do tell," I said, and he told me his own ranger war stories.

He drove me back to my car, and I drove home. I hurt all over, but I managed to eat and fell asleep just as the fireworks began to go off.

I was back to work on Monday, rested and fed but still in a daze from the experience. Still dumbstruck by what had happened. What I had heard and felt. I began to scratch it down on bits of paper. It didn't seem real. I knew I couldn't forget it. It was as though I had been dropped into my own real-life parable, and now I was processing the implications. Things were the same but different.

I headed to the other side of the branch office to meet with Ann, one of the more senior advisers there with whom I shared a client.

"Are you okay?" she asked as I sat down across the desk from her.

"Yeah, I'm good. I just, uh, well, I had this thing happen over the weekend. I was hiking in Mount Rainier, and I had to spend the night on the Carbon River Glacier, and yeah, it was amazing, but I turned around and a ranger helped me back to my car."

Ann was an avid outdoorswoman. Hiking, biking, marathons, triathlons. She was plainspoken and happy to speak her mind, rarely without words to express her thoughts. I expected her to either rebuke me, as I deserved, or offer her own story of adventure or mishap. Instead, she stared at me for a moment of unusual silence, a glimmer in her eye as she studied me.

"Something happened to you," she finally said.

"Yeah, I think something did."

15

THAT WHICH WAS NOT DESERVED

Oh, you weak, beautiful people who give up with such grace.
What you need is someone to take hold of you—
gently, with love, and hand your life back to you.
TENNESSEE WILLIAMS

I drove past the A-frame sign sitting along the street next to the large campus of Evergreen Christian Community. The sign announced simply the times of their Sunday services: eight-thirty, ten, and noon. I mentally registered the times and knew I needed to go.

I had never been to Evergreen Christian. I didn't know anyone there. I simply had a hunger—not for church, not for a Sunday service, but for the Lord. I didn't want to hear the Word preached; I needed to hear it.

I sat in the back of the large sanctuary as a contemporary American Christian service unfolded before me. Once the singing was over, a tall man named Dale approached the podium. He read Scripture, one of Paul's letters in the New Testament, and began to preach.

It was as though I had never read the Bible before, even though I had done so multiple times. The text, the Scripture, was somehow three-dimensional, holographic, alive. I didn't care about church, but I felt like a starved and thirsty stranger dunking his head in the water and, after catching a breath, throwing food in his mouth. I just wanted to hear the Word. I just wanted to hear about Jesus.

I contemplated hanging around for the next service to hear the message again but thought better of it. That put me at risk of being noticed and of having to engage in conversation, so I left.

I still drank. It was an entrenched habit by this time. Having recovered from my hike, I found myself running and playing soccer with a local league again. The exercise seemed to help my sleep, making the nightmares and agitation less frequent, though they still persisted.

I had begun cooking and eating better food as my physical activity increased and looked forward to the chance to fix a meal for someone other than just myself. Brook and I weren't divorced yet, though the paperwork had been filed. We were waiting for the final decree.

Brook and I had planned to get together on a semiregular basis for Gracie's sake. I invited them over for dinner for our first visit.

The doorbell rang, and there stood Brook and Gracie.

"Hey, come on in," I said.

Brook and I hugged briefly, and I gave Gracie a high-five.

"You guys hungry?" I asked.

"Yes, I'm starving," Brook said. "What's for dinner? Chips and salsa?"

"No. We've got grilled chicken and vegetables with rice. I've got dessert, too, if you want. Would you like a glass of wine or a beer?"

"Wine would be nice," Brook said somewhat suspiciously. "You're cooking for yourself and eating this kind of thing regularly?"

"Not every night, but yeah, I'm trying to eat healthier. I need to now that I'm playing soccer and running again."

"Oh, that's great," she said.

We ate to our satisfaction, and though the evening was meant to create some continuity from things past, this was new. We had hardly eaten together when we were married, and I had hardly bothered to cook or eat anything resembling a balanced meal. The idea of the three of us being together was familiar, but the reality of that as it unfolded at the dinner table was wholly different.

Gracie watched a cartoon while Brook and I chatted.

"How are you guys doing?" I asked.

"We're okay, I guess. Gracie is having a hard time. I didn't think this would bother her so much. I think coming over here is good for her, and I'm grateful you were up for it."

"Of course. Maybe we can do it again in a couple weeks or something. How are you doing?" I asked politely and somewhat guardedly, not wanting to be overly familiar, trying to maintain the posture of a soon-to-be-ex-husband.

"I'm okay. I just got back from New York to finish my nutrition counseling certification, so I'll start meeting with clients soon. What happened to your leg?" she asked as she instinctively reached out and rubbed a scar just below my knee before quickly retracting her hand.

Even a month later, I still had some scars on my knee and shin from the icy walk to Mowich Lake.

"Oh, I—well, I sort of went hiking on Mount Rainier and had to sleep in the park overnight. I had kind of an icy walk back to the trail."

"Wait, you were lost?"

"No, I wasn't lost. I knew where I was, I just wasn't entirely sure where the trail was located."

She rolled her eyes. "So you were lost. Who knew you were out there?"

"Well, not anyone, really."

"You didn't tell Kellen or Joel? You just went out there by yourself and got lost without telling anybody?"

"It sounds so bad when you say it," I said. "You want some dessert?"

"Don't change the subject," she said. "Don't you ever do that again. Call me if no one else."

"Okay, I will," I relented. "I'm sorry I did that."

"Good. I forgive you," she said, satisfied that she had been heard. Two weeks later the doorbell rang again, and my dinner guests entered with greater ease than their first visit. I grilled burgers on the back patio while Brook and Gracie kicked the soccer ball in the grass. We ate and played Mario Kart together. It was nice. We had never done that before.

Our wedding anniversary approached, and I tried not to think about it as I went to work that Monday. I lamented having another day of the year dedicated to remembering a failure. I already had one of those, April 22. That was a day that was almost always marked by heightened anxiety and an insatiable urge to get black-out drunk. I had endured five of those so far. I hoped August 27 would become a much more manageable, much more forgettable date.

I buried myself in work, which was easy to do given that the market news was still overwhelmingly negative and clients required a great deal of hand-holding. Markets had rallied from the lows of March but were still decidedly in the red with no end to the fear in sight. It was the middle of the trading day on Wednesday the 26th when my assistant buzzed me.

"Steven, it's Brook on line one."

"Okay, thanks," I said with mild irritation.

"Hey, what's up?" I answered.

"Not much," she said. "I just had a question about the insurance for the car. I hadn't gotten a new card yet, and this one is about to expire and, uh, excuse me," she said as she cleared her throat. "I just, uh, I just wondered—" Her voice broke and she was crying.

My heart was split in two. Part of me felt empathy and compassion, which I think I would feel for any person who began crying mid-conversation with me. The other part of me felt as though I were now in a hostage situation. I was trapped with no escape. I couldn't hang up on her, but now between me and my work was a crying woman on the phone.

"Can you hold on a second?" I asked.

"Sure," she managed in between sobs as I set the receiver on the desk, got up, and closed my door that, along with a wall of glass, provided some degree of privacy.

"What's going on? Are you okay?"

"No," she said, still crying.

"Well, help me understand what's happening."

I waited uncomfortably for her to compose herself and finally speak. "Why did you wait to change everything until after you left?" She asked the question with soft defeat as if she were a soldier surveying the battlefield after a horrendous loss, only to have the weapon that would have brought victory now placed in her hands.

"What do you mean?" I asked, though I knew exactly what she meant.

"You're exercising and eating right, and I begged you so many times to do that. You're seeing a counselor, and I asked you so many times to do that. You actually seem present and like you want to be with us when we hang out. Why did you wait until now to change?"

"I don't know," I said as the spotlight of her honest question blinded me. I talked to her about the EMDR, that maybe that was helping. That maybe all the pressure of a new home, a new job, and a new family piled on top of lots of old hurt had just been too much. I didn't have a good answer. Then I asked a question. A question posed by my heart, spoken with my mouth, and resisted by my mind.

"Do you ever think about getting back together?"

My mind objected on two counts. First, I feared rejection. If she said no, then I would just feel stupid for having seemed weak and perhaps still carrying a torch for her. I hated the thought of that. Second, I feared repeating the past. I had been a terrible husband, and she ultimately went her own way in response and became a terrible wife. Our past indicated that we weren't good for each other. Why revisit that? My heart didn't seem to care about either objection.

There was a pause. She didn't expect that question any more than I did. Any more than either of us expected a routine phone call to bring us to this place in the conversation.

"Yeah, I've thought about it," she said.

"Okay, well, would you want to go to church with me?" I didn't know what else to ask. "We could talk about it some more afterward if you want. Maybe get some lunch?"

"Yeah, that'd be nice," she said.

I hung up and stared at my computer screen, filled with stock symbols and numbers dancing silently between red and green as the market traded. *What have I done?* I thought. *What am I doing?*

That weekend I pulled up to our old house, where Brook and Gracie still lived, to pick her up for church. Gracie was with her dad in Seattle that weekend. I was picking Brook up for a date, something I hadn't done since I had been in the army. It felt familiar and dangerously new all at once.

Dale at Evergreen Christian was preaching from Genesis chapter one, the Creation story. He talked about the two Hebrew words used in the Old Testament for making something. The first was *asah*, which means to make or do, as in building something out of raw materials. The second was *bara*, which means to create something from nothing. *Bara* is what is found in chapter one of Genesis, describing the Creator speaking into the void and making things out of nothing.

In that moment, I knew that was us. Brook and I had nothing. What we had together we had managed to destroy. Not simply disassemble, but destroy. There was only ash and wreckage where a marriage once stood. But now, inexplicably, I could feel the pulse of life—life that didn't come from Brook or me. Life that neither of us had done anything to deserve.

Brook and I continued to go to church together and often ate lunch afterward across the street at Olive Garden. Bottomless soup, salad, and breadsticks was too good a deal to ignore.

On a sunny late-September afternoon, I walked across the parking lot in front of my office building to the Olympia farmers' market to meet Brook for lunch. We ordered tacos from one of the vendors and sat at a picnic table.

We chatted for a bit and then she set her taco down and asked me a question. "Why do you want to see me?"

I thought for a moment. "Because I love you," I replied. I meant it.

For the next few months, Brook and I dated like seminormal people. We didn't have some awful military drama hanging over our heads. We lived in the same town. We went out to dinner and the movies. She and Gracie came over and played video games.

At the end of a lunch together on October 17, Brook handed me an envelope. I opened it after I got home. I recognized the card. It was a letterpress greeting card that came with a letterpress piece of art we had bought in Portland a year before. On it, a rabbit sat in a field of sprouting carrots with a barn in the background. Inside she wrote,

Over the last few weeks a lot has been revealed to me. My perception towards you and our relationship has changed. My conviction on wanting to share my life with you is stronger than it has ever been before.

In such a short time I have seen so many reasons why we have been brought down this path. I have seen so many things I did that had a negative impact on us. It was easier to blame you and avoid dealing with reality before. I wanted so badly for things to change and I couldn't wait anymore, so I gave up. I'm deeply sorry for hurting you. Thank you for forgiving me. I'm working on forgiving myself.

My heart's desire is for us to share in a loving, committed relationship, devoted to serving each other. I feel incredibly blessed to get to know you again. Being with you, even in silence, feels right. You are the love of my life. You are my closest and dearest friend.

We have experienced so much grace in our relationship; I am deeply grateful. God is good.

The card was a pure, beautiful risk. I loved it. I loved her.

On New Year's Eve Brook was over with Kellen, Joel, and me and some other folks for a little celebration. She came early, around dinnertime, just after I got home and was going through the mail. I noticed a large manila envelope from the Lincoln County Clerk. I had no idea what it was.

Inside I found a decree dated December 22, indicating our marriage was legally dissolved, which was a little odd considering that we had basically been dating for the past three months. I slid the document across the granite countertop as Brook came into the kitchen.

"You win," I said.

"What do you mean? What's this?" she asked.

"You officially divorced me. You win," I said, nodding to the paper.

"Oh, this? I forgot about that."

"You forgot that you divorced me?" I said chuckling.

"It's so weird," she said. "It doesn't seem real. How do you feel about it?"

"Good. I feel good. I'm glad you divorced me. Our first marriage was way overrated."

I was already hatching plans for our second.

In January, I enlisted Gracie's help—she had just turned eight—on a top-secret mission to secure a high-value target: Brook's wedding ring. On my instructions, she sneaked into Brook's bedroom and stole the ring from the top drawer of the dresser. Brook hadn't worn it since we had split, but Gracie knew where it was. The next time the two of them were over for dinner, when Brook had left the room for a moment, Gracie delivered the goods.

"Do you have it?" I asked.

She nodded, suppressing a shriek of glee as she pulled the ring out of her little pocket.

I took the ring to a jeweler to have the large pink sapphire center stone replaced with a bloodred ruby of equal size.

On Saturday, February 13, I took Brook to Tacoma to celebrate Valentine's Day. We walked along the waterfront near the Museum of Glass. It was clear and cool as we strolled between docked sailboats and glass sculptures. We ventured onto the Bridge of Glass, which connected the museum to downtown.

We stopped, and I pulled the ring out of my pocket and held it up to her. Her eyes opened wide.

"I want to spend the rest of my life with you," I said. "Will you marry me?"

"What? How did you get that?" she exclaimed.

"Gracie helped me out."

"I can't believe it!" she said, taking the ring from my hand and examining it more closely. "Did you get a new stone?"

"Yeah, it's a ruby. I figured you needed something a little different the second time around. So, any response to that question? Now would be the time."

"Yes, I'll marry you again," she said before kissing me.

We continued our walk to El Gaucho, just down the street, where a table was waiting for us. We ate a lavish dinner, which was of course what we always did when we got engaged.

On April 15, Brook, Gracie, and I met at the Thurston County Courthouse with Evan and Rachel, who would be our witnesses. Evan revived his role as best man for an encore performance. Brook and I said our "I dos," and with that our second marriage began.

What was lost was somehow found. What was once dead somehow came to life. We did nothing to deserve it, and yet life was given to us anyway.

I couldn't explain why. I still can't.

16

TELLING THE STORY

To love at all is to be vulnerable.
C. S. LEWIS

The phone rang. I glanced at the caller ID and saw the name "Mike Fish."

Don't know who that is, I thought. *It can go to voice mail.*

As I left the office that evening, I asked our office manager if Mike Fish had left a message as I didn't see a voice mail. She said he hadn't and that he'd call back another time.

"Any idea why he called? It's not the first time I've seen the name."

"No idea. He didn't say."

I thought little of it as I drove home.

It was now late 2013, and home was a house in the country, just south of Olympia, where Brook and I had moved after getting remarried in 2010. The thirty-minute drive offered a welcome buffer between work and home. A time to think, to process, and to feel the demands of the office shrink further and further away.

Work was the same but different. A few months after our courthouse wedding, I left Smith Barney and joined my partners Pat and Sandi to form a new company called Capstone Investment Group, LLC. My core clients from Smith Barney followed me, and I had been building on that for the past three years. The people I worked with, both colleagues and clients, were incredible, but the work itself was draining as I continued to manage the money of others in a new, post–financial crisis environment.

I had chronic posttraumatic stress disorder. That was now an openly acknowledged fact in our household. The acceptance of this was helpful, as having awareness of any malady brings some measure of relief—the relief of knowing. But that knowledge in and of itself didn't make me well.

"Hey," I said tiredly as I walked into the kitchen and poured myself a glass of wine.

"How was work?" Brook asked as she fixed dinner.

"It was work. I don't really want to talk about it. How are you? How are the girls?"

"I'm okay," she said. "Gracie has a friend over and they're working on homework, and Hazel is still napping. I should probably wake her up soon; otherwise she won't go to bed until super late."

Hazel.

On May 15, 2012, Hazel Grace Elliott was born. After allowing our new baby girl to lie with Mom for a bit, the nurses had to take her to clean her up. She sat there, all six and a half pounds of her, on a baby tray, her eyes squinted shut as she cried and cried. I went to her and said, "Hazel," at which point she became instantly silent, turned her newborn head to face me, and just stared—eager, it seemed, to hear what I might say next. From that point on I was hooked.

After dinner I retreated into the dark confines of the study with a glass of wine in hand. I sat on a black leather couch set against dark green walls and stared at the books on the shelf. Many I had read. Some I hoped to read but somehow couldn't. I couldn't seem to concentrate well enough anymore to sit and read a book. Occasionally I could, but mostly my thoughts would wander. I lacked the power to focus.

My sleep was little better than before. Nightmares persisted, although alcohol seemed to make them less frequent. At least that's what I told myself as I drank.

Brook mostly tolerated my coping mechanisms, knowing that they were not a response to her. We communicated well enough, had a wonderful community of friends, and were growing in our relationships with God. The darkness had been pushed back, and more light flooded in, but it wasn't gone. Shadows still persisted.

In the shadow of a November night, unable to keep my mind on an intentional train of thought, I sat, drank, and listened to a record. Louis Armstrong, I think. The blues he played seemed so oddly happy. The crispness and trueness of his trumpet almost overrode the sadness of his songs. But the sadness was there, in some ways more obvious as it was played with such joy.

★

The intercom buzzed. "Hey, Steven. It's Mike Fish on the phone for you," our research analyst Gabe said.

"Did he say what he wants or who he's with? Is he a wholesaler?"

"I don't think so. He just said he wants to talk to you."

"Fine. I'll take the call. Thanks . . . Hi, this is Steven."

"Hi, Steven, this is Mike Fish, and I'm a reporter with ESPN."

"Hi, Mike. Why exactly are you calling me?"

"Well, as you're probably aware, this coming April will be the ten-year anniversary of the death of Pat Tillman, and we're hoping to tell a story that hasn't been told yet. We'd like to be able to talk about those events from the perspectives of the shooters, which is why I'm calling you."

"Who else have you talked to?"

"Of the shooters, not really anyone. Baker has declined to comment, Alders is still in the army and doesn't want to compromise his security clearances by speaking publicly, and Ashpole changed his name and I can't locate him."

"Anyone else from the platoon? The family?"

"Yes, we'd be hoping to get reactions from Bryan O'Neal and the Tillman family as well."

Suddenly it was all back, separated by the thinnest of veils. A past reality coming even more violently into the present. The walls that separated the parts of life I wanted to forget from the parts I was trying to live inside came crashing down.

"I don't know, Mike. I'd have to talk to my wife about this."

"Of course. Take the time you need. In the meantime, maybe I can e-mail you the piece I did back in 2006. Is it okay if I follow up in a few days?"

"Sure, I guess so," I replied.

My mind raced, my senses on high alert. When I got home, a sip of wine turned into a gulp as I sought to tame the adrenaline. The thought of talking about my experiences publicly was horrifying. The thought of handing over control of the story to ESPN or any other media outlet was unthinkable.

What's their angle? What will people think of me?

I told Brook.

"What do you want to do?" she asked.

"Nothing. I don't see the point. It feels like a huge risk, and for what?"

"I don't know," she said.

"He did e-mail me the stuff he wrote on Pat back in 2006. Maybe we should at least give it a read to see what it's like."

Mike called again the following week, and I told him I wasn't interested. He persisted, politely but firmly, and I again declined. I didn't see the point. He asked if he could check in with me in the new year, and I said that'd be okay.

In the meantime Brook read his articles from 2006, and I called an old family friend back in Kansas, a retired sports reporter named Mark Janssen. Mark had spent most of his professional life covering Kansas State University athletics. He seemed an ally in the media world who might help me make sense of the opportunity/threat being posed by ESPN.

He and I finally connected shortly after I told Mike no. I had slept little in the interim. I wanted Mark to tell me what to do, but he didn't. He asked good questions and then he shut up and listened.

Mark and I talked a half dozen times over the next few weeks. Each time it seemed obvious that the right choice was to decline. To keep it private. In late December, we were chatting yet again, this time while I was at the office, and he asked simply and pointedly, "Why would you want to tell your story in any setting? Forget ESPN or the media. Why tell it to anyone at all?"

"I don't know," I said. "To just tell it again, to go over all the details again and rehash the past seems so pointless, you know? Who wants to hear that crap? I certainly have no desire to delve into it." A thought began to stir. "But you know what? If the hook of the past, my association with Pat for arguably the worst possible reasons, could be used to talk about something else that could help people, that might be worth it."

"What would you talk about?" Mark asked.

"The whole mental health thing," I said as my mind became energized. "I know I'm not the only one. I mean, the veteran suicide stats are off the charts. Something like twenty vets a day kill themselves, and I think that's the VA's own numbers. The only reason ESPN wants to talk to me is because of Pat. The only reason they care about Pat as a news item is because he played in the NFL. Fine. I'll talk about the past if that can be a springboard for talking about veterans' mental health. If we can use the past to talk about a more constructive future, I could do that." I had talked myself into it as Mark listened patiently.

I explained my reasoning to Brook that evening and braced myself for her to shoot me down, half hoping she would.

"I think that's a great idea," she said.

"You do?"

"Yeah. I mean, so many people struggle with mental health issues, and they don't feel it's safe to talk about it. Not just people in the military, either. It could really help people. If it helps just one person, it would be worth it. And you know what? I've never been able to talk about it because it was your trauma, but it has affected all of us.

I have friends who wondered why we got divorced, and I can't really tell them the truth because I'm afraid you'd be mad at me."

"Really? I guess I never really thought about that. I'm sorry," I said. "Have you read any of Mike's stuff?"

"Yes, and I wanted to talk to you about it," she said as she pulled out articles she'd printed from his 2006 series.

I braced myself for the questions. I hadn't yet read the articles.

I answered various logistical questions about the investigations, all of which were revelations to Brook as I had never talked about them with her. This was the first time she'd read anything about the incident. All she had learned she learned from me, which was very little. She never researched it on her own. To do so would have felt like going behind my back, she would say. She was married to a man who may have killed Pat Tillman, yet she knew less about his death than the casual viewer of *SportsCenter*.

She finally came to a portion of one of the articles she had highlighted, a quote from Pat and Kevin's younger brother, Richard. He said that finding out Pat had been killed by friendly fire after having been lied to was "like losing him all over again." Brook wiped away tears as she read this.

"I can't believe what they put the family through," she said angrily. "What they put all of you through."

It was a moving yet odd thing to hear. I didn't consider myself someone who was "put through" something. I couldn't see myself on the same side of the tragedy as the Tillmans or Bryan or Jade or anyone else on the receiving end of our rounds. We were on opposing sides. They deserved all the empathy the nation could throw at them. More than that, the family deserved the truth, as does any family who loses a loved one in service to our country. I, at best, deserved to be forgotten, an accidental villain in a tragic farce.

A month later Brook and I had dinner with Mike Fish and Willie Weinbaum, both of ESPN. Mike would write the article and Willie would produce the *Outside the Lines* television segment that would accompany it. I eyed them suspiciously as we ate our appetizers.

Mike was from upstate New York and seemed a bit like a man from another era, as though he should have been covering Babe Ruth or Lou Gehrig on the train. Willie was a softhearted and quick-witted guy from Manhattan who was clearly invested in his work and passionate about the stories he told.

"Why do you want to do this?" I asked. "Why does ESPN want to use resources telling this story again?"

"It's about a different perspective. *Your* perspective. No one has heard from you or the others on your vehicle, and we want to hear what you have to say," Mike said.

"What's your angle? What story are you hoping to tell?"

"You tell us. We don't know yet until we talk to you. We won't know what story will emerge," Willie replied.

I told them why I would do it: to highlight the mental health crisis in the veteran community and hopefully show that the broken people aren't just the ones on the street asking for spare change but are also people like me. People who on the surface have it all together.

Willie replied, "If you write down why you want to do this and tell us what your hopes are for what you want to communicate, we can work with that and will seek to honor that."

We decided to do it. Brook and I didn't trust the media, but we trusted Mike and Willie.

On Thursday, March 6, Mike Fish arrived at the Capstone conference room at 6 p.m. for our interview. He came in with a laundry basket full of documents and statements from me and others in the platoon and offered to let me review any of them if that would be helpful to me. The bundles of clean white paper folded upon each other grotesquely, as if the rubber bands and binder clips that held them in place were about to give way, allowing all the terrible words they contained to spill out on the carpet. I declined the offer.

I emotionally detached and answered his questions. In two hours, we were done.

The following day, Brook, Evan, and I gathered with Mike, Willie, ESPN reporter John Barr, and other members of the production team in a conference room at the Governor Hotel in downtown Olympia. I spent two hours in front of the camera. It was emotionally exhausting. I cried and hated that I cried. I didn't want people to feel sorry for me. I didn't want people to think I was doing this just so maybe I could feel better.

I talked about following Sergeant Baker's lead in choosing to fire, and my heart broke for him. If his load had been anything like mine, I didn't want him to have to carry that. I didn't want people to think I was blaming him.

John Barr finally asked what I would say to the Tillman family. My lower lip quivered as I fought to maintain composure. "You just want to tell them how sorry you are," I said. "And how completely inadequate those words feel."

We transitioned to the afternoon to get "B roll" footage of me walking or running or whatever it was that I did that they could use in addition to the interview footage. Considering how important the church was to our life, Willie wondered if they might be able to shoot Brook and me there on a Sunday morning. They could just send a cameraman and sound guy. I told him I'd ask and cringed at the thought.

It felt good to be done with the interview, but I would have to wait to see what they'd do with it. With no creative control, we were now fully in their hands.

I talked to Paul Jones, a friend and one of the elders at our local church, Reality. No one there had any idea of my past. Few knew I had even been in the army. People there knew me as a professional in the community and as someone who occasionally preached on Sundays, as I served on the preaching and teaching team. This was a role I very much enjoyed and never thought I'd find myself in. Not long after Brook and I had remarried, Evan asked if I'd be willing to teach about money from a biblical perspective, which I did. Another friend and pastor learned that I had taught at Evan's church and asked me to fill in for him. This friend, Jake, was a friend of Paul's and was the reason I was able to serve in that capacity.

The thing was, I couldn't just ask Paul if ESPN could shoot during a service without telling him the whole story. Which I did. He listened intently.

"I'm so sorry for all that you and Brook have gone through," he said. "I'll talk to the other elders about filming on a Sunday, and just let us know how else we can support you."

Somewhat to my dismay the elders said they'd be okay with it, provided it was announced well beforehand and people were given the option of attending another service if they didn't wish to risk being filmed. We'd have to announce it to them. I hadn't thought about that.

Paul and I talked it over, and he offered to make the announcement on my behalf, but that felt unfair. He shouldn't have to do that, worrying if he was saying too much or too little about why ESPN was shooting footage. It should be me.

The following Sunday, before Paul preached his message, I stepped up to the podium to make the announcement. It wasn't unusual for me to speak in front of the congregation, and I normally enjoyed it, but that day I felt more exposed and vulnerable than I ever had. I watched people's faces as I pondered this moment—the last of my moments in hiding. Everything would be different on the other side of what I was about to say.

I told them ESPN would be coming to shoot some footage of Brook and me in a church service for a piece they were doing in which I was featured.

The congregation became noticeably interested and excited. They leaned forward.

"But it's not because of any athletic accomplishment of mine, I can assure you," I said as I fought for composure. *You just have to tell them; otherwise none of this makes any sense.*

"A few of you may know that I served in the army. Specifically, I served as a member of Second Ranger Battalion at Fort Lewis. In the spring of 2004 I was deployed to the Afghanistan/Pakistan border to conduct combat operations."

My pulse quickened. I wondered if people could see my hands shaking.

"Also in my platoon were two brothers, Pat and Kevin Tillman," I said as I choked up speaking their names.

The room suddenly felt colder, quieter.

"Some of you may have heard of Pat because he left the NFL to join the army."

The silence penetrated.

"On April 22, 2004, our platoon was ambushed, and once the smoke had cleared, it was evident that we had sustained four casualties, two dead and two wounded. One of those killed was an Afghan soldier, and the other was Pat."

The tension felt thick.

"It quickly became evident that the casualties were a result of friendly fire. That we had accidentally fired on our own men, believing them to be the enemy."

There it was. The pain of the past now brought into the present for all to see.

"We don't know for sure who killed Pat. From what we do know, it is likely that one of two men are responsible for his death." I paused. "I am one of those two men."

The words themselves didn't seem real. How could they be?

"ESPN is doing a story for the ten-year anniversary of Pat's death, and because the Lord has been such a part of our lives, they'd like to include some footage of us at a Sunday gathering, which is why they'll be shooting here."

I proceeded with the logistics as the emotion began, thankfully, to ebb. No one had expected to hear that.

After the service, a number of people approached me to offer their support. I hadn't been shunned, so that was good, but doubt still remained. *Is this really a good idea?*

Soon Mike and Willie informed me that they had just completed interviewing Bryan O'Neal for the story. Mike asked me, "Have you talked to Bryan recently?"

"No, not since I left regiment."

"Well, he's still kind of angry about all this. Just so you know."

"Oh. Okay. Well, thanks for telling me."

Finally, on Good Friday, April 18, ESPN aired the *Outside the Lines* piece that featured interviews with me and O'Neal and, briefly, Brook.

Brook and I didn't have cable, so we sat in the study and watched the piece on our computer. It was surreal. Bryan was angry. When asked if he'd been able to forgive those who fired at him, O'Neal said, "I guess to say to forgive somebody means I have to think about them. And I don't. You know, they're meaningless to me. I guess to forgive them would mean I have to acknowledge they exist. And to me, they're nothing. All of them."

Brook looked at me for a response. I looked back at her, searching for the same.

"Well," she said, "aren't you going to say something?"

"I think it was good. I think."

"What about Bryan?" she asked.

"I get it. I don't know that I'd feel any differently. I mean, of all the survivors, he was probably more traumatized than anybody. And then he was ostracized at regiment because he wouldn't sign off on the witness statement for Pat's Silver Star. He lost so much that day. I can't even imagine."

"I know, but he's so angry," she said. "I just don't like hearing him talk that way about you."

"I know, but we can't judge him for that. He's right to feel wronged. I don't know that I'd respond any differently. I'm certainly in no place to judge."

On April 22, the ten-year anniversary of the ambush, ESPN posted its main story, written by Mike Fish and titled "Enduring Guilt." I read it first thing in the morning after Mike texted me to let me know it was live. It was an extensive article that included numerous photos and links to related stories, along with a repost of the video from four days earlier. It described the ambush, shooting, and army cover-up, as well as how O'Neal and I dealt with the experience, which seemed rather similar. It also included comments from Jade Lane and Will Aker. Not surprisingly, Lane felt I should acknowledge firing on his position as well.

Hardest to read were the quotes from Mary Tillman, Pat's mom, describing the "tremendous void" left after the loss of her son, as well as how it would have meant something if any of the shooters had reached out to her. (Baker had called after Pat's death, but I hadn't.)

One more thing I screwed up.

All in all, it felt fair. It wasn't sensationalized or embellished. Mike and Willie were true to their word in honoring our intent. The video segment ended saying that I want other veterans who are suffering to know that "with help, there is hope."

Later that morning I went to do an interview for National Public Radio's *All Things Considered* that would air that afternoon. On the way out of the studio I got a call from Willie. Bryan O'Neal had contacted him and wondered if it'd be okay to contact me directly. I was pretty surprised given Bryan's comment, but I was certainly open to it. I asked for Bryan's number as well, which Willie gave me.

I didn't want to waste any more time, so I did what any thirty-something in 2014 would do. I texted. "There is so much to say that can't be communicated via text, but I want you to know how incredibly sorry I am for my decision to fire on your position. It pains me to know what you went thru and I can't imagine how difficult that has been these past years. My family and I care for you and are praying for your continued good health and healing."

Bryan soon responded: "I am very grateful that you decided to come forward and say what you said. I will have a hard time getting past the anger and frustration that I've endured these past ten years but I think it's time I do so. It will obviously be challenging to forgive you for what happened but I feel that not only do I need to do this to move on but you also deserve it. I can't imagine the hardships you've suffered over these years but I can understand the pain you've felt. I know that I can't speak for Pat's family but I am ready to let this pain go and tell you that you have earned my forgiveness."

I read those words over and over again. I hadn't earned anything. Bryan had given the gift called "forgiveness" to someone who could offer nothing but remorse in the face of a crippling debt.

I took Bryan's lead and asked Willie if he could help me reach out to Will Aker, Jade Lane, and Marie Tillman, Pat's widow. He contacted all of them, and they each agreed to provide their e-mail addresses for me to contact them.

Will and I connected. He was really glad to hear from me. It was great to know he was doing well. I apologized. He gladly forgave.

I e-mailed Jade. I told him how sorry I was for shooting him. I told him I was sorry if he felt I was hiding behind a lack of memory. I never heard back from him. That was okay. He owed me nothing.

I e-mailed Marie. It felt constantly pathetic that all I had to offer were words expressing sentiments. I expressed my remorse for Pat's death and for the possible role I had in it. I never heard from her. That was okay. Marie didn't owe me anything either.

I didn't have the guts to contact Mary. I was too scared, and her comments in the article made it seem as though that opportunity had passed.

People were contacting me through Mike, offering encouragement and sharing stories of their struggles.

My family was proud, especially Grandpa. He was dying of congestive heart failure by then, but his ailing heart was encouraged as we spoke of it.

"I'm glad you done it," he said. "You done real well. You got nothin' to be ashamed of. And I'm real glad you got to talk with that other guy. You's in the same unit, you didn't want to hurt each other, you know? I'm glad that can be behind you now."

The relief he felt on my behalf was palpable and directly proportionate to the grief he had likewise felt for me.

Overall, the week was a blur as we digested the responses and reactions of those around us, all of them overwhelmingly positive.

I sat that Friday night on the couch and watched an old James Bond movie, *Thunderball*. I loved the Sean Connery Bond films. The girls were in bed, and I drank to unwind, as was my custom. A half bottle of wine or so.

I should feel better than this, I thought. I felt relieved, but not well.

People had accepted me. People had forgiven me.

I'll be better now, I told myself.

The worst is surely behind me, I thought as I watched Bond lean backward off the boat into placid waters only to find the enemy lurking in the deep.

17

HEALING

The Spirit of the Lord is on me, because
he has anointed me to proclaim good news to the poor.
He has sent me to proclaim freedom for the prisoners and
recovery of sight for the blind, to set the oppressed free.
LUKE 4:18

I sat on a long, green, velvet couch. The walls of the room were lined floor to ceiling with bookshelves filled with old volumes that emitted the pungent aroma of must and leather. Seated across from me was a man with his legs crossed and a notepad open in his hands. He was writing as I spoke. It was a therapy session.

I was telling him about my fear that people won't believe I have nightmares. That they'd think I was making it all up.

The corpse sitting next to me on the couch was silent.

The body was missing its head and covered in damp blood. The brownish-red residue gleamed in the dim light of the desk lamp. The body wore the familiar tan desert camouflage we had worn in combat. As I spoke, the corpse slowly leaned toward me until our shoulders touched. All I could hear was my voice, the scratching of the therapist's pen, and a couch spring that creaked, betraying the movement of the headless mass.

The corpse pressed harder against my shoulder. Its weight was considerable. While continuing to talk, I gritted my teeth, took both hands, and pushed it with all my might. As I pushed, I feared I might send the body tumbling off the couch, yet all I could manage was to barely get it upright again. As soon as I released my grip from the wet uniform, the corpse once more began tipping almost imperceptibly in my direction as the couch spring creaked again.

I wanted it to go away, and I also wanted it to stay close and to know it was safe. I didn't want it to be hurt anymore.

The bloodied name tape on the uniform read "Tillman."

I opened my eyes and took a slow, deep breath as I adjusted to my waking world. I rubbed my fingers against my palms to verify that they were indeed dry. This nightmare was new and was becoming a frequent occurrence in the weeks following the interview.

After work that afternoon I met a fellow veteran named Matt. He was also an infantryman and had been a platoon radio operator in Iraq. He was now working on his master's in social work. He shared his pain and I shared mine.

He told me of the deaths he witnessed in a year of combat in Iraq, how he could still feel his hand mic on his left shoulder. I told him how I could still feel the buttstock of the 240 in my right. I couldn't solve his problems, and he didn't expect me to, but we left knowing that we were not alone.

This happened with some frequency. A friend or acquaintance knew something of my story and "referred" someone to me, invariably a guy who was a veteran and wasn't doing well. None of these guys were homeless. None of them incapable of holding down jobs. None of them leeches on the system. All of them struggling. Struggling with PTSD and the physical effects of that disease. Struggling with survivor's guilt, wondering why they lived or were unhurt and others were dead or wounded. Struggling with moral injury having seen the travesty of war and left feeling hollow that such things can happen.

Struggling from the second- and third-order effects of protracted deployments or alcohol abuse that layer more trauma on top of core trauma, making it difficult to know where the whole mess started in the first place. No two were alike and yet, in some way, all were the same.

My reconciliation with Brook was an encouragement to some as they struggled in their own marriages. The conversations themselves were mutually beneficial. It wasn't always clear who was helping whom, but ultimately both parties were always better off.

I was also given more opportunities to speak publicly as a result of the interviews. One such invitation was at our county's local veterans court. I had no idea veterans' courts existed or what they were. Essentially, they're treatment courts that allow vets charged with certain crimes—often DUIs or domestic abuse—to enter an intensive, two-year intervention program to help address wartime trauma that hasn't been treated and could be contributing to where they find themselves in the criminal justice system. If they can complete the program, they won't have a charge on their record and will actually have been forced to deal with issues they were either unwilling or unable to handle on their own.

Judge Brett Buckley said I could talk about whatever I felt was appropriate. I decided to talk a bit about one of Jesus' disciples, Peter. I felt a lot like Peter. He talked a good game: he was the one who was going to stick it to the Romans and help Jesus fight for his throne. But when Jesus was betrayed and taken into custody, Peter denied him. He denied even knowing the man who had been his friend for the past several years. He denied Jesus in his darkest hour and then ran away.

Before Peter did that, though, on the very night he would do it, Peter, Jesus, and the rest of the disciples shared a meal. At that meal, Jesus—the one who would be abandoned by his friends, tortured, and murdered—turned to Peter, the one who would deny him, and encouraged him. As recorded in the Gospel of Luke, Jesus turned to Peter and told him that Peter was going to be tried and that he was praying for him. Most amazingly, Jesus said, "When you have turned back, strengthen your brothers."

Jesus knew Peter's strength would fail. He knew that his friend would pretend to not even know him, and yet he encouraged Peter. Jesus told him there was hope and purpose on the other side of soul-crushing failure. That's good news.

I didn't want to be too preachy, but this was the most appropriate thing I could think to tell this group, many of whom were dealing with their own version of soul-crushing failure. It seemed to be received well. I was invited to serve as part of the court's mentor program, which allowed me even more opportunities to connect with vets who were struggling and now dealing with the legal ramifications of their actions. I went to court almost every Wednesday. It was a good reminder that none of us were alone.

Not long after I started serving at the veterans court, Brook and I watched the film *The Assassination of Jesse James by the Coward Robert Ford*. It is a dark and broody Western about a dark and broody man named Robert Ford. Ford was part of Jesse James's gang and ultimately killed James partly for the reward but mostly because he thought that in killing the infamous outlaw, he would become a hero. It didn't work out that way for him, but that didn't stop him from reenacting his shooting of James on stage hundreds of times. Robert Ford's sole identity became that of the man who killed Jesse James.

Watching the movie raised uncomfortable questions in me. *Is that me? Have I unwittingly become Robert Ford?* Though my actions bore none of the deliberate violence to Pat that Ford's did to James—I didn't even know if it was my rounds that killed him—and though I didn't seek out opportunities to relive the event, was my identity becoming that of "the man who may have killed Pat Tillman"? I didn't care whether I was known for anything, but what if that became all I was known for? What then?

Meanwhile, I discovered the gin martini. Dry, with olives. I was drinking a lot, at least two cocktails a night plus wine with dinner. Six drinks? Eight drinks? I had stopped counting. The need seemed to grow the more I drank. There was something inside me I was trying to get to but I just couldn't touch.

That Christmas Brook gave me a book—a book I actually wanted to read and felt like I could read, which at that time was rare. It was Shelby Foote's three-volume work *The Civil War: A Narrative*. I had watched Shelby Foote on Ken Burns's Civil War documentary and wanted to read what he wrote. The Civil War itself was fascinating to me, this great moment where the unaddressed sins of America's founding came to a head and nearly tore the nation apart. That time and the personalities of that time continued to draw me in.

A couple of months later, in February 2015, I was on a plane to Tampa to visit a client. I was now on the second volume of Foote's epic work and came to the Battle of Chancellorsville, fought in the spring of 1863. It was in some respects the high point of the Confederacy, and the battle itself was a rout of the Union forces by the legendary Southerner Stonewall Jackson.

I cared nothing for Jackson's politics or the lost cause for which he fought. I was, however, shocked to learn that on the evening of his victory at Chancellorsville, as he and his aides returned to the Confederate lines at dusk after conducting reconnaissance, Confederate soldiers mistakenly opened fire on them, believing they were a Union patrol. A number of his party were killed, and Jackson himself was struck by three bullets and had to have his left arm amputated. Jackson technically died of pneumonia eight days later, but his recent amputation presumably didn't help his already weakened condition.

I sat in the middle seat of a darkened airplane cabin while the single bulb I was allotted illuminated the words of Jackson's final moments on earth:

Jackson summoned McGuire. "Doctor, Anna informs me that you have told her I am to die today. Is it so?" When McGuire replied that it was so, the general seemed to ponder. Then he said, "Very good, very good. It is all right." After a time he added, "It is the Lord's day; my wish is fulfilled. I have always desired to die on Sunday."

At 1:30 the doctor told him he had no more than a couple of hours to live. "Very good; it's all right," Jackson replied as before, but more weakly, for his breathing was high in his throat by now. When McGuire offered him brandy to keep up his strength, he shook his head. "It will only delay my departure, and do no good," he protested. "I want to preserve my mind, if possible, to the last." Presently, though, he was back in delirium, alternately praying and giving commands, all of which had to do with the offensive. Shortly after 3 o'clock, a few minutes before he died, he called out: "Order A. P. Hill to prepare for action! Pass the infantry to the front. . . . Tell Major Hawks—" He left the sentence unfinished, seeming thus to have put the war behind him; for he smiled as he spoke his last words, in a tone of calm relief. "Let us cross over the river," he said, "and rest under the shade of the trees."

I discreetly wiped away tears. It was possibly the most beautiful thing I'd ever read. Jackson's last words were a deep comfort. The comfort lay, at least in part, in the idea of crossing over from this life to the next. The comfort of knowing that at least someday I'd die. Like Jackson, sweating and writhing in his delusion, someday I would be dead and free of all this. The thought of my ultimate death was hope.

As the year wore on, the drinking continued and my health declined. It was as though I had found a new darkness. I slept mostly on the couch by my own choice, rarely attempting to close my eyes before one or two o'clock in the morning. The pain was always right there. It was like a splinter coming to the surface that I could see and almost pluck out of the flesh, but it wouldn't budge.

One night I sat in the darkened study, on my third martini and listening to an Ella Fitzgerald record. I felt I had to get something out on the page, a feeling I never otherwise had, so I sat at the desk in front of the keyboard and let the ugly words flow. I was too drunk for formal prose. Poetry was all I could manage. I began to write:

The canyon calls and claims its victim
The canyon is our friend and foe
It is but earth and clay you know
As rock is torn and boulders flow
We fire at those we deem the foe
But those condemned are sadly friend
The friend cries out and cries again
The cries are drowned in rounds of hate
The cries grow silent in death and fate
The cries cry on in hearts of shooters
The cries cry on
Cry on
Cry on

Pages of the stuff. Pages and pages and pages flowing out of me like pus from a gaping wound. I began to see the nature of my injury in the form of drunken poems and was sickened. I continued to write:

Poisons of the heart they must be bled
Poisons wreak
I tire of the pain
The pain tires not of me
No mind can outthink it
The pain knows no thought but me
Where is the Bread of Life?
Where is the Living Water?
Heart full of putrid sulfur ever flows
Hearts' wounds of poison never close

Finally, it got to Pat. I trembled and cried as I saw his name appear on the page:

Pat is his name whose life is lost
Pat is the name that names the cost
He is no better than the rest

He stands for those who stood the test
His life shouts meaning for the others
His life is gone woe to his mother
The mother weeps the father grieves
The brothers' hearts hem and heave
The widow's mind is struck with pain
The widow's cries drown in the rain
The father reaches through the grave
The father's reach is numb but brave
The brave die in the face of danger
The brave is Patrick the tragic Ranger

After a few hours I was finally spent. Drunk, exhausted, and spent. The words were written, as if some strange force had swept in and put them there, but inside nothing had changed.

★

Some weeks later I stepped into our walk-in closet to change clothes after work. There sitting on the shelf in front of me was a small safe with an electric lock. Inside the safe was a weapon. With three electric beeps the door swung open, and I pulled the pistol from its resting place. I pulled back the slide handle of the upper receiver to ensure there was no round in the chamber. It was a Desert Eagle .45 caliber in the 1911 style. It felt heavy, cold, and nice in my hand.

How easy it would be, I thought as I put a loaded mag in the handle, slapping it into place with my left hand. I didn't chamber a round.

A pull of the charging handle and a pull of the trigger and it'd be over. The shame, the guilt, the nightmares, the incessant restlessness, the difficulty concentrating, the fear, the anxiety, the depression. All of it. Over.

I was Landry, a weak and pathetic soldier incapable of handling the weight of his choice to serve and all the ramifications of that service. It had taken longer to break me, but I was breaking, and there was no one there to watch.

I'd be a quitter. To kill a man is to kill one man, but to kill oneself is to kill the entire world. It's to say that there is nothing in God's creation worth living for. He was keeping me alive. Why?

Some poor soul would have to find me. My trauma wouldn't end; it would simply find a new form in the lives of my wife and daughters. That would be the legacy I would leave.

I pressed the button releasing the magazine and let it drop into my hand. I placed the pistol and magazine back in the safe and closed the door.

I felt out of options and willing to try anything. I went to a psychiatric nurse practitioner, someone who could prescribe meds if she deemed it necessary. I didn't know what I needed, but I knew I just needed it all to stop. Whatever was still in me, I needed it to be gone. I just needed to rest. All I wanted was to rest.

We went through the same drill to start off. Me telling her why I was there and such. Me fighting the urge to apologize for the mess I presented in her otherwise well-kept office. She got right to the point: "Do you have suicidal thoughts?"

I pondered that for a moment. "I don't want to kill myself; I just don't really want to live anymore." I grinned a bit, trying to sell the joke, but she wasn't buying it.

"Tell me what you mean by that," she persisted.

"I just . . . I'm just tired, you know? I'm so tired. I just want to rest and I don't know how. I can't turn this off. I just want to turn it off, and I don't know how else I could do that. I have so much to live for and so much to be grateful for, but I can't do this anymore. It needs to stop."

"What's kept you from doing it?"

"I guess I feel bad for the poor person who has to find me. You can't just disappear. People have to know you're dead, which means someone has to find you. Dead. And I think about the girls. I don't want suicide to be the legacy I leave them."

"Do you have any firearms in the house?"

"Yes."

"Are they in a safe?"

"Yes."

"Okay. Here's what I need from you. I need your wife to change and keep the combination, and I need you to have her call me in the next twenty-four hours to confirm that's been done. You're not allowed to have access to that weapon," she said sternly.

"Okay."

She then prescribed a couple of different medications. I don't remember their names. The first was in the same family as Zoloft, one of your classic antidepressants meant to help recalibrate your brain's chemistry. The second was a blood pressure medication that had the side effect of reducing incidence of nightmares. It was now being prescribed in the veteran community for the side effect.

"I already have kind of low blood pressure," I told her. "Is this still okay?"

"You'll just want to be careful when you get out of bed. You might feel light-headed, so give yourself a moment, and don't get up too quickly."

I stopped drinking and took the prescriptions. They helped. Sort of. The nightmares were mostly gone. Now my dreams were just super weird, and I nearly passed out every time I had to get up in the middle of the night to pee. The antidepressant seemed to help for a while, but eventually it was just depressing to take an antidepressant. I felt numb and remote, not myself. I'm not opposed to drugs. I know they can really help people. But they weren't helping me. I had traded some symptoms for others.

★

In December 2015, I sat down with an academic, a professor at Antioch University in Seattle who had taught our friend Jen in her doctoral program. After Jen saw the interviews, she suggested he and I get together.

Dr. Mark Russell was a clinical psychologist and naval veteran. He was the son of a veteran who had served in Korea and Vietnam, and he had children serving on active duty in the navy and marines. He along with other academics had founded the Institute of War Stress Injuries, Recovery, and Social Justice for the purpose of helping eliminate the mental health crisis that was raging and continues to rage among our nation's armed forces and veterans.

We connected immediately, and I was fascinated by his work and his passion. The work, though seeking to help veterans, is not focused on the veteran community. Rather, his focus is on solving how mental health care is seen and delivered while men and women are still in uniform. People are killing themselves as veterans, but the wounds that lead to that awful decision are sustained while on active duty. We began to discuss how my story could be put in the service of the academic record, which was both damning and hopeful. Damning to the armed forces for allowing the stigma of mental illness to persist and the care for service members to not be properly tracked and coordinated. Hopeful because there are tried-and-true methods that can be employed that can help people feel safe to get the care they need.

In February 2016 I tapered off from the meds. I was tired of how they made me feel. I drank some, but I was tired of that, too. Whatever benefit I had gotten from alcohol, its return was diminishing.

I read Shelby Foote's passage describing Stonewall Jackson's death every night. Often multiple times a night. I'd sit in the wooden chair next to the built-in bookshelf under a single overhead spotlight and read the words in a barely audible whisper.

"He spoke his last words, in a tone of calm relief. 'Let us cross over the river,' he said. 'And rest under the shade of the trees.'"

Calm relief. How marvelous that sounded. The text itself was strangely and strongly beautiful to me. I was drawn to it and never tired of reading it. I read it for its beauty—the beauty I saw, anyway. And I now know I read it as a prayer. It was a cry of help and a cry of hope uttered via the dying words of some dying man, a man who had been killed by others who cared for him. It was a prayer. A prayer of repentance. A prayer of desperation.

A month went by, then another. On a Sunday afternoon, Gracie's dad, Christian, stopped by the house to drop off Gracie after the two of them had been hanging out. He is a good man, and he had become my friend.

"You wanna take a walk and chat for a bit?" he asked. "There's something I wanted to talk to you about."

"Sure," I said as we walked down the sunny side of the street. "So, what's up?"

"Well, I just wanted to tell you what's been going on with me and invite you to something."

"Sure, go for it."

He proceeded to describe a retreat he'd recently attended. It was nothing special. Just something a friend of his had invited him to where people gathered to pray and meditate at a small campground. The Lord had been speaking to him, and I could tell things in him were changing. He bravely told me some of those things, risking my response to his supposed encounter with God.

Christian had been through a lot. He was a sober alcoholic and a highly functioning professional. I could see healing taking place in him as he spoke. I knew that whatever he invited me to, the answer would be yes.

"This isn't just a bunch of burned-out hippies who get together to smoke weed or do mushrooms, is it?" I asked.

"No," he laughed. "They actually don't allow any drugs or alcohol. You can't even smoke, which sucks for me, but it's a really healthy, clean environment. I'd love it if you'd come with me to check it out."

"Okay. Let's do it."

On Father's Day weekend in June, I joined Christian for a two-night retreat at the campground. About thirty of us gathered that Friday evening around a fire. Some prayed. Some meditated. Some played music. As I sat there, staring at the flames and taking in my surroundings, I began to think this was dumb. *I'm wasting a perfectly good weekend, and for what? To sit around with a bunch of strangers and sing "Kumbaya"?*

Slowly, the noise in my head and in my heart began to soften. A voice that was familiar began to speak.

I began to feel convicted. Who was I to judge these people? Who was I to demean or cheapen this time?

A familiar voice began to speak with startling clarity as I sat on the ground, my knees pulled forward toward my chest.

"I need you on your knees" was all I heard. I argued and finally acquiesced. I sat up on my knees for a few minutes. Then I heard, "I need you on your face."

Why? I thought, but I finally complied, lying flat on the ground.

I don't know what I thought would happen. At that point I was so desperate, I would have done almost anything for the prospect of relief, which is why I was there in the first place. In some respects, I wish what follows would have been different, that the events would be easier to understand and easier for me to describe. I can neither defend nor argue in favor of what I experienced. I can only tell you what happened and tell you that I can't explain it.

As I lay there in the dirt, a vision unfolded.

I saw part of a horrid, festering wound, and I thought that was all I would see, but I found myself in the dark center of that wound. It was a giant void. I was both trapped and floating in nothingness.

Though I was near the fire and warm, I began feeling an icy cold current throughout my entire body as though I were moving through the black void alone. It was impressed upon me that this was how Brook had felt throughout our entire marriage. I began to cry. His voice, his impression continued.

He said that he had created me, as he had created everyone, as an instrument to be played. He was the maestro. He was sovereign. He told me he had given me a voice, a voice that was meant to speak for others who couldn't speak for themselves. I saw the poor, the abandoned, the homeless.

I saw Brook. I saw her beauty in a way I never had before. I knew I had to make things right at home first. I knew that it all started with her. I had to repent of my selfishness and my lust. I had used porn as another escape from reality for years, and she never knew.

He showed me Grandpa, how we were a gift to each other. He had died the previous year just shy of his ninety-second birthday. It was as though I began seeing things that Grandpa had seen: dead animals, dead children, scorched earth. He put me in Grandpa's shoes as he ran for cover, rounds from German aircraft kicking up dirt in his face. Like he had healed my Grandpa, the voice said, he would heal me.

Things went dark. Images of war and my training overwhelmed me. Images of Pat, Kevin, and their family overwhelmed me. I wanted it to stop. I missed Pat and again began to cry. I saw my last moments with Kevin and my fear and regret. I just wanted to give him a hug and tell him I was sorry. I knew I must try and see them. Brook and I would be going to Northern California in August, and I knew then that the purpose of that trip was to see Mary Tillman.

Images of war returned. Then images began flashing before my eyes. Images of targets I had fired at in training and on deployment. Like a thick deck of cards being shuffled, the images were flipping fast in my mind. As this happened, my right index finger began to tremor as if every pull of the trigger was being undone. As the images flashed and my trigger finger shook, physically and mentally I felt the impression of these images leave me. It was painful, as if leeches were being removed.

I tried to get up but couldn't. A force was intensely drawing me to the ground as the visions continued.

I asked why this was happening to me, and the voice said, "Because you prayed for it."

The Lord was doing the work; I was just the instrument.

I lay there for the better part of eight hours, unable to rise from the ground as he spoke. Christian and a few others checked on me as the night progressed, and I was able to assure them I was okay as the experience continued. As dawn approached, the vision faded, and I rested in the cool of the night turning slowly to morning.

I spent most of Saturday writing down the details of the encounter. I considered the notion of being healed, and though I felt distinctly different, connected, focused, and present in a way I hadn't felt in years, I couldn't dare to trust it yet.

★

Christian and I returned to Olympia on Sunday, Father's Day. We ate and celebrated at the house with the girls. There was a newness to it all, as if I could see clearly the value of what I'd been given. A veil between the world and me had been removed. The colors were once again vibrant.

That evening I told Brook what had happened, half bracing myself for her to dismiss it as craziness. She didn't. I broke down many times as I attempted to recount what I had seen and heard, and she sat in focused silence, taking it all in.

I repented. She forgave.

"Do you really feel different?" she asked, as wary as I was of emotionally investing in the idea of me being healed.

"Yeah, I do. Maybe it'll wear off; I don't know. But I feel *here*, you know? Something has been turned off. I feel at ease. I feel like myself. I feel like how I felt and who I was before I joined the army. It's hard to explain, but yeah, it feels like whatever I had—the PTSD, the survivor's guilt, the moral injury, whatever—is gone. This sounds weird, but I can't remember in my hands what it feels like to hold a weapon. It's like all that muscle memory—it's all just gone."

"What next?" she asked.

"I have to get ahold of Mary Tillman," I said. "We have to see her."

18

THE END

From the end spring new beginnings.
PLINY THE ELDER

The next day I went to the office, and before I did anything else, I e-mailed Willie Weinbaum at ESPN. I figured he was my best shot at getting in touch with Mary Tillman. The message was short. I asked if he'd be okay passing along a request to Mary to speak with her. I made it clear that if he or she were in any way uncomfortable with that, then there was no pressure. I clicked "send" and went about my day.

A half hour later, the intercom on my phone buzzed, and I was told, "There's a Mary Tillman on the line for you, Steven."

"Oh. Uh, okay. I'll take the call. Thanks."

I picked up. "Hi, this is Steven."

"Hi, Steven," came the kind voice through the phone. "I just got your e-mail from Willie, and I could tell you were maybe a bit nervous or scared to contact me, and I just didn't want to waste any more time and have you worrying."

"Wow. Thank you," I said with mild shock.

"I'm so glad you reached out, and you need to know that I don't blame you for what happened. I can't imagine all that you've been through. We all lost."

I couldn't believe it. I was supposed to be apologizing to her.

"That's so very generous of you," I said. "I'm so sorry for what we did. I'm so sorry for all your family has had to suffer."

We chatted for a while, and I broached the idea of visiting her in August when we were in Northern California. She thought that would be great, and we agreed to schedule a time to meet once our plans were finalized.

I hung up in a daze. *What just happened?*

I knew I had to read Mary's book, *Boots on the Ground by Dusk*. I knew I had to understand more of what she and her family had gone through. I knew I had to seek to understand things that I had avoided for so long.

It was difficult, but I could do it now. It was hard reading Mary's account of what had happened: of the misinformation the family received, of being told the details of Pat's death a second time, of their having to see his remains. It was brutal but beautiful. It made me miss him. I couldn't imagine how those closer to him felt. I couldn't imagine the thousands of other families who'd experienced the same loss since 9/11. So many lives had been claimed by war and continued to be claimed.

★

"You think we should head over there?" Brook asked. "It's almost five o'clock."

"Yeah, we should," I replied.

We walked back to our car parked in the heart of Stanford University's campus. We were in Palo Alto to meet Mary, had arrived early, and were killing time. We drove back into downtown, parked, and walked to the restaurant where Mary had asked to meet us. The evening was beautiful and warm.

She sat in the outdoor courtyard waiting for us. I saw her as we approached and entered. We went to her. She saw us, stood, and extended her hand.

"Hi," she said. "You can call me Dannie. All my friends do."

"Okay," I said. "That's very kind. Thank you so much for being willing to meet with us."

"Oh, of course. I am so glad you reached out. It was time. I have to tell you, though, and I hope you won't take it the wrong way. Hopefully you'll understand it coming from Kevin. I told him I was coming to meet with you, and he said, 'Aw, Elliott, he was always such a good kid. I hope he's well.'"

I laughed. "That's really nice of him to say. That sounds like Kevin."

She didn't waste any time. "I just want you to know that I don't blame you. I don't think the situation you were put in was fair, and I'm sorry if anything we did made it worse. We were just trying to get answers."

"Thank you," I said, trying to take that all in. "That's beyond gracious. I'm so sorry for all you've been through. And I'm sorry that I may have fired on Pat. If I contributed to his death or pain in any way, I'm so sorry for that." I strained to maintain my composure.

"It's okay," she said reassuringly.

We each had a glass of wine as we munched on an appetizer and continued to talk. We swapped stories about Pat and learned more about what each had experienced along the way. We talked, laughed, and cried for the better part of three hours.

As we walked toward the sidewalk, she gave both Brook and me a hug and a kiss on the cheek.

"Anything you need," Mary said, "anything you want to talk about, anytime, please call me."

"I will. Thank you. Thank you so much."

We went our separate ways. It was getting late, and Brook and I hadn't eaten much, so we looked for something quick and as cheap as we could find in Palo Alto. I felt as though I could curl up on the cooling pavement and sleep with ease. I felt relief. Complete and utter relief. Every part of my being was at peace, and it was as though years of unrest were replaced by an intense and wonderful desire for sleep.

We got sushi and walked back to the car. I sat in the passenger seat and considered our conversation.

"You okay?" Brook asked as she started the car.

"Yeah, I'm good. It's over now. I can feel it. It's finally over."

★

Our Airbnb was a boat on the Oakland side of the San Francisco Bay. We arrived late, and after our host ensured we had all we needed, we settled in for the night.

I quickly crawled into bed and marveled as I stared at the water through a round window in the side of the boat. I closed my eyes for what seemed a moment and was suddenly staring at the gray morning light. I stretched with satisfaction.

The fog was heavy but lifting. I knew the sun would burn it all away.

Postscript

Let there be light.
GENESIS 1:3

The world we live in is beautiful but broken. On one part of that vast, broken landscape, we find those who have been sent to war and returned with wounds we cannot see, trained to fight and kill and left to deal with the consequences. Those wounds of war lie deep, and the ultimate product of that trauma is and always will be death—death of relationships, death of community, and far too often death at one's own hand. As you've read, veterans in the United States kill themselves at a rate of roughly twenty per day, more than double the civilian rate of suicide. That means that each year, suicide claims around 7,300 of those that we as a nation have sent to war. That also means that since the invasion of Afghanistan in 2001, more than 116,000 veterans have made that fateful choice, more than twenty times the number of those killed in battle during the same time frame. This is an epidemic.

Mental illness and suicide, however, are not the problem. They are symptoms of the untreated wounds of war that can be and often are just as deadly as those that we can see. Much of the blame for this and other ills suffered by our veterans community is laid at the doorstep of the Department of Veterans Affairs. While some of the responsibility may be rightly ascribed to that bureaucracy, I believe we are missing something. We are missing the fact that many active-duty service members lack a basic acknowledgment of what they are dealing with and the support they need at the point of trauma. We cannot wait until they become civilians and are the VA's "problem." I chose to tell this story in part to highlight this fact and to advocate for specific and meaningful change in how mental health care is recognized and organized for our active-duty forces.

It's also worth noting that trauma, mental illness, and suicide are not confined to those who have served in the military. Neither is the fear and stigma that can often accompany those struggles. Our society tends to not reward weakness, and yet acknowledging our broken places, places that we all have in varying degrees, is always the first step on the path to healing and strength. I don't know what that looks like for you, but I know for all of us, military or civilian, it means that we can't do this life alone. We were made for community, and it is often within community and from the helping hands of others that healing can come. I was sick with several ailments, but my greatest disease was that of prideful independence. I was so committed to my freedom that I was almost freed of the gift of life. People have and will continue to let us down, and yet we all need others to help lift us up. Whatever you're doing, don't think for a second that you're meant to do it alone. Don't think for a second that you *are* alone.

There were many times in writing the words of this book that I found it difficult to grasp all that had occurred. I have done my best to recount this story accurately, and yet I am still confronted with elements of mystery that I may never understand. I recognize that it may be even more difficult for readers to understand. For you, it may be that the "God talk" in this book is at best something to be overlooked and at worst a major turnoff. I get it. The name of God has far too often been invoked to manipulate and control, when in actuality God came as Jesus to heal the broken and destroy the kingdoms of earth that have kept and continue to keep people in chains. If you follow Jesus, I pray that you'll be encouraged by the work he has done in the life of one who could not be more undeserving. If you don't follow him, I pray that you would come to know and experience the love he has for you—a love that does not cease to be real and true in the midst of a world that is ugly and broken.

Beyond my firsthand experience, I have been fortunate to know a psychologist by the name of Dr. Mark Russell. He is the son of a veteran of Korea and Vietnam, a retired naval officer, and the father of children who have also chosen military service. Dr. Russell and his colleagues have studied and written extensively both in the popular and academic press advocating for tangible solutions to end the military mental health crisis and the suicide epidemic that has accompanied it. The notion that this is a mysterious problem with no discernible solution is ridiculous. At the heart of many of these proposals is a boringly simple solution: the military needs a Behavioral Health Corps that would centralize and coordinate efforts at meeting the demands of those suffering from the traumas of war. Those efforts are currently dispersed among so many branches and departments that they are far less effective than they could be. The military already has corps commands led by a general officer that centralize medical care, dental care, and even veterinary care, yet there is no single individual who is responsible for ensuring that adequate mental health care is provided to our service members in uniform. The creation of a Behavioral Health Corps alone will not solve the problem, but the problem cannot begin to be solved until such a corps is established and empowered.

I hope you will agree that together we can change this structural flaw and facilitate healing for wounds that otherwise continue to fester and destroy. We as the people from whom our government derives its consent to govern can advocate for this change. We are the bureaucracy, and we can change it for the better if we choose to do so. To learn more about this work and how you can be a part of ending this completely preventable mental health crisis, please visit the following website: www.elliottfund.org.

True strength can only come when we as individuals and as a society can acknowledge our weaknesses, individually and collectively. The broken places must be brought into the light if they are to be made whole. We can do that together.

Gratefully,
Steven

Photo Gallery

Here are a few photos, some new and some old, which hopefully offer additional insight into this story and the lives of those closest to me.

My grandfather, Hugo Luhman, as a new soldier in 1943. Forty years later, as a member of the local American Legion, he would help to honor the fallen on Memorial Day. The sights and sounds of that holiday and my grandfather's participation in those ceremonies are among my most vivid and cherished memories of childhood.

Me in the harvest field after riding in the combine with Grandpa.

ORU graduation night, May 3, 2003. Evan is on the left with our buddy Dan in the middle. Evan and I had been training for the army for the past year, and I would begin my enlistment just a few weeks later.

Graduating from basic training and infantry school at Fort Benning, Georgia, in September 2003. My mom, Cindy, is helping put on my blue infantry shoulder cord. I love you, Mom.

RIP graduation at Fort Benning in November 2003. I am flanked by my two friends Fischer (L) and Dustin Broek (R).

On deployment in Afghanistan in April 2004, manning the M240B, the same weapon I used the day of the ambush. This was taken less than a week before that day.

Brook and Gracie in the summer of 2004, not long after Brook and I started dating.

Brook and I on our wedding day in 2005.

Hazel Grace as a lively toddler.

Our family in 2018.
A gift.

Acknowledgments

I am because we are.
SOUTH AFRICAN PROVERB

Acknowledgments are a challenge in that it's impossible to communicate the importance of the following individuals by simply writing down their names and saying a few words. These people are likely strangers to you, but please know that each and every one was essential in this book becoming a reality and, in some instances, for me being alive. To those of you on the list, "thank you" is not sufficient. To you, the reader, please remember that you're never weaker than when you believe the lie of your own, isolated strength.

To Willie Weinbaum and Mike Fish at ESPN, thank you for integrity and compassion. I would have never sought to tell this story were it not for you both.

To Helen Dooley, Meredith Geisler, and the team at Tandem, thank you for believing in this project and for your conviction and professionalism as you supported and guided us along the way.

To Jim Lund, again, thank you for believing in this work and dedicating yourself accordingly.

To Dave Grossman, thank you for applying your heart, mind, and voice to these issues and for your support of me in this work.

To the folks at Tyndale, including Jan Long Harris, Sarah Atkinson, and Jonathan Schindler, thank you for lending your expertise to this work and for your heart to see the broken made whole and the lost found.

To Judge Brett Buckley, Stacey, Alex, Casey, Shane, and the family that is the Thurston County Veterans Court, you've demonstrated more of the gospel to me in court proceedings than I've witnessed almost anywhere else. Thank you for your heart for our veteran community and for allowing me to be a part of that family.

To Jen Hutchinson, thank you for your heart for the veteran community and for your encouragement along the way.

To Buck, RIP, and thank you for your friendship and vulnerability in the dark times.

To Dave, Sally, Rick, Jeremy, and the First ID East staff, you gave me shelter in the midst of the storm. Your simple kindness was life.

To Chaplain Jones, you gave a stranger the gift of presence and the gift of attentive silence. Thank you.

To BG McPhee (retired), you embraced me without question and supported me without fail. Thank you.

To MG Hood (retired), you helped show me what it is to lead. Your heart for our nation and its warriors is beautiful, and I'm blessed beyond words to have served under you. I'd follow you anywhere. Thank you to you and Lynne.

To our friends at Reality Church, you've accepted me in my darkest times, and I'm grateful to have walked the last leg of this journey with you. Thank you.

To Jake and Jess, the Lord has used you both to help awaken the truth of the gospel in our hearts. We love you and thank God for you and your family.

To Pat, Sandi, and our entire Capstone family, thank you for your continued love and support.

To Evan, Rachel, and the rest of the "Jewbergs," you are precious family to us and have loved us without fail. Thank you.

To Denny, thank you for loving us and for being my friend.

To Didier and Cathleen, thank you for your tireless love and support of our family.

To Daniel, Kinsey, Jerry, Susan, Marge, and David, thank you for loving us and speaking truth in the dark times.

To my grandmothers, Ida and Irene, your steadfast commitment to family and the Lord is beautiful. I love you both.

To my granddad, Keith, RIP. I felt your love for me even if it was too hard for you to say.

To my grandpa, Hugo, RIP. Thank you for being a father to the fatherless and for loving Jesus.

To Bryan and Will, thank you for forgiving.

To Mary Tillman, thank you for your forgiving embrace.

Christian, you're my brother, and I love you. Thank you for forgiving me when I deserved it least.

Mom, the heritage you've given me in knowing and seeking to follow Jesus is priceless. I love you and thank you for who you are.

Gracie and Hazel, you're beautiful girls. Thank you for loving and forgiving me as I imperfectly seek to care for you as the Lord has cared for me.

Brook, what can I say? You're God's clearest demonstration of that which is given freely and never deserved: grace. I love you.

It may seem obligatory to end these acknowledgments with a head nod to the Almighty, but please believe me when I say there is no sense of obligation. I freely acknowledge his grace and mercy that has and continues to be given without fail. It is in response to his kindness that I have repented and have sought the beauty of his law that is perfect and unchanging. My life, and by extension this work, is his creation. If there is wisdom or truth here worth learning, it is of his doing, not mine. He is the source. He is the author.

Discussion Questions

1. Do you remember where you were on 9/11? What was your reaction to that tragedy? What, if anything, can you relate to in Steven's experience of it?

2. Steven is partially motivated to join the military based on a personal relationship with his grandfather. What relationships in your life have influenced choices you've made?

3. What are some examples of leadership in this story—whether positive or negative? What do you think it means for someone to truly be a leader?

4. What was your reaction to the revelation that Steven's grandfather had also been a part of a suspected fratricide in World War II? How has your view of others changed as you learn more about their past experiences?

5. Steven's response to what he experienced included self-medicating with alcohol. When you're in pain, where do you go for relief? How have you handled grief and pain well? How have you handled those feelings poorly?

6. Steven describes God speaking to him. Do you believe God speaks to people? Why or why not?

7. How do you reconcile the idea of a loving God with the broken world in which we live?

8. How can we forgive those who have hurt us? How have you experienced forgiving others and being forgiven?

9. Practically speaking, what does it mean to love our enemies?

10. When you think of those with a mental illness or of disabled veterans, what images come to mind? Has *War Story* altered the way you think about them? If so, how?

11. What character(s) in Steven's story do you most identify with, and why?

12. What action, if any, might this story inspire you to take?

Notes

xx   *The National Health Study . . . who did not deploy have PSTD:*
US Department of Veterans Affairs, "Findings about Health from
a Large Scale Survey Study," Fall 2017, https://www.publichealth
.va.gov/exposures/publications/oef-oif-ond/post-9-11-vet-fall-2017
/new-gen-study.asp.

xx   *"It is no secret . . . He'll do for you":* Stuart Hamblen, "It Is No Secret
(What God Can Do)," Hamblen Music Co., 1952.

129   *On April 25 . . . nothing about fratricide:* Jon Krakauer, *Where Men
Win Glory: The Odyssey of Pat Tillman* (New York: Random House,
2009), 292.

129   *Bailey reportedly directed . . . making a statement:* Ibid., 297–98.

188   Washington Post *story . . . make sense of inconsistencies:* Steve
Coll, "Army Spun Tale around Ill-Fated Mission," *Washington
Post*, December 6, 2004, http://www.washingtonpost.com/wp-dyn
/articles/A37679-2004Dec5.html.

188   *"the medical examiner's report . . . in his forehead":* Robert Collier,
"Family Demands the Truth: New Inquiry May Expose Events That
Led to Pat Tillman's Death," *SFGATE*, September 25, 2005, https://
www.sfgate.com/news/article/FAMILY-DEMANDS-THE-TRUTH-New
-inquiry-may-expose-2567400.php.

210   *"head wounds . . . 5.56-millimeter munitions":* "Findings in Corporal
Tillman Death," C-SPAN video, 1:10:20, Pentagon briefing of report
on death of Pat Tillman, March 26, 2007, https://www.c-span.org
/video/?197332-1/findings-corporal-tillman-death.

210   *"During the course . . . found no violations":* Ibid.

210   *"Investigation determined . . . to defend themselves":* Inspector
General Department of Defense, "Appendix A: Summary of Army

Criminal Investigation Command Report," in *Review of Matters Related to the Death of Corporal Patrick Tillman, U.S. Army*, Report Number IPO2007E001, March 26, 2007, https://www.npr.org /documents/2007/mar/tillman/tillman_dod_ig.pdf.

210   *"critical errors . . . following his death":* "Findings in Corporal Tillman Death," C-SPAN video, March 26, 2007.

210   *"appropriate corrective action":* Inspector General Department of Defense, *Review of Matters Related to the Death of Corporal Patrick Tillman*, March 26, 2007.

225   *"Some psychiatric casualities . . . to endure it":* Dave Grossman, *On Killing: The Psychological Cost of Learning to Kill in War and Society*, rev. ed. (New York: Back Bay Books, 2009), 45.

225   *"It is the existence . . . of his pain":* Ibid., xxxv.

226   *"a reaction to . . . and sleep disturbances":* Ibid., 285.

261   *Something like twenty vets . . . the VA's own numbers:* Janet Kemp and Robert Bossarte, *Suicide Data Report, 2012*, report prepared for the Department of Veterans Affairs Mental Health Services Suicide Prevention Program, 15, accessed August 28, 2018, https://www.va .gov/opa/docs/suicide-data-report-2012-final.pdf.

262   *"like losing him all over again":* Mike Fish, "An American Tragedy: Death of an American Ideal," pt. 3, ESPN.com, 2006, accessed August 28, 2018, http://www.espn.com/espn/eticket/story?page =tillmanpart3.

267   *"I guess to say . . . All of them":* "Shooter Fears He Killed Pat Tillman," ESPN video, 11:50, April 18, 2014, http://www.espn.com/espn/otl /story/_/id/10791530/ex-army-ranger-speaks-first-former-nfl-player -pat-tillman-shooting-says-fired-fatal-shots.

267   *"tremendous void":* Mike Fish, "Enduring Guilt," ESPN.com, April 22, 2014, http://www.espn.com/espn/feature/story/_/id/10816260/pat -tillman-enduring-guilt.

268   *"with help, there is hope":* "Shooter Fears He Killed Pat Tillman," ESPN video, April 18, 2014.

273   *"When you have turned back, strengthen your brothers":* Luke 22:32.

275–276 *Jackson summoned McGuire . . . "the shade of the trees":* Shelby Foote, *The Civil War: A Narrative: Fredericksburg to Meridian* (New York: Random House, 1963), 2:319.

The Elliott Fund

All proceeds from the writing of this book that would otherwise be payable to the author will be donated through the Elliott Fund, a Washington State nonprofit. The author derives no salary or economic benefit from the Elliott Fund. The Elliott Fund exists for the sole purpose of benefiting nonprofit organizations in the business of caring for our active-duty and veterans community, including the following:

Justice for Vets is dedicated to transforming the way the justice system identifies, assesses, and treats our veterans, leading the national effort to put a veterans treatment court in reach of every veteran in need.

Operation Military Family provides world-class programs and solutions that improve the health, morale, and finances of our nation's veteran families and the industries that hire them.

The Institute of War Stress Recovery works to investigate, identify, and eliminate the root causes for repetitive crises in military mental health care and end the cycle of crisis by transforming mental health care policy and practice.

For more information, please visit www.elliottfund.org.

About the Author

STEVEN ELLIOTT graduated summa cum laude with a BS degree in international business from Oral Roberts University in 2003. Three weeks later he began army basic training at Fort Benning, Georgia. Like many others, Steven joined the military in response to the 9/11 terrorist attacks. He successfully completed the Ranger Indoctrination Program (RIP) and became a member of the elite 75th Ranger Regiment. In November 2003, at the age of twenty-two, he was assigned to the same platoon as Pat and Kevin Tillman. In April 2004, Steven deployed to the Afghanistan/Pakistan border. On April 22, in the midst of an enemy ambush, he was one of four Rangers who mistook Pat Tillman's position for that of the enemy and fired there. Steven is one of two Rangers considered likely to be responsible for firing the bullets that killed Pat Tillman (the source of the fatal bullets has never been conclusively determined) and is the only shooter to speak publicly about the incident and its aftermath.

Steven served honorably and with distinction during his remaining years in the service and completed his four-year enlistment in 2007. Today he is the president of Capstone Trust in Olympia, Washington, and an executive producer with Hero Productions in Tulsa, Oklahoma. He is privileged to serve on the board of directors of Nations Media and has also served as a volunteer veterans court mentor. Steven continues to speak about his experiences in an effort to advocate for change in how the unseen wounds of war are recognized and treated. Steven and his wife, Brook, have two daughters, Gracie and Hazel.